THE MONK'S RECORD PLAYER

Also by Robert Hudson

Four Birds of Noah's Ark: A Prayer Book from the Time of Shakespeare (by Thomas Dekker, edited by Robert Hudson)

Kiss the Earth When You Pray: The Father Zosima Poems

The Christian Writer's Manual of Style

Companions for the Soul (with Shelley Townsend-Hudson)

Beyond Belief: What the Martyrs Said to God (with Duane W. H. Arnold)

THE MONK'S RECORD PLAYER

Thomas Merton, Bob Dylan, and the Perilous Summer of 1966

Robert Hudson

Foreword by
David Dalton

William B. Eerdmans Publishing Company
Grand Rapids, Michigan

Wm. B. Eerdmans Publishing Co.
2140 Oak Industrial Drive N.E., Grand Rapids, Michigan 49505
www.eerdmans.com

Published 2018
Published in association with the literary agency of
Credo Communications, LLC, Grand Rapids, MI 49525
www.credocommunications.net
Printed in the United States of America

27 26 25 24 23 22 21 20 19 18 1 2 3 4 5 6 7 8 9 10

ISBN 978-0-8028-7520-4

Library of Congress Cataloging-in-Publication Data

Names: Hudson, Bob, 1953- author.
Title: The monk's record player : Thomas Merton, Bob Dylan, and the perilous
summer of 1966 /
Robert Hudson ; foreword by David Dalton.
Description: Grand Rapids : Eerdmans Publishing Co., 2018. |
Includes bibliographical references and index.
Identifiers: LCCN 2017048811 | ISBN 9780802875204 (hardcover : alk. paper)
Subjects: LCSH: Merton, Thomas, 1915-1968. | Dylan, Bob, 1941—Influence. |
Baez, Joan. | Popular culture—United States—History—20th century.
Classification: LCC BX4705.M542 H83 2018 | DDC 271/.12502—dc23
LC record available at https://lccn.loc.gov/2017048811

To Susan Hudson Fox,
who introduced me to the music of Joan Baez,
and Richard F. Hudson,
who first exposed me to the songs of Bob Dylan—

and to our late parents,
George "Ray" and Barbara Hudson,
who instilled in us
a deep love for books and music

La musique est une joie inventée par le silence.

—Thomas Merton

CONTENTS

CONTENTS

Part Three
The Lonesome Sparrow Sings
(July 1966 to October 1968)

FOREWORD

The Directors Have Engineered a Surprise
You Will Not Easily Discover

When Bob Hudson first told me about his idea for the book he was writing, I thought, *Oh well, we all have our eccentricities, our odd hobbies*—although some a little more odd than others. I'm all in favor of writing a book about any wild thing under the sun, bringing in whatever quirky thing floats through your mind (that's what books are). But then Bob asked if I would write the foreword. At first I thought, *Why me? Aren't we friends? Didn't we bond through our mutual obsession with the hipster saint Bob (Dylan)?* I would do anything for him—I wouldn't have been able to write my Dylan biography without him. But, I ask you, do real friends ask friends to corroborate their nutty theories?

You may think, as I at first did, that pairing a Utopian hermit monk and a demon-haunted rock star is just plain perverse or at the very least willfully paradoxical. But there you'd be dead wrong. Paradox, as Kierkegaard pointed out, is simply a great idea in embryo—and that's what *The Monk's Record Player* is, a profound meditation on apparent contradictions. With a deft, witty, and philosophical hand, Hudson shows us that Bob Dylan and Thomas Merton were at a certain point in time almost interchangeable. Well, as writers anyway, thinkers and diviners of strange truths. It's a little like String Theory—it takes a while to get used to.

I now saw the light: Thomas Merton and Bob Dylan were Siamese twins joined at the hippocampus. One an orphan (Merton), the other (liar-liar-pants-on-fire Dylan) claiming to be one—as well as a number of other unlikely things: a foundling, the son of an Egyptian king, a boy adopted by the Oglala Sioux, a tent-show kid looking after the bearded lady, etc.

After all, why *wouldn't* two people as inventive, desperate, supernaturally talented, and aghast at the temper of the times have a lot in common? Well, that's why you're reading this book.

It's too bad they never met, but we could easily arrange it at, say, the Existential Café. Dylan is perusing the menu. "What are you gonna have, Father?" Bob asks. "Tom," Merton tells him. "Please call me Tom." On another occasion Merton might have said, "Two cheeseburgers, a chocolate milkshake, and a large order of fries," because he's a true devotee of Zen masters and junk food. But these are two poets talking, and poets, as we know, talk in metaphors.

"So Tom, what's your favorite dish?" "Let me see . . . ," Merton says. "Broiled René Char, café noir à la André Breton, a taste of Rubén Darío, Miguel Hernández, Edwin Muir, and a couple of Desert Fathers on the side. And you, Bob, what do you fancy?" "Oh, the usual. A couple of French Symbolists, marinated in Rimbaud's *Seasoned in Hell* sauce, and the Comte de Lautréamont's signature dish, Spleen de *Maldoror*, hard-boiled and raving."

In 1966 Merton declared his intention to write "a new book now, in a new way, in a new language too." Rimbaud, the high priest of Symbolist alchemy of the word, had decreed, "Inventing the unknown demands new forms." So it was just a matter of finding the language for what he was setting out to do. Dylan had already kicked open that door for him, and Merton caught on to the new meta-lingo fast.

Cables to the Ace: Or, Familiar Liturgies of Misunderstanding, written in 1966, is the book, as Hudson points out, where Merton goes electric. "With the unending vroom vroom vroom of guitars," Merton insists, "we will all learn a new kind of obstinacy, together with massive lessons of irony and refusal. . . ."

Some sort of vinyl virus has got ahold of Thomas Merton; he's burning up. He's got a bad case of Dylanosis. Worse, he's deliberately infected himself with the wild mercury fever. Where did he catch it? Where else would you get Dadaist dissociation on vinyl? Dylan's liner notes to *Bringing It All Back Home* and *Highway 61*. Merton's bogged down amid "tree frogs and rain," his healer-lover can only revive him through her "distant radio-electric loving glance" (phone calls), and in section 70 of *Cables* he's really rolling down the track as he summarizes the plot of a TV show this way: "Riot woman transformed into savings bonds is traced to unforgettable swans for the entire ruin of one season." (Now that's a show I'd like to see!)

When characters with bizarre names—"Polo King," "Uncle Sled," "Jack Sound," "Miss Daisy," the "subliminal engineer," "Pocahontas a jungle nun"—start showing up in Merton's poetry, you're not sure whether they're playing cards, comic-book characters, or names out of the Bob Dylan telephone directory. He sees "Little Red Riding Hood in chains," "Coleridge . . . swimming in Walden Pond," and "The midnight express / Bringing Plato, Prophets, Milton, Blake." Well, if I can find the schedule, you'll find me on the platform waiting for *that* train.

In *Cables to the Ace*, Merton is someplace else entirely from his earlier poetry. Once you sign the register, you've checked into the Merton Motel, where they have daily, weekly, and special rates for eternity. "The realm of the spirit is two doors down the hall," the night clerk tells you. "There you can obtain more soul than you are ready to cope with, Buster." When a midget pops out of room 27 and madly cries "Hats off! Hats off to the human condition!," you don't know whether to rejoice or run.

The parallel trajectories of Merton and Dylan probably had nothing to do with angels or time spirits, and a lot more to do with the temper of the times. If you want to know what it was like to be alive in 1966, it's right there in the grooves of Dylan's LPs and on the pages of Merton's *Cables to the Ace*. They were creatures of the Zeitgeist, operating on high-tension power lines tuned in to the same oscillating wavelength. You can hear their words and phrases humming on the page, in the tracks. They were on the beam, in the moment—behind every thought there's the word NOW!

Bob Hudson's obsession with these two maniacs and his rash insistence on putting them together often made me wonder about him. How the hell is he going to pull this off? What exactly *did* they have in common? Okay, we'll make a rough list: transcendental yearnings, overamped libidos, a fascination with drugs and strange gods, and a pervert's molestation of the English language. One a hermit by disposition (you can imagine who I'm referring to), the other a hermit by profession (of faith). One of them climbed a mystical seven-storeyed mountain; the other created three albums so existentially evangelical they're often referred to as the Holy Trinity. Both were members of a perverse order of nobility. Using hieroglyphic language, they simultaneously hit upon a way of dealing with their own psychological derangements while straightening out the universe—verbally, at least. Both were willful sinners, antiheroes of mysterious virtue and reluctant saints involved in issues of street-legal theology, Symbolist poetry, radical politics, morbid psychology, women (why leave them out?), the imminent spiritual crisis, and Doom—eschatology, to use theological terminology.

Thomas Merton knew of Dylan, of course, became obsessed with him, but only after—and because—he had already found the core in himself that now needed a new lens with which to look at the world. And he found it in Dylan.

I could have warned Merton of the dangers of getting into a car with Bob Dylan, but Merton wasn't a dabbler, and when he became obsessed with something, he dived in headfirst. He knew that "one does not get 'curious' about Dylan. You are either all in it or all out of it. I am *in* his new stuff." Merton's an impulsive character, a devotee of satori—sudden enlightenment—and he jumps right in that car and he's off.

Merton and Dylan are both numinous writers—and x-ray vision was granted to both of them. They were outraged when confronted with boxes of Cheez Doodles, cigarette-smoking billboards, satanic cereal, flesh-colored Christs that glow in the dark—a "tidal wave of trademarks, political party buttons, advertising and propaganda slogans, and all the rest," as Merton described it. "An age of mass psychosis. . . . That is why some of the best poets of our time are running wild among the tombs in the moonlit cemeteries of surrealism." Given their like-minded scavenging habits, it's a wonder Tom and Bob didn't run into each other *nightly*.

It was a culture mired in hypocrisy, greed, and corruption on an industrial scale. Things were bad, very bad. The world's far worse off now than it was in 1966, the difference being that back then we at least thought we could do something about it. In this wasteland, Merton saw his antipoetry as performing a prophetic and cathartic function using phantasmagoric language—what Russian futurists called *zaum*, a parasitical language of transmutation, perversion, and verbal contortion. That was the only way to talk about an absurd world. Fired by this new word drug, pictures infused with infrared colors flooded their brains and flew out of their heads like Pentecostal postcards.

Experimental poetry here overlaps effortlessly with prophetic visions. High modernism and visionaries all share the same mantra: *Credo quia absurdum*—I believe *because* it's absurd. The intoxicated, promiscuous minds of saints and Symbolists are rag-pickers, scooping up images, words, disconnected ideas. There's no time to lose. Snatch anything you see, scavenger style. Grab a headline from a newspaper, snag an advertising jingle, predict nonsense, speak French and Dada.

Hudson's search for correspondences between Dylan and Merton—their "elective affinities," to use Goethe's phrase—is ingenious. You have to take risks when you're dealing with stuff as far-out as this. The quest has to be wildly speculative to yield any interesting results at all. It requires a nimble intelligence to see the invisible threads. This can't be achieved solely by analogy. In the end you have to rely on your intuition and cosmic coincidences.

The basic idea of *The Monk's Record Player* is to throw two eccentric characters possessed of genius in the same life raft along with himself. So now you have three men in the drunken boat. It's a sort of Mad Hatter's tea party, except instead of riddles, nonsense poetry, and a dormouse, Hudson's book mulls over a wide range of ideas, theories, and philosophies, and he obviously doesn't have any qualms about putting them all into the mix. You soon forget about specifics because Hudson's subtle observations encourage your mind to run on unexpected tracks. When you discover what Merton's run-in with Dylan's albums did for his poetry, you might begin thinking strange thoughts, like what St. Augustine could have done if he'd had a Stratocaster.

But in the end it's Bob Hudson's love for Thomas Merton and Bob Dylan that's the alchemical fire that makes it work. As curious as this cockamamie pairing is, *The Monk's Record Player* is a meditation on inspiration, contact highs, and the unknowable workings of the cosmos.

Listen, as long as you're up, put on *Cables to the Ace*. I want to hear a couple of tracks on the first side again.

David Dalton

INTRODUCTION

"Come writers and critics / Who prophesize with your pen . . ."[1]

These familiar words from Bob Dylan's "The Times They Are A-Changin'" aptly describe both the songwriter himself and a Trappist monk who, in his lifetime, was known to his fellow monks as Father Louis but to rest of the world as Thomas Merton. In the 1960s, these two were among the most outspoken writers and critics to prophesy with their pens, and they did indeed change the times they lived in. Merton expressed a sentiment similar to Dylan's when he wrote, "I think only the poets are still sure in their prophetic sense that the world lies."[2] With their penetrating minds and enormous creativity, Merton and Dylan observed the culture around them, with all its violence and greed and excess, and confronted it with truth and authenticity.

Thomas Merton and Bob Dylan were two of the most brilliant and controversial figures of the twentieth century, and their influence has shaped our century as well. In 2015, Pope Francis, in an address to Congress during his first visit to the United States, cited Merton as one of the four "great Americans" who most shaped his thought and faith, alongside Abraham Lincoln, Dr. Martin Luther King Jr., and Dorothy Day.[3] A year later, Bob Dylan was awarded the Nobel Prize for literature, the first time the coveted prize had been given to a songwriter. Professor Christopher Ricks, the former Poetry Chair at Oxford University, defended the Nobel committee's choice by contending that Dylan "is the greatest living user of the English language."[4]

The lives of Thomas Merton and Bob Dylan had some surprising parallels, especially during the summer of 1966. Not only did they experience profound personal crises, suffering from physical and emotional traumas at about the same time, but their lives radically changed direction as a result. Even more surprising is the fact that Thomas Merton, the most renowned religious hermit of the time, was an ardent Bob Dylan fan.

The idea that Dylan's prophetic poetry and lyrics powerfully affected Merton's writing—at least for a time—may seem absurd. How is it possible that a rock 'n' roll icon could have influenced a religious writer of Merton's stature? But the evidence is in Merton's own hand, scattered through his journals, letters, poetry, and essays. The younger artist cast a spell on the older. As Merton wrote to publisher James Laughlin, he was "addicted" to Dylan's music.[5] After hearing Dylan's *Blonde on Blonde*, Merton declared, "One does not get 'curious' about Dylan. You are either all in it or all out of it. I am *in* his new stuff."[6]

Poet Robert Bly once singled out Merton as one of those rare souls who are fully engaged, awake to life, whom the Sufi mystics call "pure *nafs*," perfected souls. They are, Bly explains, "what Hebrew culture has always called the remnant. There are perhaps thirty-eight of them alive at any one time, none of them visible. They are probably people like Thomas Merton, sitting in a tiny cell somewhere writing about the connection between Buddhism and Christianity."[7]

So what would have drawn a pure *nafs* like Merton to a pop musician who was the subject of a documentary that one critic described as a film about "the neighborhood's biggest brat blowing his nose for 90 minutes"?[8] That is the subject of this book.

• • •

Thomas Merton lived his life a thousand miles removed from Bob Dylan's, literally and figuratively. Merton, a celibate Catholic monk, spent half of that life cloistered in the Abbey of Gethsemani, an hour's drive south of Louisville, Kentucky. While Merton was settling into his hermit's cabin in

1965, the Jewish Dylan was living in New York, vigorously personifying "sex, drugs, and rock 'n' roll." While Merton passed his days in relative silence, Dylan played music so raucous that some audience members tried to boo him off the stage—famously without success.

Merton responded generously to requests for articles and interviews, while Dylan made a habit of razzing the media and handing interviewers what would now be called "a load of snark":

> Reporter to Dylan (who is holding a giant light bulb): "What is your real message?"
>
> Dylan to Reporter: "My real message? Keep a good head and always carry a light bulb."[9]

Although they lived their lives a thousand miles apart, their souls were next-door neighbors. Both were cultural icons of the 1960s, and both dealt with the baggage that came with such fame. Dylan found himself besieged by screaming fans and clueless reporters, scenes of which are captured in the film about his 1965 acoustic concert tour of England, *Dont Look Back* [sic].[10] A year later, many of those fans were booing him, stomping out of his concerts, and branding him a traitor because he was now playing rock 'n' roll.

Merton too was mobbed by fans—and the fanatically unhinged—albeit one at a time. Lovers of his books, often women, frequently arrived at the gates of Gethsemani hoping to talk with the famous monk. On one occasion a woman was granted a private interview and ended up sexually accosting him.[11] Once, an agitated man knocked on the abbey's front door; he had a gun and demanded to see Merton.[12]

Both Dylan and Merton were prolific to the point of compulsion. In a New York radio interview in 1962, Pete Seeger asked Dylan, "Of all the people I heard in America, [you seem] to be the most prolific. . . . Bob, do you make a song before breakfast every day, or before supper?"[13] From 1962 to 1966, Dylan copyrighted more than 120 songs. By the summer of 1966 he had recorded seven studio albums, three of which are among the most influential in rock music, and a year later he was earning a million dollars annually in songwriting royalties alone.[14]

By that same summer, Thomas Merton, twice Dylan's age, had written more than three dozen books, including a best-selling autobiography as well as poetry, theology, history, devotion, biography, criticism, and commentary. He had published more than 150 articles in magazines ranging from Catholic periodicals like *Commonweal* and *The Catholic Worker* to major newsstand glossies like *Ramparts* and *Life*.

Both men were amateur visual artists. Dylan doodled on his lyric sheets and drew whimsical sketches for his book *Writings and Drawings* (1973). He painted the covers for four of his own albums and one by the Band,[15] and in recent years he has sculpted in metal and exhibited his paintings and prints worldwide.

Before entering the monastery, Merton did graphic work for Columbia University's humor magazine, *The Jester*. He continued to sketch while in the monastery, and later in life, while exploring Zen, he took up the brush to create abstract approximations of Chinese calligraphy, which he called "strange blobs of ink."[16] These were exhibited at a college in Louisville, and some were used to illustrate his book *Raids on the Unspeakable*.

Their interest in art also expressed itself in a love of photography, both behind and in front of the camera. Some photographers have said that Dylan had an uncanny way of controlling any photo session, and in his early days in Greenwich Village, he loved to take candid photos of friends—sometimes, as a prank, without film in his camera.

Photographer and writer John Howard Griffin, author of *Black Like Me*, who took many photos of Merton, commented that Merton felt entirely natural in front of a camera. Merton, he said, was easy to photograph because "his face concealed nothing . . . he had . . . an unblemished happiness with the moment."[17] When Griffin later gave Merton a camera, the monk became enraptured by its possibilities.[18]

Throughout their careers, Dylan and Merton proved to be as inscrutable as they were brilliant. One cannot devise a unified field theory to explain what makes them tick, though the world has not lacked for writers, like myself, who have tried. As Walt Whitman once warned his readers, "I charge you forever reject those who would expound me, for I cannot expound myself."[19] Merton and Dylan are enigmas, constantly contradicting themselves, though they are not so much a series of contradictions as they are the sum of the contradictions they embody. They were gifted with the ability to hold within themselves beliefs entirely at odds with each other, dissonances usually more upsetting to their fans than to themselves. Merton wrote, "We are not meant to resolve all contradictions but to live with them and rise above them."[20] Dylan put it another way: "Chaos is a friend of mine."[21]

The two shared a fierce psychological need for autonomy. Dylan has made a career of throwing off the expectations placed on him—by family, religion, musical norms, and the fans themselves—and in the process has made an art form of reinvention and radical individuation. His fervent nonconformity is what has drawn generations of younger fans to his music. Even his famous conversion to evangelical Christianity in 1979 can be seen as a way of freeing himself from his past. For nearly a year, he performed none of the songs on which his fame was built, opting instead to sing only his newer gospel songs. In so doing, he freed himself from the oppression of his older fans' expectations, and then he freed himself from evangelicalism as well. It was like a magician vanishing into thin air—after which the thin air vanishes too.

To Merton, Dylan's strident independence seemed a glimmer of the artistic freedom he himself had strived to perfect. Throughout his career, Merton pushed the limits of his monastic vows, often testing the constraints of the Catholic Church—whether in becoming a writer and hermit, having an affair with a student nurse, or expanding his religious vision to encompass Eastern spirituality.

Lastly, both were unflagging spiritual pilgrims, perpetually restless, intense, and curious. Most people have what we call their "formative experiences" early in life—school, first jobs, travel. But the genius of Thomas Merton and Bob Dylan is that both had learned the art of allowing every moment to be formative and every experience to be inspiring in unexpected ways. Merton's journey to Asia at the end of his life was his most formative experience of all, and Dylan, now approaching his eighties, is still charting new creative territory with his recent recordings, his art exhibitions, and his highly regarded memoir. The times never stop changing.

• • •

Whether Bob Dylan ever heard of Thomas Merton is another matter. Dylan, like Merton, absorbed the influences around him at a precipitous rate. During his so-called folk-protest years, Dylan would have heard about the peace-activist monk from like-minded people opposed to nuclear proliferation and the Vietnam War, which escalated rapidly between 1962 and 1964. Merton, who was linked to the Beat poets as well as the peace movement, was a respected presence in the counterculture, and his poem "Original Child Bomb" (1962) is the kind of document that Suze Rotolo, Dylan's activist girlfriend, would have shared with him. As a powerful indictment of the Hiroshima bombing, the poem, or "antipoem," as Merton called it, circulated among antinuke protesters. Folksinger and activist Joan Baez, also close to Dylan, read Merton's poetry, and few in the counterculture hadn't heard of Merton.

More intriguing is the possibility that Dylan heard about the monk from one particularly unlikely source: comedian Lenny Bruce. Bruce would sometimes end his stand-up routines by reading in a German accent a poem called "My Name Is Adolf Eichmann," which he credited to Merton, though it is only a vague adaptation of another of Merton's antipoems, "Chant to Be Used in Processions around a Site with Furnaces."[22]

Rotolo and Dylan saw the comic perform at the Village Theater not long after the assassination of John F. Kennedy. Rotolo noted this was one of Bruce's "discombobulated" sets, when Bruce spent much of his time reading the not-so-hilarious legal documents relating to the various obscenity and drug charges against him.[23] Bruce was past the point in his career when he would have read the Merton-inspired poem, but Dylan claims to have seen Bruce "before he got caught up in all that legal stuff,"[24] which means he may well have attended a performance at which Bruce read "Adolf Eichmann."[25]

In any case, monks, as a motif, pop up in two of Dylan's songs: the "jealous monk" who is a friend of Einstein's in "Desolation Row,"[26] and the "utopian hermit monks" in "Gates of Eden,"[27] which tempts one to think that Dylan had an image of Merton rattling around somewhere in the back of his brain. But nowhere in the hundreds of pages of interviews with Dylan does he ever mention the name *Merton*.[28]

• • •

A NOTE TO THE READER

While a portion of this book focuses on Merton's relationship with student nurse Margie Smith, a caveat is necessary. This book is *not* meant to be another rehashing of that affair. Their romance factors into this narrative, but that story is better told, and in greater detail, in such books as Mark Shaw's *Beneath the Mask of Holiness*, John Howard Griffin's *Follow the Ecstasy*, and Michael Mott's definitive biography, *The Seven Mountains of Thomas Merton*. And nowhere is the story more intimately recounted than in Merton's own posthumously published journals.[29]

In his biography, Mott writes that "Merton contended often with censorship. . . . But he has suffered since his death from much the same thing in the form of selective editing."[30] I quote this by way of confessing that *The Monk's Record Player* is an intentionally selective biography in which important details have been left out simply because they were irrelevant to the themes discussed. But this book is no more selective than those that approach Merton from such perspectives as social activism, environmentalism, Buddhism, Sufism, feminism, and others. Merton's whole is larger than the sum of his parts; but each part holds a fascination of its own.

In addition to being a selective biography, this book is also a parallel biography. It juxtaposes events in Merton's life with those in Dylan's (though the Dylan portion only starts after four chapters about Merton) and shows Dylan's personal and artistic influences on the monk. Do I overemphasize that influence? Hardly. It was clearly significant and well documented and a key to Merton's poetry at the time. Even as I underscore that impact, let it serve as a counterweight to those who minimize it or ignore it altogether. Although some writers briefly note Merton's interest in Dylan, they skip over it as a quaint eccentricity. But Merton recognized a prophetic voice when he heard one, and he heard one in Dylan. While Dylan has had millions of devoted fans in his nearly sixty-year career, few were as captivating or as brilliant in their own right as Merton.

Both men continue to be cultural touchstones. They are intriguing and elusory characters, visionaries and oddballs, and artists of unusual intensity in their pursuit of authenticity, creativity, connection, and truth. That both are geniuses is clear. That their lives so nearly intersected at so many points, like Leopold Bloom's and Stephen Dedalus's in Joyce's *Ulysses*, is less well-known.

This book is about solitude and love, originality and autonomy, and the extent to which music—functioning therapeutically—touched the life of one particularly gifted and troubled thinker in a time of crisis. And it all might have turned out differently if Thomas Merton, the most famous hermit monk of modern times, had not borrowed a portable record player.

PROLOGUE

Sunday, March 6, 1966

On a chilly Sunday evening, as the winter sun sinks behind thin gray clouds and, in the east, a full moon lurks just below the horizon, a man stands on the porch of a cabin in the woods. The sky is steely blue, the air filled with the scent of wood smoke from the chimney behind him. To the east, half-way down the snow-covered slope, five white-tailed deer have just stepped from the brush beyond the fence.[1]

The man has seen signs of them all winter: their tracks in the snow, their muddy hoof prints by the creek, and the depressions in the leaves where they warm themselves at night. Recently, as he walked the path, he caught sight of their white tails flapping "like flags" as they dashed off through the cedars and pines.[2]

Slowly he raises his binoculars. Fascinated by the wide-set eyes, soft black noses, and delicate movements, he wishes he could touch them. For a quarter of an hour he studies them, and they, in turn, glance nervously in his direction, pacing cautiously across the clearing, alert and searching for food as the long winter nears its end.

One doe raises a foreleg as if to spring back toward the woods, unsure about the human farther up the hill, but she doesn't run. Gently she lowers her hoof, sniffs the air, then gracefully arches her neck toward the ground. At one point something startles the group, but they prance only a few steps away. That doe has an especially elegant trot, lifting her legs higher than the others.

This reminds the man of the day last fall when a badly wounded buck hobbled three-legged across this same clearing, when the man wept and felt a flash of anger toward the hunters who poach these woods. He remembers the incident a couple of years earlier when a deer tumbled into the local reservoir, and he watched helplessly as it struggled to climb out. He wrote a poem about it later.

The plank flooring on which he stands is often strewn with cracker crumbs, left for the juncos and chickadees, though the mice and squirrels usually get them first. An ax is propped against the wall, a broad wood stump serves as a stool and wood-splitting block, a few wooden chairs are scattered around the porch, and a stack of firewood leans unevenly against one of the three four-by-four posts that support the overhanging roof. Buckets collect the rainwater, which the man uses to wash his dishes.

He stands there gazing, peaceful though alert, full of wonder, and above all, patient. In the past two and a half decades he has had much practice in the art of patience.

Later that night at his desk, by the faint hum of a fluorescent desk lamp, he will recount in his journal his experience with the deer and conclude, "I was entranced by their perfection."[3]

• • •

For many writers, such a phrase would be a self-conscious attempt at poetry. But for Thomas Merton, the man who watched the deer through binoculars on the evening of March 6, 1966, words like *entranced* and *perfection* had spiritual significance, as if the creatures were still so warm from the forge of creation that every fleeting moment spent watching them was overflowing with the divine.

As a religious hermit, he relished such moments, when time seemed suspended, self-contained, when distractions and disappointments vanished like mist on Monk's Pond at sunrise. He had moved to this cinder-block cabin seven months earlier for precisely these kinds of moments;

they were part of his regimen of meditation and prayer. For him, simply being present in nature *was* prayer.

It had taken years to convince the church to let him move here—twenty-four, to be exact. A sort of ceaseless yearning had guided him to this place—or was it, as he believed, God's will all along?

Perhaps he identified with those deer in some way. Like him, they were venturing alone into an open, vulnerable space and yet unwilling to move too far from the security of the woods. Merton had often tried to escape the shelter of the monastery, which was just a few minutes' walk from his cabin. But escaping the protective canopy of the Catholic Church—that was something he could not do.

For now, the cabin was enough. In the cold twilight, he was here, fully awake, present, and alone, relishing this hard-won solitude.

Within weeks, he would be on the brink of losing it all.

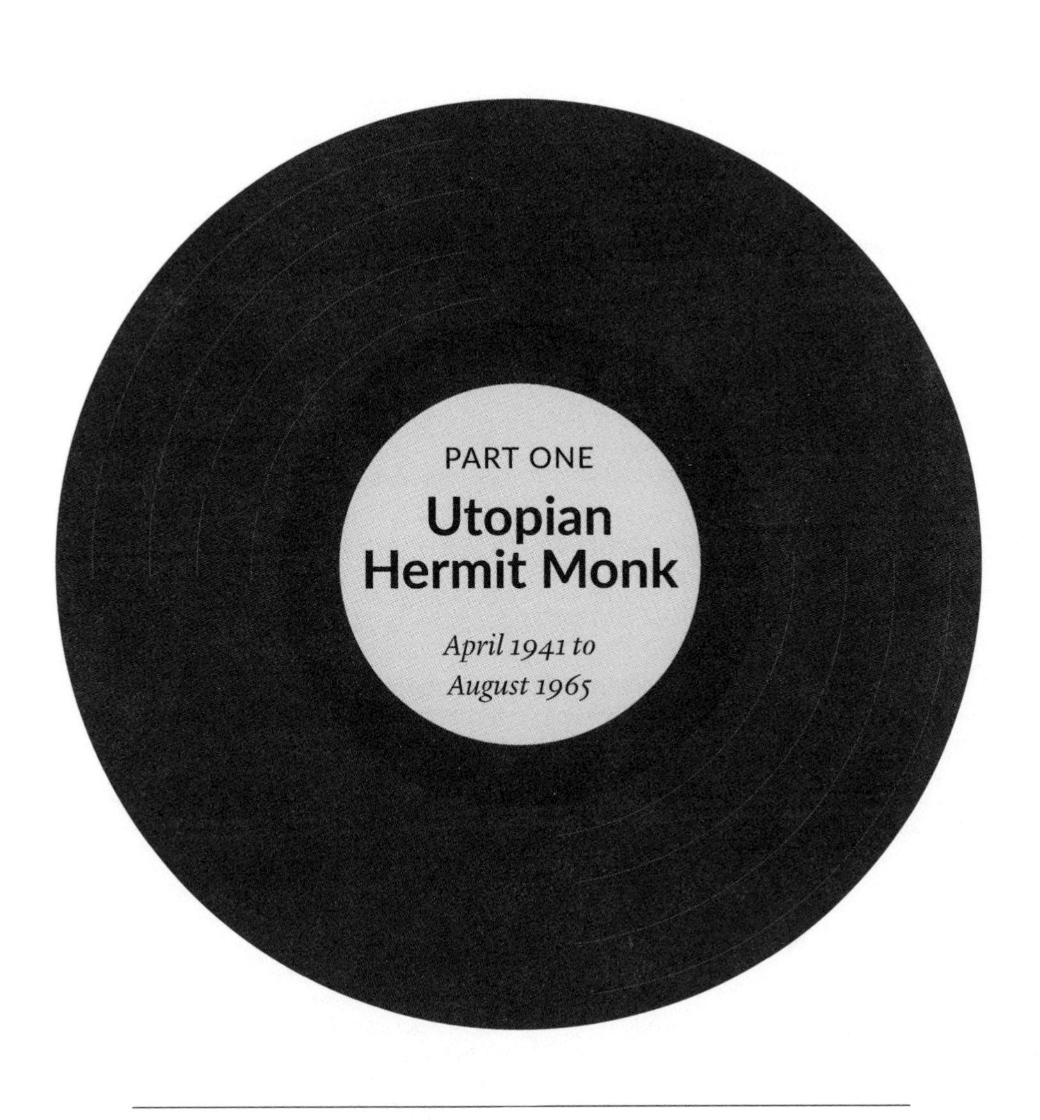

Bob Dylan, "Gates of Eden," *Bringing It All Back Home* (Columbia, CS 9128, 1965), side 2, track 2.

THOMAS MERTON	BOB DYLAN
1915, Jan. 31: born in Prades, France	
1921: his mother dies	
1931: his father dies	
1932–34: enters Clare College, Cambridge	
1935–38: attends Columbia University	
1941, April 7: visits Our Lady of Gethsemani	**1941, May 24:** born in Duluth, Minn.
Dec. 10: enters Gethsemani as a postulant	
1943, April 17: Paul Merton dies in plane crash	
1948, July: *Seven Storey Mountain* published	
Aug. 4: Dom Frederic dies	
Late Aug.: Dom James Fox becomes abbot	
1952: makes St. Anne's a temporary hermitage	
1955: *No Man Is an Island* published	**1955:** purchases first guitar
1956, July: meets with Dr. Gregory Zilboorg	
1958, March 18: has epiphany on streets of Louisville and begins writing on more social issues	
	1959, Jan. 31: sees Buddy Holly in concert
	spring: graduates from Hibbing High School
	Dec.: plays with Bobby Vee's band
1960: construction of hermitage begins	**1960:** drops out of U of Minnesota; performs in local coffeehouses
Spring: *Wisdom of the Desert* published	
	1961, Jan.: arrives in New York as a folksinger
	Nov. 4: performs at Carnegie Chapter Hall
1962, April: antiwar writings censured	**1962, March 19:** debut album, *Bob Dylan,* released
1963, April 11: Pope John XXIII issues *Pacem in Terris*	**1963, May 27:** *Freewheelin' Bob Dylan* released
	July: performs at Newport Folk Festival
	1964, Jan. 13: *The Times They Are A-Changin'* released
	March 10: Johnny Cash defends Dylan in *Sing Out!*
	Aug. 8: *Another Side of Bob Dylan* released
	Aug. 28: meets the Beatles in New York
1965, Aug. 20: moves to the hermitage	**1965, March 22:** *Bringing It All Back Home* released
	April–May: acoustic concert tour of England
	May 12: records with John Mayall's Bluesbreakers
	June 16: records "Like a Rolling Stone"
	July: purchases Hi Lo Ha
	July 25: plays "electric" set at Newport Folk Festival
	Aug. 29: Forest Hills concert
	Aug. 30: *Highway 61 Revisited* released
	Nov.: secretly marries Sara Lownds

A New Man

Imagine for a moment that you are a monk at the Trappist monastery of Our Lady of Gethsemani in 1941. Your daily routine would look something like this:

You rise at two in the morning.

Before your first meal—four hours from now—you go to the chapel to chant Matins and Lauds and to hear a homily. After spending time in meditation, you chant the Night Office, pray, chant Prime, and attend a general meeting of the community.

At 6:00 a.m., as the refectory windows brighten with the rising sun, you eat a small breakfast, called a *frustulum* ("snack"), after which you read, pray, attend Mass, work, pray some more, and attend None.

At 11:30 a.m., assuming you aren't fasting, you begin your midday dinner, the main meal of the day, during which you sit silently while the lector reads passages aloud from the Bible or other approved readings. Afterward, in summer, you lie down for *meridienne*, a short nap.

You spend the afternoon reading, praying, working, attending Mass, and chanting the remaining offices.

You speak little so as to preserve the meditative atmosphere, limiting yourself to necessary communications with your superiors and those you work with in the barns and fields. Otherwise, you use the traditional monastic sign language for basic communication.[1]

You have no supper. Before going to bed at 7:00 p.m., you examine your conscience, reflect on your sins, and pray one last time.[2]

• • •

Most people, even the most devout, would find such a regimen stifling. For Thomas Merton, it promised to be nothing short of liberating. It offered everything he had hungered for since first dreaming of becoming a monk: discipline, solitude, and an ambiance of perpetual devotion. When he first visited the abbey for a Holy Week retreat in April 1941, he repeatedly described the place as "paradise."[3]

At the time, the twenty-six-year-old Merton was teaching English at St. Bonaventure University in upstate New York. Since joining the Roman Catholic Church three years earlier, he found himself increasingly intrigued by the idea of becoming "a religious," a monastic, a monk. It was such an ancient, almost alien idea, that it seemed the perfect vocation for a man entirely at odds with, as well as wholly immersed in, the modern world—a man who adored church Latin and Thomas Aquinas every bit as much as he loved Duke Ellington and French existentialism.

He had applied to the Franciscans, renowned for their charitable works, but was rejected when he admitted that he had gotten a woman pregnant a few years earlier. It was all for the best, he thought, since the Franciscans seemed somewhat undisciplined; despite their vow of poverty, their lifestyle smacked of luxury—they were, after all, allowed to have radios.[4]

Merton then wrote to Dom Frederic Dunne, the abbot of the Trappist monastery of Our Lady of Gethsemani in rural Kentucky, and asked if he might visit. Dunne was delighted, and the retreat was scheduled for Easter week 1941.[5]

In preparation, Merton trolled through the stacks in the campus library for as much information about monastic orders as he could find. He was attracted to the Carthusians and the Trappists, both of whom placed a high value on silence and contemplation. But his imagination was particularly fired by the photographs he found in *The Catholic Encyclopedia* of the rugged mountain-cave hermitages of the Camaldolese monks of central Italy. "What I saw on those pages," he wrote, "pierced me to the heart like a knife. . . . There were still men on this miserable, noisy, cruel earth, who tasted the marvelous joy of silence and solitude. . . . In an instant, the desire of those solitudes was wide open within me like a wound."[6] He had to slam the book shut, so fiercely did he covet that life.

But Italy was out of the question. Europe, then in the second year of a catastrophic war, was increasingly under the heel of the Nazis, and Italy had aligned itself with Germany. Fascists were on the march, leaving the Camaldolese most certainly in a "miserable, noisy, cruel" place. Nor was the situation much better for the Carthusians. Their central abbey, just north of Grenoble, was in Vichy France. (A year later, in 1942, Italian forces took control of the area until the Germans occupied it in 1943.) Other Carthusian abbeys in the region were either inaccessible because of the war or on the verge of being engulfed by it, and no Carthusian monasteries yet existed in the United States. It was not a good time to become a monk in Europe. For Merton, the Trappists emerged by default.

The Trappists, a seventeenth-century subgroup of the Cistercian Order, owned several monasteries throughout the Western Hemisphere. Like the Camaldolese and the Carthusians, they promised the rigorous kind of spiritual discipline and contemplative silence that appealed to Merton. Unlike the Carthusians, who had devised their own rule, the Trappists followed the more formalized Rule of Saint Benedict, written in the sixth century, which mandates, among other things, poverty; daily routines of prayer, confession, and worship; a strict obedience to one's superiors; and stability, that is, remaining committed to the community. The Rule also provides detailed instructions on how monks should live day-to-day. Contrary to popular misconception, the Trappists do not require a "vow of silence," though the Rule does urge monks to esteem "a spirit of silence."[7] What is called "necessary conversation" is allowed. Otherwise, the Trappists zealously maintain a hushed, meditative atmosphere.

• • •

As a young musician might dream of taking center stage at Carnegie Hall, Thomas Merton pictured himself as a monk, and not just any monk, but a solitary hermit like the Camaldolese. Living as they did in those in rustic caves, they were a contemporary echo of the earliest eremites, like Anthony the Great and his companions, who, seventeen centuries earlier, sought God in the Egyptian desert. They, in turn, emulated John the Baptist and Christ himself, who went alone to the desert to fast and pray.

Why did the desert hold such allure for Merton? In a sense, the metaphorical desert had always been his home.

He came into the world without a country. Born in France to an American mother and a New Zealander father, he was brought to the United States as an infant. (He was a French citizen for most of his life, only applying for US citizenship a decade before his death, although he later considered renouncing that citizenship because of the US's involvement in Vietnam.) After his mother died of stomach cancer when he was six, he accompanied his artist father to Bermuda. At age eleven, after more displacements, he was sent to a French boarding school, where he learned to cope with his loneliness by writing, daydreaming, and poking around the old churches in the area. It was a turning point. Writing, which began as an escape from solitude, became the valued product of it. Solitude was something to be sought.

When Merton was sixteen, his father died of a brain tumor, making orphans of him and his younger brother, Paul. At eighteen, Merton attended classes at Clare College, Cambridge, where he spent the next two years in a whirl of pub-hopping, womanizing, and, as if to keep things from falling apart, writing.

Determined to make something of himself, he returned to America to study at Columbia University. As at Cambridge, he again found himself among genial peers, only these students were destined to become some of the leading intellectuals of their generation. He was classmates with Robert Giroux, who became a renowned editor and Merton's publisher; Ad Reinhardt, who became a leading abstract painter; Herman Wouk, the Pulitzer Prize–winning novelist; poet John Berryman, also a Pulitzer winner; and poet Robert Lax, who remained a lifelong friend. Merton's primary mentor at Columbia was famed professor and award-winning poet Mark

Van Doren, an intellectual of a fairly radical stripe and a spiritual bent, who later influenced such students as Allen Ginsberg and Jack Kerouac.

At Columbia, Merton developed an interest in religion and wrote his thesis on nature and art in William Blake, a study of the theological aspects of the visionary's work. Unbeknown to many of his friends, Merton joined the Catholic Church in November 1938 at age twenty-three and soon entertained the idea of becoming a monk. After running into him three years later, Robert Giroux was "stunned. . . . I had had no idea that Merton had undergone a religious conversion or that he was interested in Monasticism."[8]

• • •

No monk, least of all Thomas Merton, perceives of monastic solitude as an easy life. The desert, whether literal or metaphorical, is no place to retire. It is a demanding place, where life is lived at the sharpest possible point of awareness, where the true self, which lives in Christ, stands alone and naked before God. It is where life is lived most fully and consciously. In this way the hermit offers a living alternative to the chaos of society. As Merton later wrote,

> The Desert Fathers did, in fact, meet the "problems of their time" in the sense that *they* were among the few who were ahead of their time, and opened the way for the development of a new man and a new society. . . . [Those] hermits who left the world as though escaping from a wreck, did not merely intend to save themselves. They knew that they were helpless to do any good for others as long as they floundered about in the wreckage. But once they got a foothold on solid ground, things were different. Then they had not only the power but even the obligation to pull the whole world to safety after them.[9]

The desert is where Saint Anthony, according to his ancient biographer, Athanasius, fought throngs of demons, served the other solitaries, dispensed wisdom, and thereby became the founder of Western monasticism. The desert is where Jesus encountered Satan and resisted the temptations of bread and security and earthly power, a sojourn that immediately preceded his three-year ministry of preaching and healing as recorded in the Gospels. Moses too went to the "inner parts of the desert" to find an endlessly burning bush that spoke his name and commanded him to lead the Israelites out of Egypt—an act that altered the course of history.[10] By going to the desert, Anthony and Jesus and Moses did indeed "pull the whole world to safety after them."

Merton's Holy Week retreat opened a new world. On April 7, the day after his arrival at the abbey, he wrote in his journal, with some creative hyperbole:

> I should tear out all the other pages of this book and all the other pages of everything else I ever wrote, and begin here.
>
> This [monastery] is the center of America. I had wondered what was holding this country together, what has been keeping the universe from cracking in pieces and falling apart. It is this monastery. . . .
>
> This is the only real city in America—in a desert.
>
> It is the axle around which the whole country blindly turns.[11]

• • •

The following fall, Merton contemplated leaving his teaching position to work with Catherine de Hueck Doherty, the Catholic social worker who had founded Friendship House in Harlem four years earlier. Friendship House was an interracial community, established to promote social justice and civil rights. After growing up as a wealthy Russian baroness, Doherty received what she felt was a powerful religious calling and in 1932 sold her possessions to finance her charity work. She gave a lecture at St. Bonaventure in the fall of 1941, and her forceful personality and engaging zeal so appealed to Merton that he volunteered "a couple of weeks of evenings"[12] at Friendship House. Doherty urged him to join her.

And so Merton faced a choice. Would he work in Harlem among those marginalized by society or seek solitude as a monk? Overshadowing his decision was the fact that President Roosevelt had recently reinstated conscription. Although the country had not yet been pulled into the war, every male between the ages of twenty-one and forty-five was required to register for the draft. In March, one month before his Easter retreat, Merton, who had a low draft-lottery number, had gone for his army physical, and so certain was he of being drafted that he pondered his reply should an overbearing sergeant catch him writing and ask, "What do you think you're doing?"[13]

Throughout the summer and fall, conscription remained a real if somewhat distant possibility. All that changed on December 7. The Japanese bombed Pearl Harbor, and the time for escaping the wreckage had come.

Three days after the attack, Thomas Merton was on the bus to Kentucky. He would become a Trappist.

• • •

Merton later described this bus ride as "the last lap of my journey into the desert."[14] Although Gethsemani was in a remote part of the state, he would eventually discover that the monastery was still a long way from the desert. When he had written in his journal that Gethsemani was "the only real city in America—in a desert," he could not have foreseen the disappointment to come.

Seventeen years later, in preparing portions of that same journal for publication, he changed the phrase "in a desert" to "in the wilderness."[15] Perhaps he was clarifying that he was referring to a generalized wilderness, like Kentucky, much of which was still untouched by urban America. But another possibility is that the desert he had anticipated at Gethsemani—"the axle around which the country blindly turns"—turned out to be a mirage. The word *desert* implies something more sacred, more fundamental than *wilderness*. The *desert* was the holy ground where one could confront one's most painful yearnings for union with God, where one could show the world "a new man and a new society." By trading *desert* for *wilderness*, Merton was hinting that the abbey, while a quiet, spiritual place surrounded by rustic natural beauty, didn't offer the kind of parched, holy solitude he longed for.

On December 13, three days after arriving at Gethsemani, he wrote a farewell poem to his friends in New York, and again he uses the desert image to portray his new life:

> More than we fear, we love the holy desert
> Where separate strangers, hid in their disguise,
> Have come to meet by night the quiet Christ.[16]

These lines anticipate the tension Merton would live with for the next two decades. The desert is a holy place where Christ is encountered, but Merton sensed that those around him were strangers, hidden and disguised. In his journals, he would later rage on occasion against the "fictions and pretenses, all the façade and latent hypocrisy of the monastic community."[17] While the monastery might foreshadow the gathering of the faithful in heaven and was, in that sense, paradise, it wasn't the desert, the place where the soul takes upon itself the existential loneliness of Christ. Merton had hoped for both paradise and the desert. He found mainly the former.

Nor was this the kind of paradise that could protect him from the wreckage of war.

Manuscript Accepted

On April 17, 1943, the day before Palm Sunday, Merton's only sibling, Paul, an airman in the Royal Canadian Air Force, died in a plane crash over the English Channel. The previous summer, Paul had visited Gethsemani and expressed a desire to become a Catholic, and so he was baptized in a local church. It was the last time the two brothers saw each other. In a poem dedicated to Paul, Merton wrote, "In the wreckage of your April Christ lies slain, / And Christ weeps in the ruins of my spring."[1]

With the last of his immediate family gone, Merton, who now went by his monastic name, Brother Louis, dedicated himself to his vocation with renewed abandon. Like all monks, he began his time at the monastery as a postulant. After a few years, postulants become novices and then, upon taking solemn vows, become full-fledged members of the community. Merton knew that not all postulants make it that far, and he was determined to maintain the momentum that had propelled him through the front gates. He focused on his responsibilities to God and the abbey's superiors and threw himself into learning as much as he could about the order. He settled into daily routine, hoping that his uneasiness with the place would dissipate.

To a certain extent it did. All able-bodied monks were required to work, though Merton, by a special dispensation from the abbot, Dom Frederic Dunne, was encouraged to write for an hour or two each day, often while the other monks attended to the abbey's cheese, fudge, and fruitcake production and care of livestock. Some within the order resented Dunne's decision. The Rule of Saint Benedict clearly states that an abbot should "make no distinction of persons in the monastery. Let him not love one more than another."[2] Some also assumed that the kind of conversation discouraged by the Rule included such public conversation as writing and publishing. Merton's editor, Robert Giroux, later wrote that "Merton received hate-mail denouncing him as a 'talking Trappist.'"[3] A monk is expected to speak little and practice simplicity, humility, and inner tranquility—qualities not often associated with highly creative people.

But like all monasteries, the abbey had to support itself, and Father Dunne saw promise in the talented postulant; the arrangement might prove mutually beneficial. While the writing might bring in a small income for the abbey, it might also distract Merton from the disappointments that lurked in its shadows. So, during those early years at Gethsemani he continued to write poetry and completed two hagiographies on behalf of the order, one about an early twentieth-century Trappistine and the other about a medieval Cistercian nun. Merton disliked both books intensely. "Where did I get all that pious rhetoric?" he asked.[4]

The arrangement also gave him time to compose the first draft of a lengthy book about his own life, something the abbot not only encouraged but instructed him to do. As the writing progressed, Merton contacted an old friend from college, Naomi Burton Stone, who had been his literary agent back in his pre-Trappist days when he was writing fiction and poetry. When he entered the monastery, she had assumed his literary life was over, but when approached anew, she was delighted to renew the partnership. It was a simple matter for her to contact their mutual friend from Columbia, Robert Giroux, who was now an acquiring editor at Harcourt, Brace and Company.

But Merton couldn't completely distract himself with his writing. How often he second-guessed his vocation as a Trappist in his first five years at Gethsemani is unknown because he destroyed his journals from that time. The first mention he makes of his continuing disappointment occurs only days after he resumed his journal in December 1946. Just after Christmas, he told his confessor that his greatest desire was to leave Gethsemani and become a Carthusian, an order that encouraged, even compelled, its monks to become solitaries. The confessor responded, not unkindly, that Merton was "full of self-love and only some very extraordinary upheaval . . . would justify [Merton's] leaving." Furthermore, he advised Merton to treat it like any other "unordered appetite"—that is, try not to be too upset about it.[5]

That same day, coincidentally, during the midday meal, a telegram arrived from Stone. Dreading that it would bring the news that his manuscript had been rejected, Merton waited until later that afternoon to open it.

It read, "Manuscript accepted. Happy New Year."[6]

• • •

In 1947 Thomas Merton was an obscure monk living in an obscure monastery in rural Kentucky. Although he had already published four books—two volumes of poetry and two religious biographies, they were all issued in small print runs with little fanfare. This new book was a major project for a leading publisher, and it contained Merton's most personal writing yet.

The year was taken up with waiting, editing galleys, working on more books, and wrestling with church censors. One censor suggested that Merton was "not yet capable of writing such a book" and recommended instead that he "take a correspondence course in grammar." More to the point, wrote Merton, "he also objected to my frankness about my past."[7] Merton, like Saint Augustine in the fourth century, had had affairs with women and, also like Augustine, had fathered a child.[8] Still, Augustine's *Confessions* did not have to defer to a review board to receive imprimatur.[9] This would not be Merton's last run-in with censorship.

Apart from such distractions, he spent much of that year daydreaming about the Carthusians. Even something as simple as a chest cold inflamed his desire. On March 19, 1947, after spending part of the day sick in bed, he wrote:

> All afternoon I sat on the bed rediscovering the meaning of contemplation, rediscovering God, rediscovering myself. . . .
>
> It has been one of the most wonderful days I have ever known in my life. . . . I know this is the way I ought to be *living*: with my mind and sense silent. . . .
>
> Once again the question arises: is it possible to be quiet in an atmosphere like the one in this house? Should I move somewhere where I can find solitude and silence and peace to be alone with God in this pure tranquility that is impossible for a Cistercian? . . .
>
> God is hidden within me. I find Him by hiding in the silence in which He is concealed. . . .
>
> I go to say Matins of Our Lady of Sorrows.[10]

• • •

Merton had not yet been ordained a priest. That wouldn't happen until two years later, in May of 1949. For now he was living as a novice under solemn vows. In the usual order of things, a postulant enters the monastery under what are called "simple vows," a testing period and time of discernment. After five or six years, if the postulant proves worthy and capable of enduring the rigors of monastic life, the order invites him to become a novice under "solemn vows." Merton took his in March 1947. Solemn vows are more binding than simple vows. Some scholars of canon law argue that not even the pope can undo them. Some assert that if a monk leaves the order and abandons his vow of chastity, for instance, no subsequent marriage can ever be recognized by the church—a rule that would become more relevant to Merton two decades later, in the summer of 1966.

Merton's solemn vows were a way for the monastery to strengthen its authority over him, to reassure itself of his commitment, his stability. It was also Merton's way of convincing himself that the Trappist order, not the Carthusian, was God's will after all.

But such resolutions proved difficult. In August of that year, Merton discovered that a Benedictine monk who had conducted a workshop at the abbey two years earlier had been allowed to leave his order to go to Spain—to become a Carthusian. Merton commented, "The dog!"[11] But when one of the novices at Gethsemani left for England against his superiors' wishes, hoping to be accepted by a Carthusian abbey there, Merton's reaction was not so whimsical. "It is like having something stuck into my heart,"[12] he wrote. For the next couple of weeks, he prayed for God's will, vacillating between staying at Gethsemani and becoming a solitary elsewhere.

Then another thought occurred. Perhaps there was another solution. By late October 1947, Merton had grown curious about one particular aspect of Trappist life. Although the order had occasionally sanctioned solitaries in previous centuries, were modern Trappists ever allowed to live alone outside the walls? He had recently heard about a monk named Dom Alexis Presse, who lived as a hermit in France, but only after leaving the Cistercian order entirely. Dom Alexis had been assigned the task of repairing portions of a ruined monastery in Brittany, apparently single-handedly. The French government contributed a million francs to the quixotic project, reminiscent of Saint Francis's rebuilding of the San Damiano Chapel.

Masking the fact that the idea of being a church-refurbishing hermit actually intrigued him, Merton wrote in his journal, "I am not attracted to it, . . . a rigid imitation of the twelfth century." But the idea of living as a solitary haunted him. In that same entry, he pushed away the possibility by asserting that he had no desire other than to continue his present life as a monk, uniting himself "to God's will for here and now, and here and now it is Gethsemani and all that goes with it."[13] By stating and restating "here and now," he inserted a loophole; it was his way of saying, "Not now, but someday."

So Merton asked Dom Frederic directly: Did Cistercians have to leave the order to live as hermits, or could they remain in the order and live alone outside the walls? Dom Frederic, in his genial way, informed him that the Cistercians could indeed live as hermits, and he proceeded to give Merton several examples—all of them discouraging. One Cistercian, said the abbot, had no sooner settled into his hermitage than he came to be regarded by the locals as a holy man and was besieged by people seeking advice. He had to return to the monastery to find peace. Another Trappist in a certain

Southern state had become a hermit but soon "sheepishly" returned to the abbey "shaved."[14] Though Merton was unsure what "shaved" meant, he conjectured that it might have come about as the result of a run-in with the local hillbillies; Catholicism was still an alien sect in parts of the South. In another story, a hermit in Oklahoma returned to his abbey one day and proceeded to enlighten the abbot about how to better manage the place. The abbot quietly instructed another monk to go out into the woods and burn the proud hermit's hut to the ground. The hermit was forced to return to the abbey and, as far as Merton knew, practiced a self-imposed vow of silence by never speaking to the abbot again.

By December, Merton was understandably dejected. He decided that his urge to become a hermit was a "self-deception" and a sign of disobedience. "I have come to give too large a place to my own desires."[15] Nevertheless, he resolved to take renewed advantage of the limited solitude his life at Gethsemani afforded him. And to keep writing.

He had no idea that in a year and a half he would have an experience that would shape his life every bit as dramatically as the publication of his first best-selling book. On June 26, 1949, as Merton described the event, "I went to Reverend Father and we were talking about solitude, and quite by surprise, he gave me permission to go out of the enclosure into the woods by myself."[16]

A day outside the walls—it was a small thing, but it was life-changing. It was the first time Merton had been allowed outside the monastery alone since arriving at Gethsemani seven and a half years earlier. So excited was Merton by the prospect of this walk in the woods that he dreamed about it during *meridienne*—his midday siesta. The dream was confused and anxiety producing, which made his glee more intense when he awoke with the prospect of an afternoon's freedom before him. And "it was nothing at all like the dream."[17]

He set out. First he climbed a nearby hill to contemplate the abbey from afar—a much-needed perspective. Suddenly and unexpectedly, it seemed beautiful to him from that distance. "It made much more sense in its surroundings."[18]

The day was overcast, threatening a storm. Thunder rumbled in the west. As the wind grew gustier, he trekked across the open fields and tramped over the wooded hills and down into ravines. He knew he'd have to return as soon as the rain blew in, but as he continued to skirt the knobs and pastures, he felt the Spirit of God calling him deeper into the woods. Though he knew the danger and used to be terrified by storms, Merton now felt fearless. "As soon as I get away from people the Presence of God invades me." Seldom had he felt so happy, with "the sweet scent of the woods—the clean stream, the peace, the inviolate solitude."[19]

He pondered. A retreat center might be built on one of these hills someday, a place that could serve as a hermitage. It was a pipe dream, but a formative one. As if by a divine dispensation, the rain held off until Merton returned to the abbey for Vespers.

For one afternoon, he stood on the mountain and saw the desert spread out before him, as if God were saying to him, as he had once said to Moses, "This is the land. . . . Thou hast seen it with thine eyes."[20]

The Call to Solitude

On July 7, 1948, fame found Thomas Merton.

When an advance copy of *The Seven Storey Mountain* arrived at the abbey that day, Abbot Frederic Dunne immediately sought out its author. "I shall never forget," wrote Merton, "the simplicity and affection with which he put the first copy of the book in my hand."[1]

Even before the book was in general distribution, two book clubs and a Catholic foundation had agreed to carry it, which led the publisher to add twenty thousand copies to the original print run of seven thousand. Although the *New York Times* declined to list "religious books" on its best-seller list,[2] indicators agree that Merton's was among the five best-selling books of that year. It sold six hundred thousand copies in the first twelve months and over a million before going to softcover in 1952. It was the third most popular nonfiction book to top the best-seller lists of 1949, and the only one of those three still in print.

In this age of confessional blogs and crisp three-act memoirs, the success of Merton's spiritual autobiography is mystifying. It is reflective and chatty by turns, philosophical, self-indulgent, full of arcane references, and sometimes rambling. Although a third of it had been scissored by the punctilious church censors, it still ran to more than four hundred tightly set pages. Since Merton was unknown, without what modern publishers call "a platform," its success took even its editor, Robert Giroux, by surprise.

But times were different then, especially for the generation of young people returning from the cataclysm of the Second World War and seeking spiritual answers. "Young men and women," Garry Wills wrote of that time, "were flocking to the seminaries and convents to become priests and nuns. The number of Catholic converts surged."[3] Merton's book struck them like a lightning bolt. That was the year that Lloyd C. Douglas's biblical novel *The Big Fisherman* topped the *New York Times* best-seller list (the *Times* didn't object to religious fiction), and Cecil B. DeMille's *Samson and Delilah* was the top-grossing film, which began the craze for biblical epics. The World Council of Churches was founded, and Billy Graham was in the second year of his first evangelistic crusade. The big questions of life and faith were in the air.

The war inspired not only spiritual hunger but philosophical angst as well. Existentialism was in the ascendant. It was the age of Sartre's *Being and Nothingness*, Camus's *The Plague*, Miller's *Death of a Salesman*, and Tillich's *The Courage to Be*. Willa and Edwin Muir's translations of Franz Kafka were finding a wide audience; sculptor Alberto Giacometti was then crafting his spindly figures; and painter Jackson Pollock was at the height of his "drip period."

For Merton and many other intellectuals after the war, the metaphorical desert—the urge to separate oneself from society, from the insanity of the world—seemed an entirely rational place to dwell, a philosophical space chosen as both a rejection of society's lethal excesses and a way of showing humanity a better path forward. In the twentieth century, the desert was the only place where the religious thinker could find common ground with the existentialist, where the Christian and the atheist alike could contemplate an alternative to global annihilation.

For Merton the intellectual desert was epitomized, as always, by the Desert Fathers, who, he wrote, "were in a certain sense 'anarchists,' . . . men who did not believe in letting themselves be passively guided and ruled by a decadent state, and who believed that there was a way of getting along without slavish dependence on accepted, conventional values. The Desert Fathers declined to be ruled by men."[4]

People of earlier eras, the Georgians and the Victorians, didn't appreciate the desert in that way. Theirs were ages of optimism and progress and respectability. Hermits were seen as aberrations. Historian Edward Gibbon held a low view of the early desert monks, stating that they "were inspired by the savage enthusiasm which represents man as a criminal, and God as a tyrant."[5] Victorian writer William E. H. Lecky described the average desert ascetic as "a hideous, sordid, and emaciated maniac, without knowledge, without patriotism, without natural affection, passing his life in a long routine of useless and atrocious self-torture, and quailing before the ghastly phantoms of his delirious brain."[6] Such dismissive views, Merton felt, "degraded and corrupted the psychological heritage of . . . the Desert Fathers and other contemplatives, and prepared the way for the great regression to the herd mentality that is taking place now."[7]

But after the devastation of two world wars, many thoughtful people, religious and otherwise, had valid reasons to think that man was indeed a criminal and God a tyrant. No ghastly phantoms of a delirious brain could be any more haunting or terrible than what had transpired in the Nazi labor camps, in the obliterated cities of Japan, and all across Stalin's and Mao's communist dystopias. How could the monastic life—the desert life—*not* seem perfectly rational?

• • •

As the first printing of *The Seven Storey Mountain* was being shipped to bookstores around the country, Merton suffered a significant personal loss. Dom Frederic Dunne, his beloved abbot, died on August 4, 1948. Merton reflected, "The house is sad. . . . His sympathy was deep and real all the time he was alive. I don't know who was ever kinder to me. . . . I keep contact with God by the touch of a sort of interior hollowness and that counts as my prayer for Reverend Father and for this house."[8] The abbot represented the old, traditional Catholic Church, and Merton admired him.

In a sense, Dom Frederic invented Thomas Merton. Not only had he welcomed Merton into the monastery, but he had also bent the rules—Saint Benedict's, no less—so that Merton could write. Regarding *The Seven Storey Mountain*, Merton acknowledged that Dom Frederic "was in a certain sense even more responsible for that book than I was, even as he was the cause of all my other writing."[9]

Three weeks later, a new abbot, Father James Fox, was installed after an abbatial election. Fox had been a monk at Gethsemani when Merton first arrived in 1941, but he left in 1944 to help found the abbey of Our Lady of the Holy Ghost, near Conyers, Georgia. Within two years, Fox had been named abbot there, but now he was returning to Gethsemani. With a deliberate double meaning, Merton described him as "the Holy Ghost's candidate . . . quiet and humble,"[10] though it would be only a matter of time before Merton modified his assessment.

The morning after the election, a small exchange took place that would typify their relationship. Merton had just received a royalty check for nine hundred dollars. Since all his earnings were the property of the monastery, he promptly turned the money over to Dom James. In this gesture, Merton took pride in his accomplishment while demonstrating his dutifulness toward his superiors. Dom James simply responded, "Go on writing."[11]

Within a few more weeks Merton was able to take further measures of the man. He felt a certain foreboding, for instance, when Dom James returned from a trip to Europe, bearing for the abbey's scriptorium a book that Merton described as "flossy."[12] It was a deluxe coffee-table book about the Trappist abbey of Orval in southern Belgium, which Dom James had visited. The abbey's main product was then, as it remains today, its world-renowned Orval beer, or *Bière Trappist—Trappistenbier*, as its logo says in French and German, making Orval among the wealthiest and most modern abbeys in the world.

This slick volume served as a stark contrast to Dom Frederic's love for old books and old things in general. The late abbot had spent many hours in the same scriptorium personally rebinding some of the abbey's most fragile folios. He had a small hand press and cases of lead type brought in for small printing and repair projects.

As Merton fanned through the photos of Orval, he thought its sacristy looked "like the circular bar on the Promenade Deck of the *Conte De Savoia* [a cruise ship] which is probably long since at the bottom of the ocean. . . .

It is not . . . the conception that is out of place, but the scale on which it is done. The monks have to polish floors all day and all night." He concluded, oxymoronically, "I wouldn't be seen dead living in such a place."[13]

• • •

Where he lived continued to be much on Merton's mind. Fame had only intensified his desperation to find solitude, for with the publication of his autobiography, he had become a sought-after celebrity, an institutional commodity. While the book was not a revenue producer on the scale of Orval beer, he was still providing a supplement to Gethsemani's cheese and fruitcake production. And as his writing reached more readers, people at the abbey and far beyond were increasingly invested in his success.

By the following summer, a pattern had developed in his relationship with Dom James, a pattern typified by the visit of Dom Dominique Nogues, the abbot general of the worldwide Cistercian Order. When the abbot general learned that Merton was working on a book about Bernard of Clairvaux, an early Cistercian, he delightedly invited Merton to Rome to do research, and he offered Merton accommodations at his own headquarters, promising "a great deal of time . . . and peace and solitude and what not." When Merton approached Dom James about the possibility, the abbot flatly refused, offering the weak argument that "there is nothing so distracting as new scenery."

When the abbot general himself made an attempt, Dom James's answer was, "If I let [Merton] go to Rome, he will never come back,"[14] and furthermore, he said, once allowed out of Gethsemani, Merton would most certainly become a Carthusian. Dom James was right, and Merton knew it. Merton's only consolation was to convince himself that Rome might, in fact, be distracting; even Dom Dominique had said the traffic noise could be unnerving.[15] The abbot's goal was to keep Merton at Gethsemani, in obedience to his vows, and writing.

In 1952, as a concession, Dom James gave Merton permission to have an occasional prayer time in the woods, in an old shed used for tools and firewood. No doubt Dom James thought that since it was already September, a few months of cold afternoons in an unheated shack would most likely dampen—or rather chill—the dreamy monk's spirits. It's hard to focus on prayer when one's teeth are chattering. But Merton adored the place, which he dubbed the hermitage of "St. Anne's." After a couple of weeks of prayer in the shed, he wrote:

> Out here in the woods I can think of nothing except God and it is not so much that I think of Him either. I am as aware of Him as of the sun and the clouds and the blue sky and the thin cedar trees. . . .
>
> As long as I am out here I cannot think of Camaldoli either; no question of being here and dreaming of somewhere else. Engulfed in the simple and lucid actuality which is the afternoon: I mean God's afternoon, this sacramental moment of time when the shadows will get longer and longer, and one small bird sings quietly in the cedars, and one car goes by in the remote distance and the oak leaves move in the wind.
>
> High up in the late Summer sky I watch the silent flight of a vulture, and the day goes by in prayer. This solitude confirms my call to solitude. The more I am in it, the more I love it. One day it will possess me entirely and no man will ever see me again.[16]

Two winters later, he was still relishing the hours spent there. "Here at St. Anne's," he wrote, "I am always happy and at peace no matter what happens. For here there is no need for anyone but God."[17]

• • •

In the meantime, Merton kept writing. In the years immediately following the publication of *The Seven Storey Mountain*, he wrote in quick succession *The Waters of Siloe* (1949), *Seeds of Contemplation* (1949), *The Tears of the Blind Lion* (poetry, 1949), *The Ascent to Truth* (1951), *The Sign of Jonas* (1953), *Bread in the Wilderness* (1953), *The Last of the Fathers* (1954), and *No Man Is an Island* (1955), his next most popular success. No less a spiritual writer than Cambridge don C. S. Lewis declared *No Man Is an Island* to be "the best new spiritual reading I've met for a long time."[18]

It was an impressive run of creativity—and revenue. Not only was the abbey able to expand its operations and even donate money to other monasteries, but the Catholic Church discovered it had a vibrant public personality in its midst—a true intellectual and a compassionate face for a church that before the war had been perceived as stodgy and conservative more often than not.

Merton stood in sharp contrast to radio personality Father Charles E. Coughlin, once a prominent media spokesperson for the Catholic Church and now considered the father of modern political, inflammatory talk radio. Tens of millions of listeners tuned in to his weekly *Hour of Power* program in the 1930s—until Coughlin's Nazi-touting, anti-Semitic tirades led to his ouster from the airwaves in 1939, after which he returned to his position as a parish priest and to relative obscurity.

Even before Merton's left-leaning political writings of the sixties, he routinely faced opposition from old-school Catholics. Many inside the church objected to his seemingly privileged status in the monastery, and some would come to feel that his theological views were heretical.

So intense did the pressure of celebrity become that in 1955, Merton again asked to leave Gethsemani—to leave the country, in fact. He requested permission to go to the monastery at Camaldoli, to Italy itself, to become one of the cave-dwelling monks he saw in the photos at the St. Bonaventure library thirteen years earlier. St. Anne's had convinced him that God was calling him to complete solitude.

His request was denied.

Again he accepted it as God's will, and in that same year, perhaps to occupy Merton's mind in some more productive way, Dom James appointed him master of novices, the teacher for the new monks.

• • •

The following summer of 1956, Merton was working on an article called "Neurosis in the Monastic Life." Having long been interested in psychiatry, he was fascinated by what motivates men to seek the same spiritual disciplines that he had sought, and his piece was a perceptive overview of the sometimes misguided reasons men are attracted to monasticism. Merton drew heavily upon the work of psychiatrists who were, at that time, cutting-edge writers in the field of psychoanalysis, people like Karen Horney and Erich Fromm, both of whom were working to move psychology beyond the more astringent dogmatism of the old-school Freudians. Fromm, with whom Merton corresponded, was a friend and intellectual sparring partner.

Merton sent a copy of his draft to Giroux, who suggested that one of Harcourt's current authors, renowned psychiatrist Dr. Gregory Zilboorg, might also be interested in the piece. A year earlier, Giroux had helped to publish Zilboorg's book *The Psychology of the Criminal Act and Punishment*, which received mixed reviews. One reviewer said it "contributes more misunderstanding than improvement to the relations of law and psychiatry."[19] If Giroux could have foreseen that he too was about to cause "more misunderstanding than improvement," he would have thought twice about forwarding the article.

Zilboorg was a Catholic convert and already interested in Merton. The idea of having the monk travel to New York for a private psychiatric consultation was bandied about, but Dom James predictably nixed the idea. As an alternative, Zilboorg arranged for Merton to attend a psychology conference at St. John's University, a Catholic school in Collegeville, Minnesota, at which the doctor was to be a featured speaker. It would be Merton's most extended trip outside the monastery to date, and he was excited by the prospect of consulting with a famous psychoanalyst about his writing and, if the opportunity should arise, about his "troubles," as Merton called his longings to leave the monastery and find greater solitude.[20]

Gregory Zilboorg was born of Jewish parents in Kiev, studied medicine in Saint Petersburg, and, to escape the fallout of the Russian Revolution, came to the United States in 1919 at the age of twenty-eight. Within two decades, he became a high-priced psychotherapist for the stars—or at least for many prominent Broadway notables and New York's left-leaning elite. His patients included playwrights Lillian Hellman, who spent seven years in therapy with Zilboorg, and Moss Hart, who is thought to have based his 1941 musical *Lady in the Dark* on his sessions with the eminent shrink.[21]

Zilboorg's most noted patient was George Gershwin. Once, when that famous American composer was asked how much Zilboorg charged, he quipped, "He finds out how much you make and then charges you more than you can afford!"[22] Less amusing is the evidence that Zilboorg misdiagnosed Gershwin's various symptoms—olfactory hallucinations, headaches, and dizziness—as psychosomatic. They weren't. Gershwin died of a brain tumor within a year and a half after consulting Zilboorg.[23]

Recent research suggests that Zilboorg may have misrepresented his professional credentials from the beginning, lacking the necessary coursework for his medical degree in Saint Petersburg and his psychiatric certificate in Switzerland. He may have been neither a medical doctor nor a certified psychiatrist, and at least two of his female patients later claimed that he had had sexual relationships with them.[24]

In 1956 these details were unknown to the Catholic authorities who shipped Merton off to Minnesota in hopes that the psychiatrist would be able to fix the wayward monk, to set him straight regarding his hermit problem. The authorities wanted to know: Was Merton's obsession with solitude healthy? Was it even normal? Dom James had long had suspicions regarding Merton's mental state; earlier Dom James had written to a bishop that Merton was "temperamentally unstable, too artistically volatile to be entrusted with determining his own spiritual destiny."[25]

Unbeknown to Merton, Zilboorg had already done a psychoanalytic workup based on Merton's writings alone. As unusual as it seems, it has precedent. In 1916 Freud had psychoanalyzed Leonardo da Vinci based on his artwork,[26] and Zilboorg considered himself an expert on Freud. Only five years earlier he had published a short book called *Sigmund Freud: His Exploration of the Mind of Man*. And now Zilboorg was ready to explore the mind of a monk.

Zilboorg's diagnosis was dire. Merton, he concluded, was on the verge of mental collapse. At their first meeting, he informed Merton that the proposed article on monastic neuroses was "utterly inadequate, hastily written, will do harm, . . . should be left on the shelf." When they met the following day, Merton, who was shaken but still eager to sit at the great man's feet, decided he would confide the details of his "troubles." Zilboorg's response was swift and unremitting. After admitting that he had engineered their confrontation in order to confirm his diagnosis in person, Zilboorg said, among other things, that Merton was "a gadfly to [his] superiors," was "stubborn," and on his way to becoming a "semi-psychotic quack."

Zilboorg continued, "You like to be famous, you want to be a big shot, you keep pushing your way out—to publicity—Megalomania and narcissism are your big trends." As if that weren't enough, he added, "Your hermit trend is pathological. . . . You are a promoter. If you were not in a monastery you are the type that would clean up on Wall Street one day and lose it all on the horses the next. . . . Your writing is becoming verbological."[27] If "allowed a little liberty," Zilboorg said, Merton "would probably run away with a woman."[28]

Merton was stunned. Struggling to gain perspective, he wrote, "While he said all this, I thought 'How much he looks like Stalin.'"[29] Instead of viewing it as an open-and-shut case of psychiatric projection, Merton, as was his habit, tried to glean whatever grains of truth he could from the encounter. He was already aware of his own neuroses and had long known of his narcissism, and yet, he wondered, how does such knowledge change anything? These traits didn't interfere with his day-to-day functioning. As a successful writer, a beloved teacher, an acknowledged intellectual, and a valued friend to some of the most renowned thinkers in the world, Merton seemed to be faring quite well. Still, Merton grieved over what Dom James would think if he were to learn of Zilboorg's diagnosis.

The harshest blow was the accusation of being "verbological"—wordy for the sake of being wordy, of using language artificially to impress. Merton already secretly feared that this might be true, especially in his devotional writings, which in turn forced him to reflect on the extent to which he believed what he wrote about faith, the monastic life, contemplation, and prayer. It was not a comfortable self-evaluation, and he sensed that his own confused response was yet another symptom of neurosis.

Merton was relieved when Zilboorg recommended that they not discuss their conversation with anyone, that it remain a matter of doctor-patient confidentiality. Despite their agreement, Zilboorg took it upon himself to share his insights with Giroux, the purpose being to undermine Merton in the publisher's eyes. As if that weren't enough, when Dom James arrived at St. John's near the end of the conference, Zilboorg arranged a meeting with him to go over his diagnosis. And Merton was invited.

The ambush—the betrayal of confidences—reduced Merton to heaving sobs. While Zilboorg calmly declaimed, "You want a hermitage in Times Square with a large sign over it saying 'Hermit,'" all Merton could do was groan, "Stalin! Stalin!"[30] Zilboorg—as if with a large sign of his own—confirmed Dom James's own assessment of Merton's psychological state.

In letters to friends, Merton put a positive spin on the events, declaring that Zilboorg's bracing assessment was exactly what his soul needed to set it on the right path—and to a great extent he believed that. Whatever Merton thought about the attack, which had been conspiratorially staged by a questionable doctor and the abbot, "Neurosis in the Monastic Life" did indeed remain "on the shelf."[31]

In that essay, Merton insisted that anyone exhibiting signs of neurosis should "not be treated with indifference, patronage or contempt. We have duty of charity towards others who suffer things that we ourselves may well come to suffer someday." Such people should be approached with "kindness and understanding and infinite patience."[32] A final irony is that when Zilboorg died three years later, his obituary in the *American Journal of Psychiatry* described the possibly counterfeit doctor as being "brilliant, warm, understanding, . . . kindly" and exhibiting "a ready humor"[33]—to which Merton might well have replied, ". . . like Stalin."

This Little House

The history of the church is strewn with the wreckage of those who confused God's calling with their own mental illness. Thomas Merton was not one of them. His struggle to disentangle *vocation* from *neurosis* was a persistent theme throughout his journals and other writings, though his self-doubt was in many ways imposed upon him. In the opinion of the abbot, Merton's desire for solitude was a symptom of something—instability, volatility, rebellion, or psychosis—but hardly divine inspiration. Each time the church authorities denied Merton's requests to pursue an eremitic life, Merton would relent, convincing himself that they, not he, best knew the will of God. It was, after all, their job. And each time, Merton would eventually work his way back to the conviction that he knew God's intentions for his own life better than the church did.

This cycle came to an abrupt end in March 1958. Merton had a revelation—a vision not unlike those of the medieval mystics. While walking through the crowded shopping district of downtown Louisville, he was "suddenly overwhelmed with the realization that I loved all those people, that they were mine and I theirs, that we could not be alien to one another even though we were total strangers."[1]

His reflections about that moment of enlightenment, published years later in *Conjectures of a Guilty Bystander*, are some of the most ecstatic in all his writing. So powerful was this vision in shaping who Thomas Merton became that a historical marker was later erected on the spot where the revelation had occurred—on the corner of Fourth and Walnut Streets.[2] Below the seal of the Commonwealth of Kentucky, its brass letters read, "Merton had a sudden insight at this corner Mar. 18, 1958, that led him to redefine his monastic identity with greater involvement in social justice issues."[3]

After that point, his writing did indeed turn decidedly toward social and political involvement. "It was like waking from a dream of separateness," he wrote. "We [monks] are in the same world as everybody else, the world of the bomb, the world of race hatred, the world of technology, the world of mass media, business, revolution, and all the rest."[4]

But what, Merton asked himself, is the function of solitude in a world where separateness doesn't exist? Why would God call anyone to be a hermit? He explains, "My solitude . . . is not my own, for I see now how much it belongs to them [the people on the street]—and that I have a responsibility for it in their regard, not just in my own. It is because I am one with them that I owe it to them to be alone, and when I am alone they are not 'they' but my own self. There are no strangers!"[5]

To Merton, solitude was solidarity, a way of loving the world as Scripture had commanded. "Go into the desert not to escape other men," Merton wrote, "but in order to find them in God"[6]—counterintuitive, but in keeping with his evolving thoughts about his vocation.

On March 19, the day after his epiphany, he tramped up the hill to St. Anne's to reflect on the insights of the previous day. As he watched a hawk wheel over a neighboring farm, "tracing out a circle of silence in the sky," he was struck by the "peace and sweetness" of the place. At that moment, he had another, smaller revelation. The solitude he had been so actively seeking for years was already his, in "the silence of this little house." He wrote, "How many graces, here in St. Anne's, that I did not know about, in those years when I was here all the time, when I had what I most wanted and never really knew it."[7] This is reminiscent of T. S. Eliot's lines near the end of "Little Gidding":

With the drawing of this Love and the voice of this Calling

We shall not cease from exploration
And the end of all our exploring

Will be to arrive where we started
And know the place for the first time.[8]

Merton no longer needed to waste time waiting for that Love and Calling. They were already his. The revelation showed him that "solitude alone was not exactly what I wanted." His vocation meant nothing if he did not recognize that he was "still a member of the human race."[9]

It was as if Merton was returning to the fall of 1941, when he was faced with the choice of working in the world with Catherine de Hueck Doherty at Friendship House or traveling to Kentucky to become a solitary. He had now discovered it was a false choice. Not only could he take both paths simultaneously, but neither path could be taken without the other. He was not seeking a hermitage for himself. He was seeking it to express his unity with the whole world.

• • •

A year later, in June 1959, Merton wrote, "I really owe it to [Dom James] to propose, first of all, a request to become a hermit in the woods. I like less and less the term 'hermit.' I want to live alone—not become a member of a fictitious category. But I owe it to him to ask this permission to live alone here."[10] A few days later, he "worked out a simple plan for a hermitage behind the sheep barn in the woods, but it is too silly. Only if no other way is possible will I take that one."[11]

At that time, Merton had no less than four invitations to leave Gethsemani—among them, an offer to go to an abbey in Cuernavaca, Mexico, and another to Tortola, British Virgin Islands. He also briefly considered requesting a transfer to New Mexico to work with the Pueblo people. The idea of living in an actual desert was especially tantalizing.

With so many offers, he needed to answer one basic question first: Would the church ever consent to his transferring away from Gethsemani? In September an emissary, Father Georgio, was sent to the Vatican with a personal plea from Merton.

By Christmas, he had his answer: no. While disappointed, he also felt strangely relieved. The decision was made. Staying put—stability—was the way forward.

In January 1960, during a retreat, Merton read an article about "the canonical situation of hermits," which, he wrote, "reopened everything. The big wound bleeds."[12] Finding a way to live as a hermit at Gethsemani became his focus. With the shed of St. Anne's as a model, he again pondered the idea of a structure, a habitable shack, just outside the walls on the hills above the abbey. Ever since his afternoon hike eleven years earlier, when he surveyed the monastery from that distant, bucolic perspective, this plan had offered hope.

• • •

Ironically, Merton's new, more socially conscious writing owed as much to Gregory Zilboorg as to the epiphany on the streets of Louisville. The accusation of being "verbological" wouldn't have bothered Merton so much if he hadn't already been having doubts about his tendency to view contemplation as the solution to all problems.

Those doubts arose at a time when he was already looking beyond his roles as an income producer for the abbey and the master of novices. He was observing global realities as never before and seeing what activists and thinkers outside the monastery were seeing. And he was distressed. Although he had long been concerned about social issues, new forces had been unleashed in the world. The Cold War was now at its peak. A wall had been constructed in Berlin, spy planes were being shot down, and countries in Eastern Europe had been invaded. Merton perceived the evils of communist totalitarianism as well as the damage done by the West's overzealous backlash. He read about the emerging Civil Rights movement, the political fear-mongering of politicians, the belligerence of nuclear-armed nations, and the dangers of what Eisenhower dubbed the "military-industrial complex." Closer to home, from the Strategic Air Command base at Fort Campbell on the Tennessee border, bombers laden with nuclear payloads regularly rumbled so low over Our Lady of Gethsemani that Merton could make out the bomb bay doors on their undersides.

In the 1960s, Merton's reimagined approach to solitude and his commitment to social concerns began to feed each other, as evidenced by his newest books: *Disputed Questions* (1960), *New Seeds of Contemplation* (1962), *Seeds of Destruction* (1964), *Gandhi on Non-Violence* (1965), *Raids on the Unspeakable* (1966), *Conjectures of a Guilty Bystander* (1966), and *Faith and Violence* (1968). Even his poetry became more political and countercultural, as seen in his collection *Emblems of a Season of Fury* (1963). He contributed articles to antiwar journals and helped Catholic activist brothers Daniel and Philip Berrigan found an interfaith peace organization.

In October 1961, he published the article "The Root of War Is Fear" in *The Catholic Worker*. He was also completing a book to be called *Peace in the Post-Christian Era* and was editing a multi-author compilation of essays on the same subject. His burgeoning activism disturbed the authorities. The following April, fearful that Merton might stir up controversy among the Father Coughlin crowd, the head of the Cistercian order in France, Dom Gabriel Sortais, ordered Merton to cease all publication of his antiwar and antinuclear pronouncements. Merton, who had longed chafed at such censorship, was furious. How could he express his solidarity with those oppressed by war and political exploitation if he was not allowed to publish?

So Merton came up with a work-around. Publishing wasn't the same as writing, he reasoned, so why not keep writing? He continued to produce scores of letters and essays on the issues of war and peace, but instead of publishing them, he conscripted the abbey's novices—his monastic students—to mimeograph them. He then circulated the writings, *samizdat* fashion, among such interested correspondents as therapist Erich Fromm, Catholic social worker Dorothy Day, poet Czeslaw Milosz, novelist Henry Miller, Merton's former teacher Mark Van Doren, and nearly seventy other cultural gatekeepers.[13]

Among the recipients was Ethel Kennedy, wife of Bobby Kennedy and sister-in-law to the president. In one letter to her, after praising President Kennedy, Merton wrote, "It seems to me that the great problem we face is not Russia but war itself. War is the main enemy. . . . Unless we fight war, both in ourselves and in the Russians . . . we are purely and simply going to be wrecked by the forces that are in us."[14] Scholar James W. Douglass has suggested that Merton's letter ended up in the hands of the president himself only months before Kennedy's standoff with the Soviets over their deployment of nuclear missiles in Cuba—the Cuban Missile Crisis.[15]

Merton's views on war and peace were vindicated a year and a half later, when, on April 11, 1963, Pope John XXIII issued his influential encyclical *Pacem in Terris* ("Peace on Earth"), which was partly inspired by Merton's circulated writings. Three days later, on Easter Sunday, Merton wrote a testy letter to the abbot general who had censored his antiwar writings in the first place. "Now the Holy Father clearly says that war can no longer be used as an instrument of justice in a world where nuclear arms are possessed," wrote Merton. "Fortunately, he does not need to be approved by the censors."[16]

Merton's antiwar articles, essays, and letters were published posthumously in such volumes as *Thomas Merton on Peace* (1971, revised in 1980 as *The Non-Violent Alternative*), *Passion for Peace* (1995), *Cold War Letters* (2006), and, the book that was originally censored by the church authorities in 1962, *Peace in the Post-Christian Era* (eventually published in 2004). Those writings remain some of the most important documents in American literature on the subjects of war and nonviolence.

For Merton, the late fifties and early sixties offered an unusual convergence of circumstances—Zilboorg's attack, his epiphany in Louisville, his dissatisfaction with his own devotional writing, and the state of the world at large. It was a unique historical moment. His vocation had given him exactly the foothold he needed to climb from the wreckage, and, like the desert hermits he so admired, he was able to "pull the whole world to safety" after him.

• • •

Strong desires have a way of shaping the world around them.

At the beginning of 1960, Merton's dream of a hermitage coincided with the suggestion from someone in the community that a retreat house might be built where group instruction could be offered, important conferences held, and special guests lodged. It was tacitly assumed that Merton would be the chief beneficiary, since, as the master of novices, he could use the structure as a classroom and private meeting space—not a personal living space at that point, but a communal one.

For the next six months, the question was not *if* such an edifice would be built but *when*. The plan took shape "unexpectedly and *without* premeditation."[17] In July, after someone floated the idea of asking some major corporations for financing, it was decided that there should be no corporate strings attached, and the structure should be simple, functional, and cheaply built. After that, things moved quickly.

In September, the monks cleared the brush from the site. In October, Merton and three novices dug the shallow trench for the foundation, and a few days later, while Merton daydreamed about planting fruit trees to the east of the building, the concrete slab was poured. By the end of the month, the cinder-block walls had been raised and the roof added.

Dom James tried to tamp down Merton's excitement by "intimating," as Merton wrote, "that it is something he does not want me to have or even use except in a very restricted way. I mean, he is very clear about my not *living* in it, or sleeping in it."[18]

That did not deter him, late one afternoon, from walking up the hill to the empty structure. "Sat on the porch of the hermitage," he reflected, already conceiving of it as *the hermitage* rather than *the retreat center*, "and watched the sunlight fade in the valley, and saw the moon rise over the little maple sapling we planted on the east side yesterday. If I have any desire left in the world it is to live there and die there."[19]

• • •

Over the next two years, Dom James granted Merton permission to spend an occasional afternoon meditating at the new structure. By late 1964, Dom James eventually warmed to the prospect of Merton's moving there permanently someday, though Merton was cautious and had good reason to be. Dom James had a different vision of what a hermit's life entailed, which Merton summarized like this: "*No* contact with *anyone*. . . . *No* letters. *No* visits. *No* talking. To do any kind of productive work 'would spoil the purity of intention.'"[20] The abbot's view was the one traditionally held by the church.

Merton's vision was more expansive. A few years earlier he had compiled *The Wisdom of the Desert*, and the alternately winsome and austere anecdotes in that collection directly challenged the stereotype. The desert solitaries of the fourth century were vibrant characters, wise, waggish, and, Merton insisted, "eminently social."[21] They had relationships. They ministered to the poor. They talked to each other, received visitors, and did productive work, like weaving mats and baskets to sell in the nearby towns. It was simply that they spent most of their time alone praying in the desert.

Within the abbey, circumstances began to conspire in Merton's favor, and many of the old obstacles fell away. In October 1964, Dom James gave Merton permission to sleep overnight in the retreat center on rare occasions, and shortly after that, a letter arrived from the abbot general of the order, stating that he was "not opposed on principle to experiments in the hermit life within our Order. . . . Gethsemani would be a reasonable place for such an experiment."[22]

By mid-December, Dom James seemed so supportive of Merton's spending more time at the center that he went so far as to hire a contractor to install electrical wiring. While Dom James still clung to his image of a largely isolated hermit, Merton wisely took things one day at a time, letting the situation evolve.

After more disputes, reversals, anxieties, internecine politics, and health issues, Merton was finally granted permission to live in the structure full-time. While he was still expected to attend Mass at the abbey every day, have his midday meal there, and give occasional talks to the novices, his dream of becoming a hermit was about to become a reality.

• • •

The official date of his relocation was Friday, August 20, 1965. On that day, as part of the official relinquishing of his duties as master of novices, he told the assembled monks that his move would be an unceremonious affair, nothing like the Coptic Rite for "putting away a hermit." In that ancient rite, the religious community processed to the foot of the cliff below the hermit's cave, where prayers were recited and the *Missa pro defunctis*—the "Mass for the Dead"—was sung. The hermit, in essence, was being declared dead to the world. The bishop then read from the psalms and blessed the proceedings, after which the hermit climbed the rope to his cave and pulled it up after him. "So there *are* possibilities in this racket," Merton joked. The novices laughed. Still, such caves had held special meaning for Merton ever since he had dreamed of joining the Camaldolese.

Merton explained to the novices the purpose of the solitary life, and all monastic life, for that matter: "It is possible in this kind of life to put away all care, to live without care, to not have to care. . . . It is a life in which you no longer care about anything because God has taken care of everything."[23]

With that, he boxed up a few books and manuscripts and moved to the hermitage. A week later, he wrote, "I am beginning to feel the lightness, the strangeness, the desertedness of being really alone."[24] The word *desertedness* contained a double meaning: "being alone" and "being in the desert."

• • •

The hermitage stood (and still stands) on top of a hill, about a half-mile north of the main buildings of Gethsemani—a ten-minute walk. A few footpaths forked off into the trees. The surrounding woods, mostly evergreens with a few maples and sweetgums, lay east of Nelson County Road 247, called Monk's Road. To visit Merton, friends would sometimes park on the shoulder of that road and hike across the field and through the trees rather than going through the abbey's front gate, as officially required. Directly in front of the porch, where Merton would visit with guests, a clearing sloped downward to the east, and well beyond that flowed Monk's Creek. A dirt access road zigzagged between the abbey and the hermitage.

The floor plan for the three rooms was simple: immediately inside the front door was a large main room, with a desk and a few chairs; to the left toward the back was a small kitchen; and through the kitchen to the right was the bedroom, more precisely called the cell.[25] The central fireplace, which opened to the main room, burned only wood during that first winter of 1965, which proved difficult for Merton because chopping wood inflamed the bursitis in his elbow. Behind the hermitage was an outhouse, which he approached with dread because of the king snake that lived there. Before entering, he would ritually shout, "Are you in there, you bastard?"[26]

The building was christened the Mount Olivet Retreat Center, after the Mount of Olives, the lengthy ridge just east of Jerusalem's Old City where Jesus wept over Jerusalem and prophesied the destruction of the temple. It also overlooked the garden of Gethsemane, where Jesus prayed on the night of his arrest, and where he predicted that Peter would deny him three times. It is also the place from which Jesus is said to have ascended to heaven. Merton had discovered this place when he first hiked the surrounding hills to get his salutary, distant perspective. Mount Olivet was the perfect name.

Still, the formal name faded, and the place was called simply "the hermitage."

• • •

On Sunday, July 25, 1965, less than a month before moving to his new quarters, Thomas Merton was meditating at the abbey. The long journey was nearly over; he was approaching his dreamed-of desert solitude after nearly two and a half decades. When he began, he was twenty-six. He was now fifty-one and full of anticipation.

That evening he picked up a copy of Kierkegaard's *The Present Age*, which he declared to be "one of the best and in some sense most hopeful treatments of the individual in mass-society." One line from the book struck him as unusually "fine and completely prophetic." Kierkegaard wrote, "It is in fact through error that the individual is given access to the highest if he courageously desires it."[27]

Individuality "in the present age," explained Kierkegaard, is universally stymied by society's leveling influence, by too much second-guessing, stultifying self-consciousness, and over-concern for the opinions of others. Only when, by some fluke of fate or personality, a courageous person is able to move, or perhaps stumble, beyond such constraints, can he or she achieve something extraordinary.

The idea was prophetic in a way that Merton could not have imagined.

• • •

On that same evening, nearly a thousand miles away, a young man less than half Merton's age was tuning the strings of a guitar in front of a cheering, or perhaps jeering, crowd. Something startling and unprecedented was about to happen, an event that would be talked about for decades. As the rock band exploded into a descending blues riff behind him, the young man, guitar in hand, shouted to the musicians, "Let's go!" Then he turned to the microphone. The next words out of his mouth were a chilling declaration of defiance that has resonated through the decades for anyone who has ever wrestled with authority, who has ever kicked against the oppression of society's leveling influence. In a year's time, those words would resonate with Thomas Merton as well.

The young man sang, "I ain't gonna work on Maggie's farm no more . . ."[28]

DYLAN INTERLUDE NO. 1

Bringing It All Back Home

Far from Kentucky, far from a tiny cabin in the woods near an obscure monastery, folk-music-and-protest icon Bob Dylan was, like Thomas Merton, busy bringing it all back home. Though for him, home was rock 'n' roll.

According to the accepted narrative, he "went electric" on the evening of July 25, 1965, when he and members of the Paul Butterfield Blues Band blasted out the opening riff of "Maggie's Farm" on the main stage of the Newport Folk Festival in Rhode Island. The performance had a buzz-saw intensity. It was a take-no-prisoners moment that separated the once-hip folkies from the newly hip folk-rockers. While press reports claimed that Dylan had been booed from the stage, those who were there said that while a few complained that the amps had overpowered Dylan's vocals, the rest were complaining about the complainers.[1]

Boos can be heard on the official recording, though they are mostly evident at the end of the performance because the set was so short—only three songs.[2] To pacify the crowd, Dylan returned to the stage to cheers and applause—without the band and having traded his solid-body Fender Stratocaster for a folk guitar. He performed two more songs, both acoustic, the final one being, significantly, "It's All Over Now, Baby Blue." It was a farewell in more ways than one.

The set was so short—five songs total—not because Dylan was capricious, but because all the day's performances had run late, and there were still four to come. The festival, by local ordinance, had a time limit.

A host of related tales emerged. Pete Seeger was rumored to have tried to cut Dylan's amplifier cables with an ax. It didn't happen. It was also said that Dylan's manager, Albert Grossman, one of the festival's founders back in 1959, got in a fistfight with famed folklorist and festival board member Alan Lomax over Dylan's performance. This is partly true. The men did fight, but it happened two days earlier, immediately after Lomax introduced Paul Butterfield's blues-rock band by essentially disparaging them.[3] Grossman, who was planning to sign the band as clients, resented the comments and charged over to confront Lomax as he exited the stage. Push led to literal shove, which led to the two men wrestling on the ground like schoolyard toughs.[4]

Another myth is that Lomax, one of the world's great collectors of acoustic folk music, had railed against electrified music in general. But Lomax wasn't upset by Butterfield's amplifiers. He had long endorsed urban blues artists like Muddy Waters who performed with electrified bands. Instead, Lomax felt that Butterfield and his band were simply white boys pretending to be black.

But the fact remains that Butterfield rocked Newport with full-tilt electric blues two days before Dylan did. Even so, nothing quite approached the all-out mayhem Dylan unleashed in 1965. The performance is justifiably one of pop music's great folktales, in which Dylan is portrayed as the lone prophet wailing in the wilderness, misunderstood by the suburban Philistines. It has been retold and rehashed, but the truth is more complex.

While it's true that in 1965 Dylan publicly came home to the rock music he had loved as a teenager, in another sense, he had never left home; he had never *not* been electric. As Dylan himself has said, "We've been playing this music since we were ten years old. Folk music was just an interruption, which was very useful."[5]

The teenage Robert Zimmerman, as Dylan was known in 1956, was as zealous a rock 'n' roll fan as any kid his age. "Hearing [Elvis] for the first time," he said later, "was like busting out of jail."[6] At fifteen and living in Hibbing, Minnesota, he was pounding three-chord piano accompaniments to such songs as "Let the Good Times Roll" and "Lawdy, Miss Clawdy." In the spring of 1958, on the earliest known tape of him playing music, a sixteen-year-old Zimmerman runs through a fragment of an original song called "Hey, Little Richard" before barking out Richard's own "Jenny Jenny." The next spring, he wrote in his senior yearbook that his ambition was "to play with Little Richard"[7]—and he played in a series of high school bands, including his own Golden Chords.

On January 31, 1959, Zimmerman attended a Buddy Holly concert in Duluth. Four days later, Holly died in a plane crash, along with Richie Valens and the Big Bopper, in what musician Don McLean later dubbed "the day the music died."[8] The concert had a long-term effect on him. Decades later, in 1998, as part of his Grammy-award acceptance speech for his album *Time Out of Mind*, he said, "When I was sixteen or seventeen years old, I went to see Buddy Holly play at Duluth National Guard Armory, and I was three feet away from him . . . and he looked at me. And I just have some sort of feeling that he was—I don't know how or why—but I know he was with us all the time we were making this record in some kind of way."[9]

In December 1959, Zimmerman nearly got his big break in show business. Ever a self-promoter, the eighteen-year-old talked his way into pop star Bobby Vee's backup band, the Shadows—although Vee himself, in an interview decades later, used the word *wormed*.[10] Under the name Elston Gunnn (yes, he spelled it with three *n*'s), Zimmerman pitched himself to Vee's brother as the perfect pianist for the band. The Shadows were searching for a keyboardist, and Zimmerman claimed he had just ended a national tour playing piano for country star Conway Twitty. Needless to say, Twitty's band never had a pianist.

Vee's brother, needing to audition Gunnn quickly and get back on the road, found a radio studio with a piano. Liking what he heard, he hired the teenager on the spot. But after playing one performance in Fargo, North Dakota, Gunnn was fired when the Shadows realized he played passably well, but only in the key of C—only on the white keys of the piano.[11]

Still, Zimmerman's transition from star-struck teenage rock fan to folk prodigy took place with dizzying intensity and speed. In January of 1961, a little over a year after his micro-stint with the Shadows, the newly self-christened "Bob Dylan" (most likely in honor of poet Dylan Thomas) told his friends he was going east to meet Woody Guthrie, then in the hospital with Huntington's disease. Having dropped out of the University of Minnesota the previous semester, Dylan was betting it all on becoming a folkie. Woody Guthrie, for the time being, had replaced Little Richard.

Dylan was a quick study. He absorbed his folk sources well, listening to everything from regional radio to Harry Smith's *Anthology of American Folk Music*. As Dylan once said, "Open your eyes and your ears and you're influenced"[12]—a phrase that sums up his creative process then as now.

Intensity and speed also epitomized his first year in New York. Between January and December of 1961, he not only met Woody Guthrie, performed at most of the hip coffeehouses, and met or played with many of the major folk acts, but also signed a recording contract with famed jazz producer and talent scout John Hammond at Columbia Records and recorded his first album, a collection of eleven traditional songs and two originals. When Dylan returned to Duluth in December, his old friends were dumbfounded.

Even as Dylan plied the folk trade, rock 'n' roll was on his mind. In recording the traditional songs for his first album, his intention, as he told an interviewer years later, was to do them in "a rock way." Worried that he was not as technically proficient as other folkies in the village, Dylan felt that his strength might be in bringing a rock sensibility to the songs. He said, "On the first album, I did 'Highway 51' [an old blues song] like an Everly Brothers tune because that was the only way I could relate to that stuff."[13]

In New York, Dylan found work as a studio musician, playing blues harmonica with plugged-in bands. In September 1961, he joined a guitar-and-bass combo to accompany folk singer Carolyn Hester on her third album. In February 1962, he played a chugging blues harmonica on Harry Belafonte's twenty studio takes of Leadbelly's "Midnight Special." A month later, Dylan was in the studio with Big Joe Williams and blues diva Victoria Spivey. Williams, who christened Dylan "Little Junior," was a Mississippi blues artist whose chosen instrument was a driving, down-and-dirty nine-string electric guitar. For an acoustic folkie, Dylan rubbed shoulders with a lot of electrified musicians.

Somewhere inside Dylan was a pent-up Elvis waiting to "bust out of jail." Sensing this, producer John Hammond arranged for him to record several rockabilly numbers—with a full backup band—for his second album, *The Freewheelin' Bob Dylan*. Among the songs attempted was Arthur Crudup's classic "That's Alright, Mama." The song had been Elvis Presley's first single back in 1954, and some critics have called that 45 rpm disc from the legendary Sun Records studio the first true rock 'n' roll record ever made.[14]

In October and November 1962, accompanied by Hammond's session crew, Dylan attempted to nail "That's Alright, Mama" and some other songs, including his own composition "Mixed Up Confusion." They laid down more than twenty-five takes of the latter, each sounding as mixed up and confused as the one before.[15] Finally, after Hammond decided that he and Dylan were unlikely to achieve the "Sun Records sound" they had hoped for, they sent the musicians home. It was a lucky move because, shortly after the band shuffled out of the studio that day, Dylan recorded one of his most beautiful solo acoustic hits, "Don't Think Twice, It's All Right," in a single take.

As *The Freewheelin' Bob Dylan* climbed the charts on its way to Platinum status, with its powerful, memorable songs like "Blowin' in the Wind," "A Hard Rain's A-Gonna Fall," "Masters of War," "Girl from the North Country," and "Don't Think Twice," other musicians began to record Dylan's songs. Peter, Paul and Mary's mellow take on "Blowin' in the Wind" landed at number two on the pop charts, and Dylan nudged closer to household-name status.

Dylan recorded two more acoustic albums in the next year and a half (*The Times They Are A-Changin'* and *Another Side of Bob Dylan*), and his reputation as the leading songwriter on the folk scene was firmly established. He all but originated the term *singer-songwriter*. As songs like "The Times They Are A-Changin'," "With God on Our Side," "Chimes of Freedom," and "It Ain't Me, Babe" entered the American consciousness, Dylan became one of the highest royalty earners in the music business.

He recorded *Another Side of Bob Dylan*, his fourth and final all-acoustic album,[16] in June 1964. The session took place four months after the Beatles took America by storm on *The Ed Sullivan Show*, when the country was reeling from Beatlemania. Dylan too took notice. A new, more hip attitude is evident on *Another Side of Bob Dylan*. Gone is the hobo minstrel, the work-shirted folkie troubadour, replaced by someone more swaggering, more flinty-edged. On the album cover, he looks more like a Beatle than like Woody Guthrie. The "other side" of Bob Dylan, the image implied, was rock 'n' roll.

One song on that album, "My Back Pages," is Dylan's unambiguous valediction to his folk-protest persona. No longer is he the Bob Dylan who sang civil rights anthems in front of the Lincoln Memorial the day Martin Luther King Jr. delivered "I Have a Dream." "My Back Pages" was Dylan's declaration that time had moved on and he had moved with it.

Dylan opened the recording sessions for *Another Side* not by strumming a guitar, but by pounding a hard-driving piano on an original blues number called "Denise." Later in the session, another song signaled Dylan's shift from folk-blues to blues-rock. After he had recorded two fairly pedestrian guitar versions of "Black Crow Blues"—the first sounding folkie, the second somewhat more bluesy—some intuition inspired him to move the song to the piano. Suddenly the song found its rock 'n' roll pulse. The old high school barrelhouse piano was back, including some Jerry Lee Lewis–style glissandos. It clicked. That take of "Black Crow Blues" ended up as the second track on the album. The closing track on *Another Side*, conventionally interpreted as a lover's farewell, can also be read as Dylan's own cryptic memo to his folk fans in general—"It Ain't Me, Babe."

As if to underscore folk's transition to rock, the Turtles' pop version of "It Ain't Me, Babe," with no less than three electric guitars and two percussionists, reached number eight on the pop charts the following year. In addition, the Byrds' electric version of Dylan's *Another Side* song "All I Really Want to Do" went head-to-head in a pop-chart skirmish with Cher's recording of the same number.

Although *Another Side* was his final solo acoustic album of the 1960s, it wasn't a folk album by a long stretch. One critic called it "a rock album without electric guitars."[17] Dylan was dead; long live Dylan.

• • •

For his next foray into rock, Dylan wasn't even present.

Tom Wilson, Dylan's current producer, had an idea. What if he were to take one of Dylan's old folkie vocal tracks and overdub it in the studio with electric instruments?

Wilson had followed with interest the rise of a gritty British-invasion band called the Animals, whose electrified version of the traditional American song "House of the Rising Sun" had been released that summer. The song hit number one in the UK in July 1964 and was number one in the US by September.

So, on December 8, 1964, Tom Wilson took a tape of Dylan's own vocals for "House of the Rising Sun" from his first album, along with a couple of others, and overdubbed them with a rock accompaniment provided by session musicians. Having scheduled studio time the following month to record a batch of new Dylan songs with a band, Wilson thought he would make a trial run. The December session, without Dylan, would give him some insight into how to manage a session with rock musicians compared to the jazz musicians he was used to producing, people like Sun Ra and Donald Byrd. While the overdubbed "House of the Rising Sun," released as an archival recording thirty years later, has a muddied sound and comes nowhere near the intensity of the Animals' take, it was enough to give Wilson confidence when entering the studio in January.[18]

The concept for the new album, which would be called *Bringing It All Back Home*, was to record Dylan's new songs in acoustic versions, or with only a single guitar or bass accompaniment, then to rerecord some of them with full rock-band backup. It worked. In fact, the January sessions were brilliant. Side A of the record gathered the best of the band versions, while Side B carried the acoustic songs. The album introduced such Dylan classics as "Subterranean Homesick Blues," "Love Minus Zero/No Limit,"

"Mr. Tambourine Man," "Gates of Eden," "It's All Over Now, Baby Blue," and "It's Alright, Ma (I'm Only Bleeding)." *Bringing It All Back Home* would be Bob Dylan's best-selling album to date.

Within weeks of the album's release, the Byrds issued their own jangly electric-guitar version of "Mr. Tambourine Man," and the concept of folk-rock was born,[19] melding Dylan's lyrical bravura with the Beatles' pop sensibility. The Byrds' single shot to the top of the charts, and any radio listener who may have missed Peter, Paul and Mary's "Blowin' in the Wind" two years earlier certainly knew who Bob Dylan was now.

• • •

In late April and May 1965, two months after the release of *Bringing It All Back Home*, Bob Dylan made a nine-concert tour of England, ending with a televised performance for the BBC on June 1. They would be the last solo acoustic concerts he would ever give. The sold-out shows were a critical and popular success, garnering high praise from such audience members as the Beatles and the Rolling Stones.

Fans mobbed Dylan as he went to and from the concert halls—a sort of Dylan mini-mania, documented in D. A. Pennebaker's film *Dont Look Back* and mirroring in a much smaller way the Beatles' first triumphant visit to the United States. In one scene, Dylan is seen briefly jamming in a Newcastle hotel room with Alan Price, the Animals' keyboardist, and in another scene, Dylan is quizzing Price about his views on playing in a rock band.

On May 12, just after his final concert appearance, Dylan stopped off at Levy's Recording Studio in London. Dylan had heard a single called "Crawling Up a Hill" by an up-and-coming British rock-and-blues group, John Mayall's Bluesbreakers, and he wanted to meet them. With Dylan's single of "Subterranean Homesick Blues" climbing the charts in England and the US, his management thought a joint session might also be a good chance for him to identify himself publicly as a full-fledged rock musician.

The ostensible occasion was to record a musical greeting for Columbia's next sales conference, but some people were hoping the session would blossom into a full-blown meeting of the musical minds. Tom Wilson was at the controls. Mayall's band included a relatively unknown twenty-year-old guitar phenom named Eric Clapton.[20]

The bootleg recording tells the tale.[21] After taping a short, hysterically deadpan message for the Columbia sales team, thanking them for selling so many albums and ending with "God bless you all," Dylan is at the piano, ready for action, with the Bluesbreakers standing by.

Dylan hastily counts off, "*One*, two, three . . . ," which is followed by a puzzled silence. The band is thrown off by the odd count-in. Amid the hilarity that follows, one band member cajoles, "Do it in *time*." Another scoffs, "Haven't worked much with bands, have ya?"—a particularly galling jab.

But Dylan, largely immune to being disconcerted, responds, "Naw, I won't do any count-in. You just start—you come in." After those two bits of contradictory instruction (how does a band both "start" and then "come in"?), Dylan begins banging the chords to "If You Gotta Go, Go Now," a straight-ahead rock number he'd recorded for *Bringing It All Back Home* but had not released. Again, it's the old hammer-and-tongs piano style he used when he was fifteen. Mayall's drummer, Hugh Flint, makes a few tentative tapping noises, but despite Dylan's directive, the band neither starts nor comes in. Did they even know what key he was playing in?

After one valiantly miserable verse, Dylan yells to Tom Wilson in the control booth, "Okay. We'll fade it out here . . . Tom? . . . Fade out . . . *Fade it out!* . . . Did you fade it out?"

A weary Tom Wilson, who had himself learned how not to be disconcerted, drawls back, "Yeah, it's faded out, man."

• • •

One month later, Dylan and Wilson are back in New York. After the tour of England, Dylan is exhausted, recovering from the flu, and sick of being a "folk icon." He's ready to quit. He's fed up with the fans, the same old demands, the grind. Still, he's written one new song since his return—a song Dylan perversely says began as "a long piece of vomit about twenty pages long"[22]—and he wants to try it out in the studio.

On June 15, he and Wilson assemble six crack musicians in Columbia's Studio A, four of whom had played on *Bringing It All Back Home*. Also included is Mike Bloomfield, a guitar phenom in his own right, whose regular gig is with the Chicago-based Paul Butterfield Blues Band. (A month and a half later, he will join Dylan on stage at Newport for the infamous electric set.)

With Wilson at the controls, Dylan and company start laying down tracks. After warming up with repeated takes of a couple of throwaway blues jams, they're ready to take a swing at the new song. They rehearse it but it flops. The song was written in a somewhat galumphing waltz time, and the words don't sync up. Dylan doodles at the piano and ponders. Later, not long after Dylan announces his "voice is shot," Wilson sends everyone home.

When they reassemble at 2:30 the next afternoon, things have changed. They try the new song again, but this time in a straight-ahead rock tempo—*one*, two, three, four—heavy on the downbeat. It clicks. The musicians feel—and sound—exhilarated. By the second complete take, they've nailed the definitive version of a song that Dylan would later say "changed it all. I mean it was something that I myself could dig."[23] It convinced him not to give up on music.

The song became what many consider to be the greatest rock anthem ever cut on vinyl, "Like a Rolling Stone."[24]

Yes, Dylan had worked with bands before.

And he had most definitely brought it all back home.

Bob Dylan, "Love Minus Zero/No Limit," *Bringing It All Back Home*, LP (Columbia, CS 9128, 1965), side 1, track 4.

THOMAS MERTON	BOB DYLAN
1966	
	Jan.–March: records *Blonde on Blonde*
March 6: watches the deer from his porch	
March 25: has neck surgery in Louisville hospital	
March 30: meets Margie Smith	
	April: Australian concert tour
April 9: returns to Gethsemani	
April 19: receives first letter from Margie	
April 26: meets Margie in Louisville	
	April 27: arrives in Europe for concert tour
May 5: James Laughlin and Nicanor Parra visit	
May 14: discusses Joan Baez with Margie	
	May 17: the "Judas shout" concert, Manchester, England
May 22: returns to hermitage	
	May 27: final European concert, London
May 28: Thich Nhat Hanh visits	
June 14: admits the affair to Dom James	
June 25: gives *Midsummer Diary* to Margie	
	July: *Blonde on Blonde* released
July 16: goes to Cherokee Park with Margie	

The Invented Backbone

Sunday, March 6, 1966

He lowers the binoculars. The deer have wandered off in the direction of Monk's Creek. As the full moon rises, flooding the woods with shadows, the wind feels colder. Time to go inside.

Right now, down in the abbey, the monks are praying before bed. But he will stay up, sitting in the glow of the fire, and then he will turn on his desk lamp and jot some thoughts in his journal. He will write about the deer. The incident seems significant somehow, not just because they seldom linger so long in the clearing, but because some kind of connection was made. They were as aware of him as he was of them, but it was more. They looked into his eyes and he looked into theirs. It was unearthly. Like knowing and being known.

Inside, he tosses a log on the fire, stokes it, and there it is—the pain. A disc in his neck has disintegrated, leaving the vertebrae to grind against each other like broken cinderblocks. It's unbearable at times. The numbness in his hands often keeps him from writing. He was in Louisville this past Wednesday for X-rays, and the doctor said surgery was the only option. A spinal fusion. It's scheduled for the twenty-fourth, just two and a half weeks from now, though he's supposed to register at St. Joseph's Infirmary the day before.

Things seem so fragile. Since moving to the hermitage, one problem has followed another. The dermatitis sometimes gets so bad he has to wear dermal gloves to protect his chafed, bleeding hands. The bursitis flares up regularly, especially when he chops wood. One of his eyes has been giving him problems ever since it got poked with a tree branch. And there's that odd lump—a tumor?—on his stomach. He'll get all of this checked at the hospital. Last November, a bout of dysentery deferred his dream of visiting the Solentiname community in Nicaragua to work with Ernesto Cardenal—one of his own former novices, now a celebrated poet and revolutionary. He can't risk dysentery again. And the abbot probably won't let him go anyway.

No wonder he's been thinking about death recently, not in a morbid way, but simply the raw actualness of it. The inevitability. How do you prepare for it, "set your house in order," as people say?[1] He has no idea.

It's not about legacy either. Poet Thérèse Lentfoehr, that dear Salvatorian sister, has taken care of that.[2] She's been writing him about where to archive her collection of his manuscripts. She even has an unpublished novel he wrote before entering the monastery.

He stands and walks to the kitchen to pour a glass of water from one of the jugs he hauls from the abbey each day. It tastes wonderful. "As the deer pants for the water brooks . . . ," he thinks.

The deer. How peaceful it all felt, and how hopeful. There was something intimate in those eyes, a reciprocity. He used to coach the novices about the *theoria physike*—"the contemplation of God in and through nature, in and through things He has created."[3] It was like Meister Eckhart's famous pronouncement, "The eye with which I see God is the same eye with which God sees me."[4] And that, in turn, reminds him to pack some Eckhart to read in the hospital.

He wants to remember to mention the deer in his letter to Jacques Maritain tomorrow—a letter he's been meaning to write for days. Jacques is brilliant about our perceptions, our "intuition of being" and its relation to the senses, but he lives in his head much of the time. Jacques would love this place, so different from the Little Brothers of Jesus in Toulouse, where Jacques has lived since Raïssa's death. The hermitage would reconnect Jacques to Nature, its visceral reality. Yes, remember to mention the deer. And chopping wood. And the cold.

All this—the deer, the pain, the unwritten letters—has roused in him something that he finds hard to admit, something so hulking and obvious that it's the easiest thing in the world to miss.

The other side of solitude is loneliness.

• • •

That Merton felt isolated is certain. He had complained that the brothers were ignoring him or had forgotten him completely. For their part, they were keeping their distance because they assumed that's what someone with a hermit's vocation would want.

He wrote Jacques Maritain the next day. Maritain, a major Catholic philosopher, had been a mentor to Merton ever since Merton first heard him lecture at Columbia. Maritain's last visit to the States had been five years ago, a year after his wife Raïssa's death. Now, at eighty-three, the great French thinker was contemplating a sort of farewell tour in the fall, to visit old friends while his health was good. Gethsemani would be on the itinerary.

In his letter, Merton complained about the controversies sparked by Vatican II and confessed it all made him "feel a thousand years old,"[5] though his illnesses and pending surgery as much as the new English liturgy made him feel that way. And he mentioned the deer: "Through field glasses I could look right into their huge brown eyes and it seemed I could touch their big black noses with my own."[6]

In hindsight, the experience with the deer was pivotal, a moment around which many emotions revolved. The deer embodied Merton's longings for connection. Nowhere else in his journals before then does he mention looking so deeply into eyes that look back into his own, nor does he write elsewhere so much about the physical act of touching. The deer are as much about relationship as about Nature. The previous September, from that same vantage point, he had watched a doe and two stags cross the same clearing, and then too he "longed to touch them." He wrote, "The deer reveals to me something essential in myself!"[7]

As someone who prayed the Psalms, Merton would have often been reminded of Psalm 41: "As the hind pants for the water brooks, so my soul pants after thee, O God."[8] The deer that traipsed across the abbey grounds on the night of March 6 were no doubt looking for "water brooks." The farm ponds on the other side of County Road 247 from the hermitage were frozen. February and March had been exceptionally cold, and a layer of snow still covered the ground. The deer were heading in the direction of Monk's Creek, where the water was still flowing, just a few hundred yards east of the hermitage.

Merton's own "panting after God" is something he hints at when writing that he was "entranced by [the deers'] perfection."[9] Ten years earlier, in a small chapbook called *Praying the Psalms*, he had composed a meditation about that very passage from Psalm 41. He wrote, "the sufferings of the soul that thirsts for God are blended with mystical joy."[10] The cover of that first edition of *Praying the Psalms*, not coincidentally, showed a stylized drawing of a leaping deer.

The seventh-century mystic Isaac of Nineveh, whom Merton considered his favorite writer to read in the hermitage,[11] wrote about the importance of eyes, and of seeing Nature, in the contemplation of God: "What the eyes of the body are for physical objects, faith is for the hidden eyes of the soul. Just as we have two bodily eyes, so we have two spiritual eyes, and each has its own way of seeing. With one we see the glory of God hidden in creatures: with the other we contemplate the glory of God's holy nature when he deigns to give us access to the mysteries."[12] A passage from Canticles, the Song of Solomon, even describes a human lover as a deer: "My beloved is like a roe, or a young hart. Behold he standeth behind our wall, looking through the windows, looking through the lattices."[13]

Five days later, Merton was still thinking about the deer. On Friday, March 11, he wrote to Argentine poet Miguel Grinberg, "The woods here are where I belong. The deer were out the other night and I was looking at them (in the evening light) with field glasses, looking right into their big brown eyes. They could see me just as clearly as I could see them and they did not run away."[14]

That mutual locking of those eyes was a moment that explains much about what was on the verge of happening to Thomas Merton, about his desire for God on one hand and for human love on the other—and the interconnection between the two, a form of intimacy, a way of knowing and being known. Those two loves are inextricably bound together in much of Merton's writing and much of traditional Christian theology, especially in mystics like Saint John of the Cross and Teresa of Ávila.

All winter, he had been reading the poetry of Rainer Maria Rilke, one of the master poets on the subject of the spiritual aspects of love. Four days earlier, on March 2, while in Louisville for his medical exam, Merton had found a copy of Rilke's *Letters to a Young Poet* at the University of Louisville Library. He was astonished by what he read. The letters, he felt, "complete and deepen some of the things said about love"[15] in Rilke's poems. He was referring specifically to the seventh letter, in which Rilke outlines his personal philosophy of love. The letter's recipient was Franz Kappus, a young poet friend of Rilke's.

At the time, Rilke and his young wife, sculptor Clara Westhoff, were living in Paris, though Rilke was visiting Rome when he wrote this particular letter. Kappus, envious of Rilke's marriage, had mentioned experiencing a certain amount of loneliness, a lack of female companionship, so Rilke explained the connection between love and solitude. Imagine how these lines of Rilke's would have resonated with Merton:

> It is good to be solitary, for solitude is difficult; that something is difficult must be a reason the more to do it.
>
> To love is good, too: love being difficult. For one human being to love another: that is perhaps the most difficult of all our tasks, the ultimate, the last test and proof, the work for which all other work is but preparation. For this reason young people, who are beginners in everything, cannot yet know love: they have to learn it. . . . But learning-time is always a long, secluded time, and so loving, for a long while ahead and far on into life, is—solitude, intensified and deepened loneliness for him who loves.[16]

As he read Rilke, Merton incorporated these ideas into the Zen-infused meditation he was writing as a preface for the Japanese edition of *Thoughts in Solitude*. A little more than two weeks later, three days before going to the hospital, Merton again thought about Rilke's *Letters to a Young Poet* and wrote, "There seems to be something to his ideas on love."[17] A month later, in his journal, Merton would again echo Rilke's words about love and solitude, though by then, the object of Merton's love would have a human face and a name.

• • •

The medical term for Merton's condition is *spondylosis*, a wearing out of the cartilage between two vertebrae. While Merton's complaints were of acute back pain, the degeneration was actually in his neck—a *cervical* spondylosis—with chronic numbness radiating to his arms and hands. He was uncomfortable sleeping in certain positions. The treatment was a procedure called an anterior cervical fusion, in which a small piece of flat bone is cut from the hipbone and inserted into the neck as a wedge-like replacement for the collapsed disc. The pieces are screwed together until the bone fragment and the surrounding vertebrae grow together. A spinal fusion. Merton later referred to it as his "invented back bone."[18]

On Wednesday, March 23, Merton rose, as usual, four hours before dawn and took up his journal. His mood was reflective: "I know I have to die sometime and may this not all be the beginning of it? I don't know, but if it is I accept it in full freedom and gladness. My life stands offered with that of Christ my brother."[19]

He then wrote short appreciations of some of his fellow monks, such as Father Chrysogonus, the choirmaster, and he took care to praise Dom James as "an extraordinary man, many sided, baffling, often irritating, . . . but who honestly and in his own way really seeks to be an instrument of God." Although his assessments were heartfelt, he was hedging his bets against the possibility of not returning from the hospital. He wanted the journal's final entry to be conciliatory, no doubt to compensate for his many fulminations directed at the abbot and others. He leaned heavily on terms of approbation in describing those in the community—they were "excellent ... good ... excellent ... fine ... good ... extraordinary ... excellent ... good ... extraordinary ..."—as if he were anxious to make amends.

In the final paragraph, he expressed his gratitude for the hermitage itself. Should he die at the hospital, his greatest regret would be the "loss of the years of solitude that might still be possible."[20]

Then he shut the journal, gathered a few things, including his volume of Eckhart's *Sermons*,[21] and walked to the abbey for morning Mass. Afterward, the abbot's brother, Bernard, another monk at Gethsemani, chauffeured Merton one hour north to Louisville in a heavy downpour. "Man is the saddest animal," Merton wrote in a poem a few months later, perhaps remembering this drive to the hospital. "He drives a big red car called anxiety."[22]

They drove to St. Joseph's Infirmary in Louisville, run by the Sisters of Charity. It was a 324-bed Catholic hospital, the largest in the area.[23] There, the doctors pronounced Merton's eye healthy and determined the growth on his stomach was benign.

Although the operation was planned for Thursday, March 24, it didn't take place until the following day, Friday, which happened to be the Feast of the Annunciation; in Catholic tradition, that is the celebration of the angel Gabriel's message to Mary that she would bear a child. The timing appealed to Merton because not only was it a holy day, but he annually performed a private ritual of his own every March 25: "In the old days I regularly renewed my resolution to become a Carthusian."[24] The surgery began midmorning, and when he came out of the anesthesia at eleven that night, he thought it was the following day and that he had missed Saturday Mass.

He spent the next few days recovering, coping not only with his pain but with the sterile hospital environment and the routine prodding and pestering. He secretly wished the ever-efficient staff wouldn't disturb him quite so much. Knowing that he preferred anonymity and privacy, the nurses tried not to bother their famous patient more than necessary—a deliberate routine of mildly depersonalized attention. Amid the insensate chatter of medical machinery, his pain, and the alienation that comes with hospitals, Merton thought, "I wonder who the hell I am."[25]

He immersed himself in Eckhart's *Sermons*, making notes and copying passages from the book, hoping to eventually write something about the famous German scholastic and mystic. He later referred to Eckhart as his "life-raft" while at the hospital.[26]

• • •

As he lay there "bleeding in a numbered bed,"[27] as he described it, one day followed another—until on Wednesday, five days after the operation, something out-of-the-ordinary happened. Absorbed in his Eckhart, trying to distract himself from his discomfort, he was interrupted by a young woman in hospital garb, someone he hadn't seen before. Unlike the other nurses, this one chatted openly and volubly. She explained she was a student nurse and would be taking care of him for the week, checking his bandages, dispensing medication, and giving him sponge baths. Her name was Margie Smith, and she was honored, she said, to be his caregiver. She knew who he was.

Though initially put off by her talkativeness, he found her fresh and attractive, and to his surprise, he eagerly anticipated her next visit. When she returned later that day, they talked freely. She was Catholic and had spent time in a convent. In the next twenty-four hours, their discussions broadened to include their views on Vatican II, the liturgy, their favorite gags from *Peanuts* cartoons and *Mad* magazine, their family backgrounds, and Merton's life at Gethsemani.

Out of curiosity she asked why anyone would want to live as a solitary. In an effort to explain, he loaned her the typescript of his new preface for the Japanese edition of *Thoughts in Solitude*, the one that expands upon Rilke. In it, Merton wrote somewhat mystically: "The paradox of solitude is that its true ground is universal love—and true solitude is the undivided unity of love for which there is no number. . . . He who is alone and is conscious of what his solitude means, finds himself simply in the ground of life. He is 'in Love.'"[28] In this play-on-words, he is saying those who are solitaries are not only grounded in "Love"—that is, in God—but also find themselves "in love" with all people.[29] It was a reiteration of the solitude-and-solidarity epiphany he'd had in Louisville eight years earlier.

The conversations energized Merton. By Friday, he had recovered enough strength to attempt a short walk. With Margie gripping his arm, he took his first shaky steps down the hallway and outside to the hospital grounds. It was painful, but her encouragement inspired him. They walked to the Grotto of Our Lady of Lourdes, just a short distance behind the hospital and the most impressive feature on the grounds. It was a large concave shrine, about fifteen feet high, made of mortared rocks and stone, with a statue of the Virgin Mary inside and a beautifully manicured, walled garden leading up to it. Margie would have pointed out the nurses' dormitory, Lourdes Hall, where she lived, just beyond the grotto.

The next day, when Margie called in sick, Merton grieved. Her absence and an uptick in his pain aroused his despair. Still, he was determined to say Mass in the hospital chapel the following day, Palm Sunday, which he did, but it proved to be an ordeal. Perhaps Margie might attend, he thought. She didn't. Upon returning to his room, he was convinced this young nurse was somehow essential to his healing.

That afternoon, he was permitted to take a walk by himself outside. Treading carefully because of discomfort, he selected the path that led past the Grotto to Lourdes Hall. Not unlike a love-struck teenage boy bicycling past a girl's house, Merton hoped he might run into Margie by chance or that she might look out her window and see him. She admitted later she had indeed seen him but had decided not to disturb his time alone.

He was overjoyed when she returned to work on Monday. That day and the next, they shared more confidences, to the point that her supervisor had to remind her not to neglect her other patients.

On Wednesday, a week after their first meeting, Margie dropped by his room before she left for a few days' vacation. Since this might be the last time they'd see each other, they were unusually subdued. She knew she wouldn't return before he was released. She was flying to Chicago, she explained, to see her fiancé, who was about to be shipped off to Vietnam.

Silver Dagger

That Thomas Merton fell in love is not nearly as surprising as it would have been had he not fallen in love.

Here was a man who had lost his mother when he was six and grew up with few nurturing females. In his journals he periodically regretted his youthful dalliances, and now that he was capable of loving more maturely, his vows imposed limitations.

Here was a man who had been feeling lonely for months, who had been reading Rilke's poetry, meditating on the role of love in the context of solitude, so much so that he had found comfort in the soft eyes of passing deer.

Here was a man who, after living without a woman's touch for two and a half decades, suddenly found himself personally cared for by an attractive, vivacious woman in her twenties. He leaned on her as he walked. She gave him sponge baths and checked his bandages.

• • •

Three days after Margie left for Chicago, Merton returned to Gethsemani. By the time he stepped back through the front gates—over which a sign read *Pax Intrantibus*, "Peace to those who enter"[1]—he was feeling anything but peace. He was aware of being in love and mindful of the risks. On Easter Sunday, April 10, the day after his return, he resumed his journal. "Though I am pretty indifferent to the society of my fellow monks . . . ," he wrote, "I do feel a deep emotional need for feminine companionship and love, and seeing that I must irrevocably live without [that,] it ended by tearing me up more than the operation itself." He wondered if he and Margie had perhaps become "too friendly."[2]

Although he had given Margie one of his books with a note inside explaining how he could be reached, he assumed their acquaintance was over. Perhaps he might run into her when he returned for checkups—at least, he hoped so—but his main concern was to continue healing and to cope with his tangled feelings. Although he shuffled up the path to the hermitage most days after his return, he slept in the infirmary because he was still experiencing pain, night sweats, and numbness in his leg. But he was improving.

As spring unfolded, he was ready to resume his daily disciplines of prayer, writing, and reading. The redbuds were in bloom along the edges of the woods, and the pink buds of the dogwoods would soon blossom into white. Wildflowers could be seen in every direction, bringing a refreshing sense of renewal.

On Tuesday, April 19, a letter arrived. From Margie. In it, she affirmed her friendship and confessed to feeling lonely, referencing their discussions about love and solitude. She enclosed a cartoon of Snoopy and expressed her regret that they probably wouldn't see each other again. Like a man grasping a lifeline, he penned a response in which he openly declared his love. It was one of those Rubicon moments from which there was no turning back. He could well lose the hermitage—and his vocation—should his superiors find out about his letter. "I responded positively," he wrote later in his journal, "because I already loved her."[3]

For her part, Margie was terrified. She was engaged, and Merton, more than twice her age, was a renowned writer, esteemed by the church, and someone she personally revered. But here he was, opening the door to a romantic involvement. She consulted a priest, who exhorted her to break off all contact immediately.

Three days later, Merton was at the abbey, helping to host a visiting abbot. After dinner, unsure of how Margie was reacting to his letter, he managed to find a phone with an outside line and surreptitiously dialed her number. Although she didn't answer, he had crossed another boundary; after the first illicit call, the others were easier. He tried again the next morning; again, she wasn't in. When he tried that afternoon, she finally answered. In that conversation, they acknowledged their feelings for one another, and, knowing he would be going to Louisville for a checkup in four days, he asked her to meet him outside the doctor's office.

In the interim, Merton agonized about his motivations, about the inevitability of things ending badly, and about the guilt he felt for stooping to stealth in contacting her. In his journal, he repeatedly couched his feelings in spiritualized terms. Although Rilke had said that loving another human was "the ultimate, the last test and proof, the work for which all other work is but preparation," Merton knew his infatuation was too powerful and too frankly sexual to be easily dressed in pious trappings.

On Tuesday, April 26, he returned to Louisville for a post-op checkup. Beforehand, he met with Dr. James Wygal, the psychiatrist he had been seeing for the past five years. Wygal was the first person in whom Merton confided the details of his feelings for Margie, and, clearly alarmed, Wygal advised him against seeing her that day. But the encounter had already been arranged. As soon as Merton emerged from the surgeon's office after the checkup, Margie appeared as if out of nowhere. Merton introduced her to Wygal.

The three of them went to lunch at Cunningham's, an old Louisville institution three miles north of the hospital—and a mere four blocks from the corner of Merton's life-changing epiphany. Merton and Margie, who were left alone for half an hour while Wygal ran an errand, discussed their relationship, including the level of intimacy people in their unusual situation could expect. Sex, obviously, was out of the question. Of that they were sure.

Wygal returned, and after he and Merton dropped Margie off at the hospital for her shift, Wygal warned Merton that his involvement was extremely dangerous and could have tragic results. That evening, Merton tried to justify his situation, writing that the relationship was "beautiful," like that between Jacques Maritain and his late wife, Raïssa.

Over the next few days, more letters were exchanged and more phone calls were made while Merton vacillated between justification and pangs of conscience. He knew he could never abandon the hermitage or his vocation, but he was determined to find a way to incorporate a platonic though passionate relationship into his life—though he despised the word *platonic* in relation to Margie.

On Thursday of the following week, Merton would have a second opportunity to confide in a friend. He was expecting a visit from his longtime publisher, James Laughlin.

• • •

In 1936, at the age of twenty-two, and with the help of family money, James Laughlin founded New Directions and soon grew the publishing company into a formidable literary powerhouse. Over the decades it issued pioneering literary works by Ezra Pound, Tennessee Williams, Franz Kafka, James Joyce, Albert Camus, and Pablo Neruda, to name only a few, and by the mid-sixties, few students graduated from college without owning a well-thumbed copy of Lawrence Ferlinghetti's *Coney Island of the Mind* (1958), Dylan Thomas's *Collected Poems* (1953), or Hermann Hesse's *Siddhartha* (1957)—all iconic publications from New Directions.

Laughlin had published Merton's first book, *Thirty Poems*, in 1944—well before the publication of *The Seven Storey Mountain*—and had subsequently issued more than a dozen other Merton titles, including *Seeds of Contemplation* (1949), *Selected Poems* (1959), *The Wisdom of the Desert* (1960), and *Original Child Bomb* (1962). At the time Merton first met Margie, New Directions was in the process of publishing what would become one of Merton's most admired books, *Raids on the Unspeakable*.

Laughlin arrived at Gethsemani on May 5, accompanied by Chilean poet Nicanor Parra, then a visiting professor at Louisiana State University. Only months before, New Directions had issued a bilingual edition of Parra's *Poems and Antipoems*, originally published in Spanish in 1954. Parra's collection was a favorite of Merton's and had influenced many of the Beat poets, including Allen Ginsberg and Lawrence Ferlinghetti. Merton had long admired Parra and written in the "antipoem" form, which is characterized by a deliberate rejection of traditional poetic technique. Merton had even translated some of Parra's antipoems for this new collection. Although the two had corresponded, Laughlin was eager for them to meet in person.

After their arrival, Laughlin and Parra treated Merton to a scenic drive and a meal. As they meandered north toward Louisville, Merton asked them to stop periodically. He wanted to call someone. Not finding a payphone, he suggested they simply continue driving to see if his friend might be at home. So as not to arrive completely unannounced, Merton finally located a payphone and called Margie to tell her to expect them in twenty minutes.

At Lourdes Hall, introductions were made, and, though understandably puzzled, Laughlin offered to treat everyone to lunch. If there was ever a premise for an intriguing one-act comedy, it must certainly be the day that James Laughlin, Thomas Merton, Nicanor Parra, and Margie Smith had lunch in the Luau Room at the Louisville International Airport.

How different the thoughts of each person must have been. Laughlin, no doubt wishing to play the gracious host, was hoping to cement a closer relationship between Merton and Parra, and Margie might have seemed something of a fifth wheel. Parra, in his poetic way, was delighted with everything—the attractive young woman, the monk who was clearly in love with her, the conversation, and even the airport itself. Parra, a thoroughgoing Communist, was amused by the well-fed bourgeois Americans teeming through the concourse in preparation for the Kentucky Derby, which was to take place in two days. For their part, Margie and Merton, while delighted to be together, were guarded, sticking to safe topics of conversation. Sensing their reserve, Parra eventually nudged Laughlin under the table, indicating they should let Merton and the young woman talk privately. Excusing themselves, Laughlin and Parra said they could all meet up later.

Now on their own, Merton and Margie strolled to a secluded grassy area outside the terminal, where they could talk as they distractedly watched the planes come and go. Later Merton wrote, "It was beautiful, awesomely so, to love so much and to be loved and to be able to say it all completely without fear and without observation."[4] It was their most intimate conversation yet.

On the drive back to Gethsemani that night, Parra, in an impish mood, told Merton he should "follow the ecstasy," a comment that caught Merton up short. He wrote, "By which he meant evidently right out of the monastery and over the hill. This of course I cannot do."[5]

The following morning, before leaving, Laughlin told Merton he understood the monk's attraction to such a lively and intelligent young woman, but he expressed reservations about his own part in the events of the day before. He didn't want to get Merton in trouble or endanger their relationship.

Laughlin's qualms did nothing to prevent Merton from immediately suggesting yet another deception for which he needed Laughlin's help. Merton wanted to mail him his growing catalog of love poems for Margie—with the intention of having Laughlin publish them posthumously. Since his mail was often screened, Merton wanted to avoid arousing suspicion. His solution was to refer to the poems, which eventually numbered eighteen, as translations of obscure Latin American poets, for Merton was, in fact, translating a number of them at the time.[6] The code name Merton devised for use in their correspondence was "the Menendez file."

• • •

Even as Merton and Margie spoke at the airport, they knew they would be seeing each other two days later, on Derby Day. The abbot had given Merton permission to invite some friends to Gethsemani on Saturday to enjoy a picnic and to listen to the race on the radio. As a personal favor, Merton asked these friends, philosophy professor Jack Ford and his family, to bring along another guest, one who was unknown to the Fords. It was Margie.

The night before the Derby, Merton wrote a Menendez poem about their airport tryst, titled "Louisville Airport, May 5, 1966," intending to read it to Margie the next day, though he worried he wouldn't be able to contain his emotion. The deer he had watched from his porch two months earlier returned again in his imagination. He wrote:

> [God's] alone and terribly obscure and rare
> Love walks gently as a deer
> To where we sit on the green grass[7]

Rilke's themes of solitude and desire are again echoed in God's "alone and . . . rare / Love." When Merton looked into this woman's eyes, he couldn't help but echo Shakespeare;[8] he writes of his and Margie's

> . . . solemn love
> Now for the first time forever
> Made by God in these
> Four wet eyes and cool lips
> And worshipping hands[9]

• • •

During the Derby Day picnic at the abbey, Merton and Margie, to the Fords' surprise, disappeared over the hill and were gone for a couple of hours. The two walked to the creek at the foot of Vineyard Knob and had a long talk. They discussed their options, which they narrowed to three. First, Margie suggested she could live in Louisville after her graduation from nursing school and visit him regularly. This would mean more illicit meetings and whispered phone calls, possibly for years. Second, Merton could leave the monastery, which was his only path to "marrying"—Merton himself put the word in quotation marks because he knew the church would never recognize such a marriage, and he could be excommunicated.[10] Finally, a distant hope: perhaps, in light of Vatican II, the church might eventually allow its priests to marry. But this possibility was as remote then as now, more than fifty years later.

A few days later, Margie wrote to him, suggesting that their only option was simply "to be ourselves." The problem, Merton observed, was, "This is not allowed."[11]

• • •

On Saturday, May 14, a week after the Derby, Merton was back in Louisville to get a shot for his bursitis. He met Margie at Cunningham's and read another poem he had written for her, "Aubade on a Cloudy Morning," in which he grieves he cannot sleep next to her and watch her as she wakes each day. They talked about their situation, about the possibility of Merton's leaving the order so they might simply live together without marrying, which was implied in the poem. They knew this was unrealistic.

At one point, the conversation turned to Joan Baez, whom the media had dubbed "the Queen of Folk" and a *Time* magazine cover story had called a "Sybil with a Guitar."[12] Margie adored her music, and Merton had recently been listening to Baez's first album on the recommendation of Gethsemani's choirmaster, Father Chrysogonus. Baez's version of the folk song "Silver Dagger" seemed so poignant to Merton and Margie that they made a resolution. They vowed to listen to the song every morning at 1:30—just as Merton was rising from his bed to start his day and as Margie was settling into hers after her late shift fifty miles away. One biographer refers to it as their "binding song."[13]

The idea is a variant of the old lovers' vow involving the moon. Henry Fielding described it in *Tom Jones* when the title character tells a friend, "Two Lovers . . . agreed to entertain themselves when they were at a great Distance from each other, by repairing, at a certain fixed Hour, to look at the Moon; thus pleasing themselves with the Thought that they were both employed in contemplating the same Object at the same Time."[14]

The "Object" in this case—Baez's plaintive ballad—had a cathartic quality for Merton and Margie.

Don't sing love songs, you'll wake my mother,
She's sleeping here right by my side
And in her right hand a silver dagger,
She says that I can't be your bride.

All men are false, says my mother,
They'll tell you wicked, lovin' lies.
The very next evening, they'll court another,
Leave you alone to pine and sigh.

My daddy is a handsome devil
He's got a chain five miles long,
And on every link a heart does dangle
Of another maid he's loved and wronged.

Go court another tender maiden,
And hope that she will be your wife,
For I've been warned, and I've decided
To sleep alone all of my life.[15]

What the lover does after this rejection is not explained. Perhaps he will murder the mother. Perhaps he will elope with the girl. But none of this is hinted at in the version Baez gives us. Hers is not about the lover; it's about the girl and her rejection of the man before he betrays her.

One can picture Thomas Merton, in May 1966, sitting alone in the abbey's dimly lit library in the early hours, seated by one of the record players with headphones on.[16] He has risen a half hour before the other monks so he can keep his 1:30 listening date with Margie. He hunches slightly over the phonograph. Gently, he brings the phonograph needle down on the edge of the record, called simply *Joan Baez*.[17] She had recorded it, her debut, in 1960, and the first track is "Silver Dagger."

In the song, Baez projects a heartbreaking innocence as well as an astonishing power. A rapid acoustic-guitar accompaniment creates a tension, impelling the narrative forward in a headlong way, as if anticipating a train wreck. Baez, as always, sings with flawless conviction. Four decades later, Bob Dylan could still remember the impression Baez's recording of this song made on him: "She made your teeth drop." She had the ability, Dylan wrote, "to make you believe what you are hearing. . . . I believed that Joan's mother would kill somebody that she loved. I believed that. I believed that she'd come from that kind of family. Folk music, if nothing else, makes a believer out of you."[18]

The song itself is only two and a half minutes long, but in its four verses, a whole world of inexpressible emotion opened for Merton, just as it had for Dylan. A month later, Merton summed up his own feelings in his *Midsummer Diary*, the private journal he kept for Margie. He wrote, "All the love and death in me are at the moment wound up in Joan Baez's song 'Silver Dagger.' I can't get it out of my head, day or night. I am obsessed with it. My whole being is saturated with it. The song is myself—and yourself for me, in a way."[19]

For Merton and Margie, the song was talismanic, mysteriously evoking their situation. They would have equated the mother with the church itself, or perhaps with Dom James, who would certainly disapprove of their relationship. The dagger represented not the redemptive cross of Christ, but the powerful symbol of the Church of Rome's ultimate authority over its clerics in such matters.

The girl's warning to the lover not to sing love songs must have been especially significant for Merton. He had already conspired with Laughlin to hide his own "love songs"—his poems for Margie—from the abbot and anyone else who might be intercepting his mail. Metaphorically, if Dom James were to wake up to the sound of love songs being sung outside the abbey window, he would most certainly take up the cross, the church's authority, to end the relationship. He would have reminded Merton, as he eventually did, that Merton had already "decided to sleep alone" when he took his simple vows twenty-five years earlier.

In the short term, Merton and Margie found some small comfort in the fact that the song ends, as one writer said, "inconclusively." But few listeners would mistake that for a happy ending. The ominous, modal melody and Baez's heartrending delivery leave little doubt that things will end badly—and soon. Whatever happens, the listener knows the lovers will part—just as Merton and Margie must have known they would eventually have to. For them, like the lovers in the song, their situation was impossible.

Perhaps even more apposite is the song's finely pitched sexual tension, which comes as much from the edgy guitar pattern as the singer's luxuriant voice. Baez herself has referred to "Silver Dagger" as "by far the most erotic song in all of my repertoire."[20] More than a month later, one of Merton's fellow monks, who may have overheard him listening repeatedly to "Silver Dagger," chided Merton, saying, "The songs of Joan Baez had 'sensuality in them.'" But Merton was in no mood to be lectured. In the *Midsummer Diary*, he vented his fury: "My eye. I told him that he was hearing the deep archetypal symbols and resonances that come from the love and death planted deep in our hearts: things the monks would rather not hear. . . . There is no sensuality in them."[21]

After a few moments' reflection, Merton sensed he had overstated things and, in a seemingly defeated tone, added, "There are no archetypes in them either. Maybe there is a kind of death in them, and maybe even a life comes out of them." Then he reminded himself why he and Margie were listening to "Silver Dagger" in the first place: "No one can ever prevent us from thinking of each other and from loving each other."[22]

• • •

For those few weeks, Merton's world contracted. Due to the physical and emotional "tearing up," his focus narrowed to the thin geographical corridor between Gethsemani and Louisville. Where his journal used to overflow with a wide array of topics—presidents, poets, Nature, the peace movement—the writing now became a catalog of his conflicted feelings about Margie. His once voluminous correspondence slowed to a trickle, and when he did write, it was usually to say, cursorily, he'd had an operation, had returned to the abbey, and was recovering.

World events that would have formerly compelled his attention now remained largely unmentioned. On March 23, for instance, the day he was driven to the hospital in the pouring rain, Archbishop of Canterbury Michael Ramsey made a landmark visit to Pope Paul VI in Rome, initiating a rapprochement of the Anglican and Roman Catholic Churches after four hundred years of estrangement.

Before the operation, Merton noted that an antiwar demonstration was to take place in New York on March 26. Twenty thousand people gathered. After his return to Gethsemani, he mentioned neither the protest—the largest to date—nor the follow-up march in Washington, D.C., on May 15. Nor did he mention that on April 12, the US expanded its strategic bombing of North Vietnam in an operation ominously called "Rolling Thunder."

On March 16, a week before the surgery, Merton expressed outrage about the January crash of a US military B-52 off the coast of Spain. During a routine refueling, the plane broke apart with a nuclear payload—the infamous "Palomares incident." Three of the four bombs were recovered near a small fishing village, and though none exploded, five hundred acres of Spanish coastline became uninhabitable due to plutonium contamination. The fourth bomb was fished out of the Mediterranean on Good Friday, April 7. After returning from the hospital, Merton didn't mention the incident again.

Also on that Good Friday, *Time* magazine issued what was probably the most controversial edition in its history—the famous "Is God Dead?" issue.[23] It sparked years, if not decades, of debate and misunderstanding. The article outlined the complex issues philosophers and theologians were discussing at the time—the fact that traditional conceptions of God were becoming functionally irrelevant and that theologians were positing the need for a "God above the God of theism."[24] Merton had been writing intensely about the death-of-God movement for many years already, but the publication of that issue of *Time*, which suddenly brought the discussion into the public square, passed unacknowledged by Merton until months later.

More personally for Merton, on that Easter Sunday, Catholic writer

Evelyn Waugh died. Noted for his lyrical novel *Brideshead Revisited*, among many others, Waugh had edited the British edition of *The Seven Storey Mountain*, which was retitled *Elected Silence*. He also edited Merton's subsequent book, *The Waters of Siloe*, a history of the Cistercian order.

Waugh had been a personal writing coach for Merton and, as such, something of a poke in the eye to those Catholic censors who had once recommended that Merton take a correspondence course in grammar. Merton did them one better by apprenticing, by mail, with one of the greatest English stylists of the twentieth century. Waugh first exposed Merton to such classics on writing as Graves and Hodge's *Reader Over Your Shoulder* and Fowler's *Modern English Usage*. Waugh, whom Merton respectfully addressed as "*Mr.* Waugh," had visited Merton at Gethsemani in 1948. But the level of Merton's distraction was such that he never mentioned Waugh's death in his journals or letters until much later. While it was not uncommon for him to get the news of the world weeks late, in this case, Merton simply had other things on his mind.

His life had gone underground. Secrets needed to be guarded. Merton regularly made illicit phone calls, arranged private trysts, and smuggled love poems out of the abbey under a code name. In his journals, he refers to Margie only as "M."

Though problematic, this new life had its advantages. The surgery offered Merton a much-needed respite from the daily grind of church politics, monastic rules, writing deadlines, and world affairs. The romance offered him a chance to reclaim a part of his life that had been overshadowed by his fame, his vows, the church's high expectations, and his own enormously high ideals. He was entering a new kind of aloneness, existential and visceral. Not unlike the young Sebastian in Waugh's *Brideshead Revisited*, Merton found himself in a situation that was now "Thomas *contra mundum*"—"Thomas against the world."

His recovery at the abbey gave him a different sort of desert experience—one in which he was suddenly forced to focus wholly, if stealthily, on his own emotional needs, which now had enormous relevance to his spiritual development. His vision that "there are no strangers" became personal in a different way. He found a new kind of solidarity with the world. Now, being in love, he was dealing with ethical and romantic issues he'd not dealt with this intensely since before entering the monastery, and though not without its agonies and anxieties, this new life—this *vita nuova*—energized him. It made him feel alive as never before.

And all it took was the tender gaze of one caring human being.

The Absurd Man

Sunday, May 22, 1966

The thinnest of crescent moons settles through the trees to the west, and ahead, the faint glow of Bardstown rims the horizon. As he walks the path to the hermitage—his first overnight there since the operation six weeks ago—he breathes deeply, relishing the quiet. The birds fall silent. The air feels clearer, less oppressive.

He reaches the porch and looks back. As he leans against a post, fireflies flicker in every direction, and he spots the constellation Scorpius rising above the trees to the south, showing what one imagines to be the scorpion's pincers. No lights in the abbey, so the southern sky is dark and crystalline and full of stars.[1]

Two and a half months ago he stood on this porch and watched the deer cross the clearing in the snow. Ten weeks, and so much has changed. Now he is feeling more like himself, back home at the hermitage. He thinks, "I am a solitary and that's that."[2]

• • •

The previous Thursday, three days before his return to the hermitage, he and Margie attempted to reprise their memorable Derby Day picnic. The plan was for her to come to the abbey with a basket of food, but, a basket not being handy, she used paper bags, which started to disintegrate as the ice in one of them melted. So a long hike to their secluded spot by the creek below Vineyard Knob was out of the question. They found refuge instead in the shade of some nearby bushes, feasted on ham and herring and wine, and, as on Derby Day, the sexual temptation was intense.

The next day Merton wrote in his journal that he "refused to be disturbed by it." He told himself that their attraction "purified" him, made him "real and decent again," though by Saturday, he regretted the whole thing, describing it as "a great wave of . . . love [that] subsided slowly and left a rather stark expanse of mud-flats!!" The whole situation "was absurdly impossible."[3] By the next day he was thoroughly confused and looking forward to settling back into the hermitage.

He called Margie that Sunday morning, May 22, and again that night, just before hiking up to the cabin. The second conversation was hurried because she was expecting another call, which Merton suspected might be from her fiancé; and after hanging up, Merton also feared that she may have misinterpreted his apprehensions as a veiled rejection. He was anxious. He stepped out of the abbey door, inhaled the cool air, and trudged up to the hermitage. Whatever happened, that was where he belonged.

The place had its advantages. He could be more alone with his thoughts there, though he soon found prayer and meditation difficult. He was freer to focus on resolving the situation with Margie and would have more time to write her letters and poems with less risk of discovery. He occasionally had friends post his letters to her from outside the abbey. The Menendez file continued to grow.

The main disadvantage was the cabin's lack of a telephone. In the next three weeks, the abbey's phone system would become a major character in the drama, not unlike the farcical chink in the wall in Shakespeare's *Midsummer Night's Dream*, through which the lovers Pyramus and Thisbe whisper. During those weeks, Merton surreptitiously called Margie, on average, more than once every two days. The risks were considerable. Apart from a few "safe lines," which were private phones in administrative offices, the abbey had a primary phone line, which was more accessible. The disadvantage was its multiple extensions—a call on one receiver could be overheard on the others. Merton used both kinds of phones.

Face-to-face meetings involved the most risk, but Merton was undeterred. He and Margie planned another rendezvous for the next week, Saturday, May 28, but at the last minute, she was unable to find transportation, so she went home to Cincinnati instead. Merton was relieved, not so much because they might be observed but because he feared temptation would finally overcome them, and in his journal that evening he continued to vacillate between self-justification and regret, at one point confessing, "I should never have got in love in the first place."[4]

• • •

But something else happened on that Saturday, the day of the canceled tryst. The outside world abruptly forced itself upon Merton in the form of an encounter that would have widespread, even global, implications. Minister and peace activist John Heidbrink, who four years earlier had helped organize the Catholic Peace Fellowship (CPF), was scheduled to visit Gethsemani with someone he wanted Merton to meet, the Vietnamese Zen Buddhist monk Thich Nhat Hanh. Although familiar with Nhat Hanh's writing, Merton had never met him.

The two monks mirrored each other. Like Merton, Nhat Hanh was a prolific writer on issues of faith and nonviolence, having edited Buddhist publications and having founded a peace organization in Saigon. In the early 1960s, Nhat Hanh had studied at Princeton, taught at Columbia, and was now teaching a symposium on Buddhism at Cornell. Just as Merton looked with curiosity toward Eastern spirituality, Nhat Hanh looked with hopeful expectation to the West. Though critical of Christianity, he was interested in Western thought and philosophy, which led Merton to assess him as being "like Camus, . . . a Buddhist existentialist."[5] Both men were poets and teachers, and both had lost brothers to war.[6] Even Dom James liked him because, wrote Merton, "he looks like such a kid and is yet so smart."[7] Nhat Hanh was thirty-nine at the time.

Nhat Hanh was currently in the midst of an important but quixotic project—to convince the US government to forgo its destructive policies in Vietnam. His letters to public figures were in some cases as influential as Merton's Cold War letters. A year earlier, Nhat Hanh had written to Dr. Martin Luther King Jr. to urge the Civil Rights leader to declare publicly his opposition to the war, which King did two years later when he delivered his "Beyond Vietnam" sermon.[8] Nhat Hanh was now at Gethsemani to connect with another influential American, and Merton welcomed the distraction.

The visitors arrived Saturday evening, May 28. Exhausted from his travels and hoarse from a throat infection, Nhat Hanh had to cancel his address to the monks scheduled for the next day, Pentecost Sunday. Instead, he and Merton had a lengthy, presumably *soto voce* conversation while they were driven around the countryside, visiting Bardstown and Abraham Lincoln's childhood home. Later that day, Merton spoke to the assembled monks, acting as Nhat Hanh's intermediary, explaining what he understood about Buddhism and Nhat Hanh's views. Years later Nhat Hanh wrote warmly of Merton's understanding of Eastern religion, especially his ability, rare among Christians, to get beyond Western dualisms.

Although Nhat Hanh intensely disliked the French Catholics who had done so much to suppress Buddhism and support the corrupt South Vietnamese government during France's war with the north between 1946 and 1954, Merton was among those who eventually persuaded Nhat Hanh that much could be achieved by Buddhists and progressive Catholics working together. The conversations at Gethsemani that weekend were fascinating and revelatory, and many writers have declared the meeting to be a decisive convergence of the antiwar movements of the East and the West. For Merton, it was also another milestone in his own journey toward bridging the gulf between Western and Eastern monasticism. A far-reaching dialogue had begun.

So moved by the Zen monk was Merton that in the weeks that followed he wrote one of his most famous essays, "Nhat Hanh Is My Brother,"[9] and he also wrote to the Nobel committee in Oslo to recommend Nhat Hanh for the Nobel Peace Prize.[10]

But absent from most discussions about that momentous encounter was one painful, unspoken subtext.

• • •

On that same Pentecost Sunday—significantly, the day on which Christians commemorate the fire of the Holy Spirit descending on the disciples—nine thousand miles distant from the Abbey of Gethsemani, something happened that powerfully affected both monks in different ways. Merton noted it only briefly in his journal, but for a writer as hypergraphic as he was, his very brevity was telling. While listing some books he was currently reading, he inserted this apparent non sequitur: "A Buddhist nun burned herself to death in Vietnam."[11] This simple, tragic phrase contained a world of meaning.

The incident occurred in Saigon, outside one of the city's three main Buddhist pagodas, and the nineteen-year-old woman who set herself on fire did so as a statement of protest against the South Vietnamese regime. That day a Buddhist monk also burned himself to death in Da Lat, a mountain town two hundred miles northeast of Saigon, and two days later, a seventeen-year-old Buddhist nun would do the same in Hue City.[12]

These and at least two other similar incidents that week were inspired by the death of Thich Quang Duc, an older Buddhist monk who, three years earlier, had burned himself to death at a busy crossroads in downtown Saigon. The photograph of his last moments, widely distributed by the Associated Press, remains one of the most haunting images of that decade.[13] It shows Quang Duc sitting peacefully in a lotus position as the flames, blown laterally by a buffeting wind, engulf his head and body. Shocked and helpless onlookers stand in the background. Quang Duc had been a friend of Nhat Hanh, and Merton was shaken by the photo, once commenting, "Symbolism of the Viet Nam conflict, the burning Buddhists!"[14]

The American and South Vietnamese governments were outraged by such acts, not so much by the suffering involved as by the sympathy they garnered for the antiwar cause. On Monday, May 30, the day after the nun's death, President Johnson declared in his Memorial Day speech at Arlington

National Cemetery: "This quite unnecessary loss of life only obscures the progress that is being made toward a constitutional government. It only clouds the sacrifices of thousands of lives that have already been made for the cause of independence and political hope in South Vietnam."[15]

For reasons quite different than Johnson's, Merton too regarded these deaths as an unnecessary loss; he opposed self-immolation as a tool of protest. Six months earlier, on November 9, 1965, a peace activist named Roger LaPorte, the day before his twenty-second birthday, soaked his clothing with gasoline and set fire to himself in front of the United Nations building in New York. He died later in the hospital. A week earlier, a thirty-one-year-old Quaker named Norman Morrison had set himself on fire outside the Pentagon offices of Defense Secretary Robert McNamara as part of an antiwar protest. Like the Buddhists, LaPorte and Morrison had been inspired by Thich Quang Duc.

While Merton endorsed nonviolent protest, he was appalled by self-immolation, which he considered an implicitly violent and coercive act. He was a founding member of the CPF, but in November 1965, after learning that LaPorte had died in connection with a demonstration by the group, Merton resigned his membership, explaining that such tactics possessed "an air of absurdity and moral void."[16]

Merton's defection prompted dismay among those in the group. Some were angry. Some wondered if Merton was rejecting the peace movement altogether and reneging on his support. Especially disturbed was Heidbrink, who, Merton feared, felt it was like "a knife in the back."[17] Though the rift was largely repaired in the months that followed, these events provided an important subtext for his meeting with Heidbrink and Nhat Hanh.

In bringing Nhat Hanh to Gethsemani, Heidbrink was confronting Merton with an alternate view, for Nhat Hanh's take on those deaths was quite different. In his famous letter to Dr. King the previous year, Nhat Hanh referenced such burnings as an argument for the moral rightness of the antiwar cause. Religious men and women would never consider such measures, he argued, if the situation were not so dire, and he denied that such actions were protests or suicides. They were a form of self-expression.

"To burn oneself by fire," Nhat Hanh wrote to King, "is to prove that what one is saying is of the utmost importance." From a Buddhist perspective, death is the next step in the cycle of life. "In the Buddhist belief, life is not confined to a period of 60 or 80 or 100 years; life is eternal."[18] For Merton, and in Christian belief, by contrast, self-murder is an unacceptable rejection of a divine gift. Merton, though he agreed with Nhat Hanh on much else, would have had a hard time viewing it any other way.

Three days after leaving Gethsemani, Nhat Hanh issued a statement to lawmakers in Washington, D.C.: "The demonstrations, the self-immolations, and the protests . . . are dramatic reflections of the frustrations which the Vietnamese people feel at being so effectively excluded from participation in the determination of their country's future."[19]

As far as we know, that difficult topic was not broached at Gethsemani that Pentecost weekend, or at least none of the participants reported it. The only reference is Merton's, written within forty-eight hours of Heidbrink and Nhat Hanh's departure: "A Buddhist nun burned herself to death in Vietnam."

• • •

Merton didn't mention Nhat Hanh in his journal again until several months later. As enlivened as Merton was by the visit, he put an end stop to the events of that weekend with these simple words in his journal: "Getting back to M."[20] After that he returned to writing about their increasingly untenable situation.

But why did he mention the Buddhist nun at all? Was it bewilderment or sorrow? Or was there something paternal and pastoral in his empathy for her and for all young women faced with impossible choices? Did he connect the young nun with Margie in some unconscious way? Margie had once briefly considered becoming a Catholic nun, and only a week earlier, Merton had written a Menendez poem for her in which he said, "I will no longer burn your wounded body. We do not need to weary ourselves grasping anything, even love: still less the bloody jewel of desire."[21] In Merton's mind, her complicated relationship with him was, in a sense, a burning.

The idea of *sacrifice*—even the word itself—recurred regularly in his discussions with her and in his journal entries. Several times he had warned her that their relationship would ultimately involve sacrifice, and as recently as the day of Nhat Hanh's visit, Merton had written a letter in which he told Margie, "The only answer is sacrifice."[22]

Merton, shaken and aware of his responsibility, sifted through his conflicted feelings like an obsessive inner archaeologist. He so overintellectualized his emotional minutiae that in one phone call Margie chastised him for it. But he knew, on the most basic level, he would eventually hurt her. Though each of them would make sacrifices, hers would be the greater.

Two years later, in a sad irony, there would be a burning: Merton would burn all of Margie's letters before leaving for Asia.

• • •

On the Tuesday after Pentecost, Margie returned from Cincinnati, and she and Merton had a long phone conversation. They devised a plan to meet in Louisville the following Saturday, when Merton would be in town for another bursitis shot. By Friday, anxious with anticipation, he wrote, "There is a real danger in my cracking up under the pressures and contradictions of love in my absurd situation." His use of the word *absurd* triggered another association: in that same entry he resolved to reread Camus, because from Camus he could learn "to prefer happiness, or the taste for it, even though absurd."[23]

On Saturday, in Louisville, he headed to Cunningham's, where all his anxieties evaporated when he saw Margie walking toward him in a light summer dress, with "her long hair flying in the wind."[24] The day went beautifully. They spent most of the afternoon in a semi-private room in the restaurant, talking, drinking wine, reading Menendez poems, and being completely absorbed in each other. Merton was an hour late for his ride back to Gethsemani, and that night they spoke again on the phone.

As often happened, Merton's misgivings disappeared in her presence, but back at the abbey, the anxieties reemerged. By Thursday of that week, while he was concelebrating Mass on Corpus Christi Day, the incongruity of his situation struck him: "I stood there among all the others, soberly aware of myself as a priest who has a woman,"[25] becoming what Albert Camus called an "absurd man."

• • •

Like an allegorical figure, the notion of the Absurd stalked through Merton's journals during these weeks. He was a monk in love with a woman with whom he could not pursue a relationship—unless he was willing to break the vows he knew he would never break—so that he could marry her in a ceremony that the church he belonged to would never recognize.

Along with Søren Kierkegaard, Camus was a formulator of the philosophy of absurdism, which posits that humans are instinctually drawn to find significance in circumstances even—or especially—when no inherent significance exists. The Absurd is an untraversable desert that stands between our need for meaning and our inability to discover it. Camus's solution is to create our own meaning—the absurd man must start trekking across that desert even in the face of hopelessness. Merton took comfort in the idea that he should choose "to prefer happiness . . . even though absurd."

Merton began rereading *The Myth of Sisyphus*, Camus's influential collection of essays. Its central metaphor is the Greek tale of Sisyphus, the ill-fated Titan who was condemned to push a boulder up a hill only to have it break free from his grasp and roll back to the bottom—over and over again for eternity. The myth resonated with Merton, if only because this was not the first time he had suffered the agonies of an impossible love. At age sixteen, aboard an ocean liner bound for the US, he became infatuated with a woman who was, coincidentally, twice his age—just as he was now twice Margie's age. The event, which he described in *The Seven Storey Mountain*, was at once prophetic and ironic:

> I would rather spend two years in a hospital than go through that anguish again! That devouring, emotional, passionate love of ad-

> olescence that sinks its claws into you and consumes you day and night and eats into the vitals of your soul! . . . No one can go through it twice. This kind of a love affair can really happen only once in a man's life. After that he is calloused. He is no longer capable of so many torments. . . . He is no longer capable of such complete and absurd surprises.[26]

The word *absurd* predominated then as now. With Margie, Merton was rolling the boulder back up the hill. One can only imagine how he must have paused over this arresting line in *Sisyphus*: "The more one loves, the stronger the absurd grows."[27]

• • •

Shortly after the Corpus Christi Mass, Merton walked to one of the monastery offices to call Margie, only to discover that the direct line to Louisville had been disconnected. He briefly wondered if he might be under suspicion. Putting that thought aside, he called her on the main phone system instead. A new plan was underway. Since he had to return to Louisville the next Saturday, June 11, he arranged with Jim Wygal to meet Margie privately in Wygal's office, with poems and champagne in hand. The meeting took place, and, as before, the temptations were strong.

That evening, after returning to Gethsemani, he called her on one of the abbey's main lines, and in that conversation, they again enumerated the unlikely outcomes of their love—his leaving the abbey, their living together, their getting married. . . . The next morning, after sleeping poorly, he wrote in his journal, "Something has to be done. We can't go on like this."[28] Only one outcome was inevitable—discovery. It was at this point that the telephone took center stage.

As soon as Abbot Dom James returned from a trip abroad on June 13, one of the brothers asked to speak with him. The monk said that while in the gatehouse recently, he saw a light blinking on the phone console. Thinking that one of the extensions might be off the hook, the monk picked up the receiver. He heard voices. One was Merton's; the other, that of a woman. The two were on intimate terms.

Merton got wind of the discovery that evening from another one of the brothers—ironically, while Merton was in the abbey, poking around for a phone on which to call Margie. He didn't know which conversation had been overheard: the one on Thursday, during which he and Margie had arranged their meeting, or the one afterward, when they had discussed marriage. Perhaps on an unconscious level, Merton precipitated the discovery through his own lack of caution, as the only practicable way out of the situation. He called Margie quickly to let her know what had happened. "She was desolate, and so was I," he wrote.[29]

The next morning, June 14, rather than waiting to be summoned, Merton went to the abbot to make a preemptive confession—though providing as few specifics as possible. The abbot was unexpectedly understanding. While sympathizing with Merton's "powerful emotions,"[30] he demanded that all communication with the young woman cease. The abbot blamed the hermitage, suggesting that Merton had been too lonely and should return to the abbey. Merton bargained him out of it by agreeing to do extra training for the novices.

Over the following days, Merton responded variously with resignation, anger, shame, consuming heartache, but above all, relief. While he grieved for Margie, he knew he couldn't forgo his calling as a solitary. It was one of the first things that she had asked him in the hospital—how could anyone live as a hermit? The hermitage was home; he knew it back then, and he knew it on the night, just three weeks ago, when he stood on the porch watching Scorpius rise over the trees.

On the day of his confession to the abbot, he wrote in his journal, "I am better and freer in solitude, total and accepted, including loneliness and sorrow for M. . . . I am going to write maybe a new book now, in a new way, in a new language too"[31]—a declaration reminiscent of Søren Kierkegaard, who felt compelled to break his engagement to Regine Olsen. While Kierkegaard knew the separation would make him miserable, and make Olsen miserable as well, he also sensed that to accomplish his best writing, to achieve his goals, he would have to avoid such complacent middle-class joys as marriage. The next day, Merton quoted Kierkegaard in his journal: "The self is the relationship to oneself."[32] A reaffirmation of solitude.[33]

At the time, Merton was also reading Camus's novel *The Stranger*, in the final chapter of which the book's antihero, Mersault, is awaiting execution for murder. When a visiting priest asks Mersault why he never addresses him as *père*, "father," Mersault responds, "I told him he was not my father; he was with the others."[34]

Two days after his talk with the abbot, Merton copied that ominous line in his journal—"He was not my father; he was with the others"—for it expressed his own disaffection. At that moment, nearly everyone—the monks, the church, Dom James—belonged to "the others."[35] That was the same distancing phrase he had used on Corpus Christi Day, standing at the altar, a priest with a woman, celebrating Mass alone among "the others."

But as strongly as Merton identified with Camus, he was about to embrace another artist equally able to articulate the absurdity and estrangement he felt. On the day of his confession, feeling vulnerable and exposed, Merton gloomily paced the fields around the abbey. That evening he drank brandy from a marmalade jar and confided to his journal: "Invisible. 'Like a rolling stone.'"[36]

His reference to a line from Bob Dylan's "Like a Rolling Stone"—"You're invisible now, you got no secrets to conceal"—provided a remarkably cogent summary of Merton's situation.[37] Like countless other fans, he had discovered how intensely personal Dylan's universalities could be, though some secrets did remain, with Merton choosing not to tell the abbot about a number of things, like the Menendez file and the extent of his contacts with Margie.

In that same entry, he wrote, "Lately borrowed from Fr. Chrysogonus records of Joan Baez (especially 'Silver Dagger'!!) and Bob Dylan, which I like a lot ('Tombstone Blues' and 'There is something happening here and you don't know what it i-i-s, Do you, Mister Jones?')." Although Merton slightly misquoted the refrain from Dylan's "Ballad of a Thin Man," he caught the acerbity in the descending melody as Dylan sings, ". . . *i-i-s*."

As Merton commented: "Very pointed and articulate."[38]

The Soundtrack

Once, one of the brothers—perhaps the same one who dismissed the songs of Joan Baez for having "sensuality in them"—decided that the cows would give more milk if sacred music instead of classical was played in the barn. Liturgical chants and hymns would have the added benefit of keeping the brothers more "recollected," that is, better focused on things spiritual while they milked the cows and shoveled the stalls. Later, Merton wryly noted that the plan resulted in neither more milk nor more recollected monks. The scheme was quickly abandoned, and "the hills resounded with Beethoven" once more.[1] But no one could have foreseen the kind of music that resounded across those hills in the summer of 1966.

Among the books that explore Merton's romance with Margie Smith, few chronicle his musical interests at the time, but if ever a story needed an audio accompaniment—a soundtrack—to be fully appreciated, it is this story. In the months after the discovery, the music that filled Merton's head had a cogency that none of the books he was reading at the time, except for Camus, quite possessed. Music was now comforting him, influencing his writing, and reshaping him more than at any other time in his life.

And for that, Merton had "Fr. Chrysogonus" to thank.

• • •

Father Chrysogonus was born Thomas Waddell in 1930 in the Philippines, the son of a US Army officer. When Waddell was eighteen, his musical talent took him to the Philadelphia Conservatory, where he studied with composer Vincent Persichetti, whose distinguished career spanned nearly six decades. Persichetti later moved to Julliard, where he would teach such extraordinary talents as the enigmatic Philip Glass and the redoubtable Peter Schickele, better known as P.D.Q. Bach. Schickele would eventually work with Joan Baez on three of her albums.[2]

In 1950, at the age of twenty, Waddell became a postulant at Gethsemani in hopes of using his gifts in service of the church, which he did, first as a choir monk and then later as choirmaster. Under his monastic name, Chrysogonus, he became a noted composer of English liturgical music as well as a respected scholar of medieval chant and the early Cistercians.

In 1962, as the English Mass was replacing the Latin after Vatican II, Waddell was sent to Rome to study theology with a view toward helping to shape the new liturgy. When he returned in September 1965, he was still a young man of thirty-five, a decade and a half younger than Merton, and as a composer, he immediately took the temperature of American music. Though folk and pop music were hardly new to him, what *was* new was Beatlemania. The Beatles' records had started climbing the US charts in late 1963, and with the band's arrival on American soil in February 1964, the face of popular music changed forever.

But an American-grown response to the British invasion was also taking the radio by storm: folk rock, the next big thing, was tuneful, powerful, rooted in traditional song, with lyrics that reached beyond the well-worn themes of romance and teen angst, which even the Beatles were still singing about. In 1965, the Byrds had number-one hits with Bob Dylan's "Mr. Tambourine Man" and Pete Seeger's "Turn, Turn, Turn," which took its lyrics from the book of Ecclesiastes. Barry McGuire charted with "Eve of Destruction," a chip-off-the-Dylan-block protest number, replete with shaky Dylanesque harmonica solos. The very week of Waddell's return from Rome, the top two songs on the *Billboard* chart were the Beatles' "Help" and Bob Dylan's "Like a Rolling Stone" from *Highway 61 Revisited*, an album released two weeks earlier.[3]

That this music grabbed Waddell's attention is only natural, for in light of the demands of the new liturgy, he heard potential in folk music and jazz as ways to reinvent worship. While most of Waddell's compositions were firmly grounded in Gregorian chant, he briefly experimented with choral pieces in the folk mode, writing hymns like "Jesus Lives" and "He Is Risen!"[4] He even wrote a hymn with guitar accompaniment, folk-style. These melodies had the advantage of being memorable, easily adapted to small instruments, and extremely popular with congregants. Eventually, however, after finding that folk music's strong melodies detracted from the textual emphasis he loved in Gregorian plainsong, Waddell abandoned the style, but not before he had gathered a sampling of folk records for the library at Gethsemani.[5]

Waddell purchased Joan Baez's eponymous debut for the abbey in the winter or spring of 1966 and recommended that album, along with Bob Dylan's *Highway 61 Revisited*, to Merton sometime during his convalescence. Merton had fully absorbed the *Joan Baez* album by mid-May, when he and Margie pledged to listen daily to "Silver Dagger," but Merton doesn't mention Dylan until a month later, on June 14, the day of his confrontation with Dom James.

• • •

Imagine the scene as Waddell handed *Highway 61 Revisited* to Merton. The first thing Merton would have noticed, aside from Dylan's hyperborean stare in the front-cover photo, would have been the title's cheeky, deadpan reference to Evelyn Waugh's *Brideshead Revisited*. Unlike most record buyers then and now, Merton wouldn't have missed the allusion. Not only did Merton know the novel well, but its author had been both an acquaintance and a mentor.

In Waugh's unmistakably Catholic story, the narrator, Charles Ryder, a British Army officer during World War II, finds himself unexpectedly bivouacked at an English country estate. It was formerly the home of Sebastian Flyte and his sister Julia, with both of whom Ryder had been in love. Waugh's flawlessly crafted novel is a heartbreaking look back at the bucolic, heady days of England between the wars.

The title of Dylan's album implies that he too is looking back at an irretrievable past, but in his trenchant, ironic world, Dylan isn't revisiting an English country house but a gritty, 1,400-mile-long piece of concrete that winds from New Orleans, the birthplace of Dixieland and the home of the blues, to Duluth, Minnesota, an hour-and-a-half drive from Dylan's childhood hometown of Hibbing. Along the way, that highway passes through

- Vicksburg, where General Grant finally broke his losing streak in the Civil War;
- Clarksdale, Mississippi, where bluesman Robert Johnson is said to have sold his soul to the devil—at the famous crossroads of Highways 61 and 49;
- Como, Mississippi, the home of Fred McDowell, composer of "61 Highway Blues," which partly inspired Dylan's own song;
- Memphis, the home of Beale Street and of Sun Studios, where Elvis Presley first recorded;
- St. Louis, subject of W. C. Handy's "St. Louis Blues," the first blues song to become a national hit;
- Davenport, first stop on the Rock Island Line, which the great bluesman Leadbelly declared was "a mighty good road";
- Redwing, home of the Minnesota State Reform School, about which Dylan wrote a powerful song in 1963;
- and Minneapolis, where Dylan attended a semester of college before heading to New York to meet Woody Guthrie.

While Route 61 bisects the country geographically, it bridges the country racially, for it was along this highway that rural Southern blacks traveled north to find factory jobs in the big Midwestern cities.

Merton may not have been aware of these resonances, but in listening to the album, he was immediately struck by Dylan's kaleidoscopic images of our cultural landscape, our pop heroes, our shared history, poetry, art, and religion—what Merton later referred to admiringly as Dylan's "baroque obscenities."[6] Dylan, wrote Merton, "bravely jumbles together all the mad collection of cultural ikons that have been stuffed into the heads of our kids in high school."[7]

The album's title track is like a car trip down a surrealist highway while loud blues music blares on the radio; flying past the windows are such off-beat characters as Georgia Sam, Poor Howard, Mack the Finger with his shoestrings and telephones, the seventh son, and a roving gambler intent on starting World War III. And how could Merton not love a song that begins, "Oh God said to Abraham, 'Kill me a son'"?[8] Every song on the album is an existential patchwork, a slideshow of some bizarre demimonde Mardi Gras.

After putting the vinyl disc on the abbey's record player and dropping the needle on the first track, "Like a Rolling Stone," Merton scrutinized the back of the record jacket, where he found Dylan's own album notes, a baffling surrealist prose-poem beginning, "On the slow train time does not interfere & at the Arabian crossing waits White Heap, the man from the newspaper & behind him the hundred inevitables made of rock & stone—the Cream Judge & the Clown . . ."[9] For a monk who loved the resonances and mystifications of words, a deeper study of Dylan's cryptogram would come later.

Merton also noted a small blurb on the bottom right-hand corner of the back cover, which read: "Other albums by Bob Dylan you might enjoy: *Bringing It All Back Home*, *Another Side of Bob Dylan*, and *The Times They Are A-Changin'*." One week after his difficult meeting with the abbot, Merton wrote his friend Ed Rice to request those three albums, listing them in precisely the same reverse-chronological order.[10]

Initially Merton was impressed with Side One, for he references three of its five songs in his June 14 entry: "Like a Rolling Stone," "Tombstone Blues," and "Ballad of a Thin Man"—songs that touched upon the chaos and alienation he was then feeling: "You're invisible now . . ." and "Something is happening here. . . ." For Merton, it was pure poetry, new and thrilling and immediate.

In the monastery, he had been limited to experiencing poetry almost entirely on the page. No jazz poetry readings in smoky coffeehouses for him, and no vinyl LPs of Dylan Thomas's booming recitations. Though Merton read poetry constantly, it was in the two-dimensional medium of print. He was not without spoken poetry, however. He compensated by wandering the hills surrounding the hermitage with a book in hand, reciting aloud whatever poems he was currently enjoying. For Merton, like a man suddenly emerging from a dark room into full sunlight, hearing Bob Dylan was a profound jolt of poetry. For perhaps the first time since entering the monastery, he was actually hearing a poet (and Merton considered Dylan a poet) deliver powerful words directly to his ear rather than to his eye. A third sensual dimension suddenly became part of Merton's aesthetic life.

Although Merton's thoughts were largely about Margie over the next several months, Dylan's music, to judge from Merton's writings, was usually playing in the background. His enthusiasm for it enlivened him and contributed to his emotional recovery. While he was reading a variety of books—from Camus, about whom he was writing a major article, to German and Italian poetry, which were among the books he read aloud in the woods—Merton's fascination for Dylan became a valuable distraction, if not an outright obsession.

• • •

But, to borrow Merton's phrase, "Getting back to M . . ."

On June 14, when Abbot Dom James forbade all further communication with the "young woman," Merton understood this to mean that his letters were sure to be inspected and the phones monitored. Once again, as with the Cold War letters, he would find detours around the censors because further communication was still necessary. There was, above all, the matter of explaining to Margie what had taken place in his meeting with Dom James.

The opportunity arose two days later when Dr. Wygal, who had gotten wind of the goings-on at the abbey, arrived to take Merton for a drive and a chat. When Merton suggested they stop at a liquor store so he could call

Margie from a payphone, Wygal tried to dissuade him, warning that he was on a "collision course," but Merton prevailed. He said he was "tapering off, gradually."[11] That night, reflecting on his first conversation with Margie since the discovery, Merton wrote: "For me solitude is not a problem but a vocation. For her it tends to be *the* problem. And she knows that for me it is a solution."[12]

He ached to write a note about Margie to James Laughlin—who was Merton's next-closest confidant after Wygal—but Merton knew better than to entrust details of the recent developments to the mail. So, the day after calling Margie from the liquor store, Merton wrote Laughlin a generic, newsy letter about his health, what he was reading, and Nhat Hanh's visit, and asked Laughlin to send some volumes of Camus in French. He made no mention of the Menendez file, made no veiled references to his "Peruvian inspirations" or "the situation," as he had in previous letters[13]—but noted only that he was "getting back to real work," ready to "buckle down to work on a book . . . after a period of being more or less fallow."[14] He was hoping that Laughlin would read between the lines and sense that something had happened.

In that letter, just before requesting the Camus volumes, Merton wrote, "Incidentally I heard a record of Bob Dylan lately and like him very much indeed. Respond extremely to that, very much at home in it." He wrote Laughlin again the next day: "I finally got to hear something of Bob Dylan's and like his stuff immensely. Can you get me a copy of the *New Yorker* of Oct. 24, 1964 with a profile of B. Dylan by [Nat] Hentoff? . . ."[15]

Ordinary letters to friends, like the ones he wrote to Laughlin, posed no problem should they be inspected, but letters to Margie were another matter. So, Merton hit upon the idea of keeping a private diary addressed to her alone. He had already asked various visitors to smuggle letters out to her, but now he had decided to put all his epistolary eggs in one basket, a rambling thesis on the subject of their relationship. He referred to the document as his *Midsummer Diary*. The title, partly a nod to Shakespeare, refers to the week of its composition, starting on June 17 and ending on Midsummer's Day, June 24, the Feast of Saint John the Baptist. Originally he conceived of the diary as the final communiqué in their relationship, his definitive apologia. He wanted to finish it by that date because he had arranged to see her one last time on June 25 while he was in Louisville for X-rays. He could give it to her in person.

In the diary, in agonizing detail, he discussed their situation and his often volatile and confused feelings. It is loving, tormented, apologetic—newsy and analytical by turns. It is in this diary that he tells Margie about his confrontation with the monk who had said the songs of Joan Baez "had sensuality in them," and Merton describes how much the song "Silver Dagger" meant to him.

At one point, while explaining the absurdities and contradictions of being "a priest who has a woman," he wrote,

> All the things a hermit should not do I have done. Should a hermit like Bob Dylan? He means at least as much to me as some of the new liturgy, perhaps in some ways more. I want to know the guy. I want him to come here, and I want him to see one of my poems, he might even use it. . . . I should be writing the new English version of some hymn nobody is ever going to sing.[16]

It was a bold confession. Having heard only one Dylan record, he declared that it had affected him as profoundly as the English liturgy. Bolder yet was his desire to have his own poems set to music—by Bob Dylan, no less. A month later, Merton wrote Ed Rice to say that his poem "The Prospects of Nostradamus," which Merton had begun after returning from the hospital, might be a good one for Dylan to start with.[17] Musical settings of his poems, Merton seemed to be saying, might prove provocative enough to startle the church the way Dylan had startled the world of pop music.

Merton also meditated on "lostness" in the *Midsummer Diary*, an extension of his reflections on absurdity and alienation. At one point he wrote, "As long as a single person is lost I am lost. . . . [T]he way one begins to make sense out of life is taking upon oneself the lostness of everyone." The concept parallels the apostle Paul's command to "bear ye one another's burdens,"[18] but Merton refurbished it for the age of Sartre and Camus—that we must bear each other's alienation. One person's alienation is everyone's, and Merton saw our existential distance from God and each other as the result of humanity's deep-seated inauthenticity: sin. Merton asserted that "Dylan has a better intuitive realization of it than the bishops and the clergy"—essentially implying that Dylan was aware that our sense of lostness, of being out of place, is universal, and that our absurdity is shared. Yet, argued Merton, when Dylan sings, "Something is happening here and you don't know what it is, do you, Mister Jones?" Dylan seems to be assuming a superiority to Mr. Jones; Dylan is shaming people precisely for being lost. Dylan "has rejected the sin of being Mister Jones," wrote Merton. "Even Bob Dylan is not perfect."[19]

A few days after writing that portion of the diary, Merton received a response from Laughlin, confirming that he had ordered the Camus books and the back issue of the *New Yorker*. Laughlin added, "Bob Dylan is extremely interesting, both as a poet in his own right, and as a social phenomenon. His influence on the young is tremendous." Laughlin went on to say that he'd heard Dylan had written a book, soon to be released. "I will order two copies, so there will be one for you,"[20] wrote Laughlin.

• • •

The June 25 rendezvous in Louisville came off without a hitch. Merton and Margie found each other near the hospital's first-floor elevator, and after he gave her the manuscript of the *Midsummer Diary*, they sought out a secluded spot on the fourth floor. "I realized once again," wrote Merton, "not only that our love was the deepest thing in our lives, but was growing deeper."[21] He invited her to lunch with him and Dr. Wygal at Cunningham's, an idea that met with Wygal's disapproval, but, as before, Wygal relented and let them have time to themselves.

Grief-stricken, Margie informed Merton that her fiancé had been reported missing in action over North Vietnam. She also told him that she would be transferring to a hospital in Cincinnati after her graduation from nursing school in August—a decision prompted by her grief over the end of her relationship with Merton. She felt her life was falling apart. It was a heartbreaking meeting that roused Merton's sympathy and renewed their passion. "We fell on each other," Merton wrote, "in desperation and love, kissing each other over and over, swept with love and loss."[22]

Believing he would never see her again, Merton was in agony for the next few days. On June 28 he wrote what he thought would be his final letter and mailed it during a short trip outside the monastery. The next day, he believed he had turned the corner on his despair, and his clearest indication was that "Silver Dagger" was no longer running through his head. Instead, he was chanting the French children's song "Sur le Pont d'Avignon" with its gleeful "On y danse" refrain ("Everyone dances").

Merton began the following week with renewed energy. He was more able to focus on his reading and prayers. The end of that week saw the arrival of a Canadian woman named Linda Parsons, a spiritual seeker who, after exploring a variety of traditions, was eventually led to write to Merton. They had been corresponding, and now she had come to visit.

She took him for a drive, and when they stopped for drinks at a restaurant, Merton couldn't resist the temptation of a payphone. He called Margie. They arranged for her to come secretly to the abbey the next week, but her overeagerness alarmed Merton—she wanted to meet the next day, July 9, instead. Sensing not only the danger of sexual temptation but the prospect of losing his vocation, Merton said no.

After Parsons left, Merton wanted to explain to Margie the reasons for his refusal, so he began a sequel to the *Midsummer Diary*, which he called *Retrospect*, a document as yet unpublished. He was also tempted to write her a letter of explanation but thought better of it. Again he was in agonies. Despairingly, he wrote in his journal, "'Silver Dagger' is back and I know all the words."[23]

Four days later, as he sat on the porch, he admitted to himself that if he had to choose between life with Margie and life in the hermitage, it was no contest. Solitude was his first love. Aware of the elemental sexuality in their relationship, he knew that if Margie had visited the abbey, he wouldn't have been able to resist. He again vowed to end the affair.

But, as Saint Augustine famously said, not quite yet. Later that week he sprained his ankle while hiking and had to be taken yet again to Louisville. Again he called Margie, who met him at the hospital, after which they headed for a picnic at Cherokee Park, a mile east of downtown. Merton regarded this encounter as "one of the most lovely days" they had spent together. Again they discussed their feelings, raged about those who opposed their love, reaffirmed their intentions to remain in touch, and, just as before, reluctantly said good-bye. Merton said that as they kissed, she kept repeating, "I am happy, I am at peace now!"[24]

After a few days back at the hermitage, he felt calmer, more able to work and concentrate. One of his first thoughts was that he might try writing about Dylan. So Merton dashed off a letter to his friend Ping Ferry to see if there was any chance of talking with Dylan in person; could he perhaps be persuaded to come to the monastery? The response was disappointing. On July 19, Ferry wrote that there were simply "too many managers and handlers to deal with" and that none of his appeals were likely to get "through the Inscrutable Barrier."[25]

The next day, coincidentally, another letter arrived. In it, Ed Rice promised to send him the three Dylan records that Merton wanted and also asked him to write a feature article about Dylan for *Jubilee*, a Catholic magazine edited by Rice, which discussed contemporary culture and post–Vatican II issues. The request couldn't have come at a better time. Not only would the assignment distract him from the current turmoil, but it would further immerse him in the world of an artist he already admired. Conveniently, ten days earlier, Father Chrysogonus had received the abbot's blessing to allow Merton to borrow the abbey's record player.

The hermitage was now wired for sound, and the Kentucky hills were about to resound with the music of Bob Dylan.

DYLAN INTERLUDE NO. 2

I Do Believe I've Had Enough

On the morning of July 29, 1966, Bob Dylan's life took an abrupt turn—every bit as sharp as the one Merton's had taken on the day when Margie Smith walked into his hospital room. And a very literal turn it was.

Dylan was riding his motorcycle south on Striebel Road in Bearsville, New York, two miles west of downtown Woodstock. The one-mile-long road is heavily wooded and lined with picturesque fieldstone fences, and the long country driveways on either side lead to a handful of elegant homes. Sara, Dylan's wife of seven months, had just dropped him off at his manager Albert Grossman's house on Striebel to pick up his Triumph Speed Tiger T100SR, which had been stored there for the duration of his recent concert tours.[1] Dylan loved those bikes. A year earlier, he had been photographed wearing a Triumph T-shirt for the cover of *Highway 61 Revisited*.

The plan was for Dylan to take the motorcycle to the Bearsville Garage for repairs, less than a half mile down the hill, and for Sara to follow in their Ford station wagon and drive him back home. Albert Grossman wasn't at his house that day, but his wife, Sally, was. (She, in a hipster Madame Récamier pose, appears with Dylan on the cover of *Bringing It All Back Home*.) After Dylan climbed on his bike and rumbled down the long driveway with Sara trailing behind, Sally phoned her husband, no doubt to tell him that his star performer had just stopped by. Not long into the call, there was a commotion outside. A frightened Sara was at the door, and Dylan was sitting in the car, apparently hurt.

After a short conversation with Sally, Sara decided to drive her husband to his doctor's office, more than an hour away. The doctor would know what to do. No ambulance was called, nor were the police informed. No accident report was filed. Exactly what happened between the time Dylan left with his motorcycle and returned in the car a few minutes later has long been a matter of debate.

News reports variously stated that Dylan was near death, had broken his neck, was disfigured, or had a serious brain injury. For fans and those in Dylan's tight circle, it was déjà vu—only three months earlier, Richard Fariña, a songwriter, performer, and friend of Dylan's, had died in a motorcycle crash in California.

But Dylan didn't die, and in the absence of a medical report, the most common story, based on Dylan's testimony, is that he "ended up with several broken vertebrae and a concussion."[2] All very dramatic but, like so many truths, susceptible to variation.

According to Victor Maymudes, Dylan's friend and sometime bodyguard, Dylan was going slowly—too slowly—on his motorcycle. "One mile an hour," Maymudes said. When Dylan's bike started to tip, he turned the wheel in the direction of the spill, but the cycle went over anyway. Dylan fell and banged his head, according to Maymudes, but wasn't thrown.[3]

In his book *The Ballad of Bob Dylan*, poet and scholar Daniel Mark Epstein goes even farther. According to his anonymous sources, there was no crash. The tires on Dylan's motorcycle were flat, which is why he was taking it—walking it—to the repair shop. According to Epstein's sources, Dylan was pushing the heavy, wobbly machine with underinflated tires when it simply fell over, knocking him down and scraping him up.[4] Though designed to be lighter than many motorcycles, the Speed Tiger still weighs 370 pounds—almost as much as a real tiger.[5]

Other people close to Dylan insist a major accident occurred. Robbie Robertson of the Band, who was Dylan's guitarist for the spring tour, has little patience for the no-accident theorists: "People say, 'Oh, he didn't have an accident, this was just so he could kick heroin or whatever.' No, no, no! He fell off the motorcycle and fractured his neck."[6]

Still, Robertson and Maymudes would have agreed on one thing: Dylan's life took a U-turn at that point.

• • •

We may never know the extent to which Bob Dylan's backbone problem was life-threatening or, to use Thomas Merton's word, "invented," but if Dylan had done no more than stub his toe, a serious accident took place, one that involved the high-speed collision of his fame, his drug and alcohol abuse, and an impossible number of commitments that had been foisted upon him. The tour nearly killed him—literally. Robbie Robertson tells the story of a strung-out Dylan nearly drowning in the hotel bathtub after the last London show in May. Robertson pulled him from the water at the last second.[7] Not for nothing has that spring tour been dubbed "the Amphetamine Tour."[8]

While Dylan has never wavered in asserting the motorcycle accident as a fact, he has repeatedly stated that exhaustion, not cracked vertebrae, was the larger problem. In 1978, he told an interviewer, "I was straining pretty hard and couldn't have gone on living that way much longer."[9] A few years later, he said, "I woke up and caught my senses. I realized that I was just workin' for all these leeches. And I didn't want to do that."[10] In his 2005 memoir, *Chronicles*, he again hints at the reason: "Truth was that I wanted to get out of the rat race."[11]

The rat race was largely the creation of Dylan's manager, the wily and audacious Albert B. Grossman. Aggressively tending to his stable of clients—including Peter, Paul and Mary; bluesman John Lee Hooker; and later, the Band and Janis Joplin—hyper-entrepreneur Grossman was known for driving them hard.

Grossman's immediate chore for Dylan was the promotion of *Blonde on Blonde*, which had been released a month before the accident.[12] Media outlets were clamoring for interviews, and Grossman was urging his star to get out there and start promoting. But after the frenzied European tour, Dylan was in no mood to answer such inevitable questions as "What do you think about the controversy surrounding your new sound?" and "Does being booed bother you?" Dylan had spent the last year straight-facing reporters with his absurdist answers, but now those reporters had plenty of snarky ammunition to fire back with. For Dylan, to muster the energy to respond must have seemed tedious beyond description.

More stressful yet was the prospect of yet another tour. Grossman had scheduled a grueling series of sixty-seven US concert dates, due to start in a matter of weeks. That was more than three times as many gigs as Dylan's death-defying European tour—and anyone who has seen the videos of those European shows knows how close to the edge that tour pushed him. The footage shows an angular figure in tight pants, with heavy eyelids and a spectral, detached expression on his face. The new US tour was immediately canceled after the accident.

D. A. Pennebaker was also waiting in the wings. Having filmed the 1965 acoustic tour of England, which resulted in the acclaimed documentary *Dont Look Back*, he had been called upon to film the 1966 tour as well—a film already optioned for television in the fall. But this time around, Dylan insisted on editing the footage himself.

Though not quite as pressing, a new record would have to be made, and Dylan didn't need Grossman to remind him that most of the material still needed to be written. Dylan had tinkered with some new song ideas while on the road—with titles like "What Kind of Friend Is This," "I Can't Leave Her Behind," and "On a Rainy Afternoon"—but even if he could still remember them, they needed fleshing out.[13]

If that weren't enough, Dylan had to finish writing a book. More than a year and a half earlier, Grossman, without consulting Dylan, had signed him to a major book deal with Macmillan. As Dylan later explained, "These things happened in the old days."[14]

When Dylan had first learned of the deal, he had asked poet Allen Ginsberg for advice, and Ginsberg recommended that he immerse himself in the works of the French Symbolists, especially Arthur Rimbaud's *Season in Hell* and Comte de Lautréamont's *Songs of Maldoror*. It was astute advice, for Rimbaud and Lautréamont were progenitors of Dylan's own brand of barmy poetic synesthesia, along with French surrealist poet André Breton, one of Dylan's favorites. So, in early 1965, sometime between the sessions for *Bringing It All Back Home* in January and *Highway 61 Revisited* in July, Dylan managed to pound out a book-length, free-associative prose-poem in the same surreal style as the back-cover notes to *Highway 61*. At the end of the European tour, when a London reporter asked him about the rumored book, Dylan deadpanned, "It's about spiders, called *Tarantula*. It's an insect book. . . . My next book is a collection of epitaphs."[15]

When the Macmillan editors saw the manuscript, they must have thought Dylan was putting them on with its 160 pages of lines like "i am gazing into the big dipper with silver buttoned blouse in my nostrils—i'm glad Marguerita's all right—i Do feel expensive."[16] In light of the substantial advance he received, Dylan was expensive indeed.

Tarantula was largely finished and had progressed as far as galley proofs by the time of the motorcycle accident, but the vexations of reviewing it, tweaking it, and responding to the editors' queries were simply more unneeded stressors. By then, the book seemed like ancient history to Dylan, a moment in time, something that had rattled around in his brain more than a year before—so, what was the point?

Then there were the fans. They were perhaps the biggest reason for taking time off, for wanting to go underground and stop being Bob Dylan. The Newport controversy of the previous summer had stung. So, in preparation for the fall 1965 US tour, Dylan and his crew rehearsed for a week before the opening concert at Forest Hills Stadium in New York, scheduled for August 29. They worked up a formidable set list, perfected their arrangements, and checked and double-checked the sound system to make sure the instruments wouldn't overpower the vocals.

The evening started well enough. Dylan opened with a solo acoustic set of seven songs, ending with "Mr. Tambourine Man" to take advantage of the popularity of the Byrds' recent hit version. Then, after a short break, he returned to the stage with his backing band—which is when the yelling began. "Scumbag!" someone shouted between songs, and the crowd chanted, "We want Dylan! We want Dylan!"[17]

With a few rowdy exceptions, the other forty-two concerts of that US tour that fall went better than Forest Hills, but the raw hostility returned in May when he landed in Europe. He was heckled, slow-hand clapped, booed, and handed notes telling him to ditch the band. In Bristol, people yelled, "Turn it down," and many others angrily stomped out. He was even heckled during the acoustic set in Paris, and in Manchester, an audience member shouted, "Judas!" One heckler in London was so annoying that Dylan challenged him to a fight from the stage: "Come up here and say that!"[18] The concerts were a back-alley brawl on tour.

But the hostile fans weren't the only problem. They were at least energizing, part of the performance, a spontaneous spur to creativity. When Dylan was slow-hand clapped in Sheffield, for instance, he mumbled mysteriously into the microphone until the audience thought he might be saying something worth hearing, which made them stop clapping. In Paris, the audience was heckling largely to protest US involvement in Vietnam, so, in response, Dylan, pugnacious as ever, performed the second half of his show in front of a wall-sized American flag. When accused of being "Judas" in Manchester, he snarled, "I don't believe you. You're a liar!" and told the band to "play f—— loud" before they launched into a venomous eight-minute-long performance of "Like a Rolling Stone."[19] The sparring only fueled Dylan's intensity—which resulted in one of the most critically acclaimed concert tours in music history.[20]

It wasn't just the hecklers. The others—the true believers, the addled fanatics, the hippy adulators—were also a problem. They had elevated Dylan to the status of a promethean Titan, a druggie demigod, a stoned prophet bringing stone tablets down from the mountain. No one, not even the Rebel King of Rock 'n' Roll (as *The Saturday Evening Post* had christened him), could live up to such high expectations and stay sane. In response, Dylan dryly told reporters, "I think of myself more as a song and dance man, y'know?"[21]

Whatever happened on Striebel Road, what mattered to Dylan was to take control of his life, to slow down—something he hadn't done for years. Now that Jesse, his first child, was six months old, Dylan realized that he had spent nearly half that time on the road, either recording in Nashville or on tour. Now was his chance to put down roots, to focus on Sara and baby Jesse and his five-year-old step-daughter, Maria. Now was the time to find out what it felt like to be a family man, a patrician farmer, a father who was there for his kids. You can take the anarchist troubadour out of the Midwest, but you can't take the Midwest out of the anarchist troubadour.

So, after recuperating at his doctor's home, he returned to his secluded house in Woodstock, ready to find new meaning in the phrase *bringing it all back home*. And so began Bob Dylan's own search for solitude.

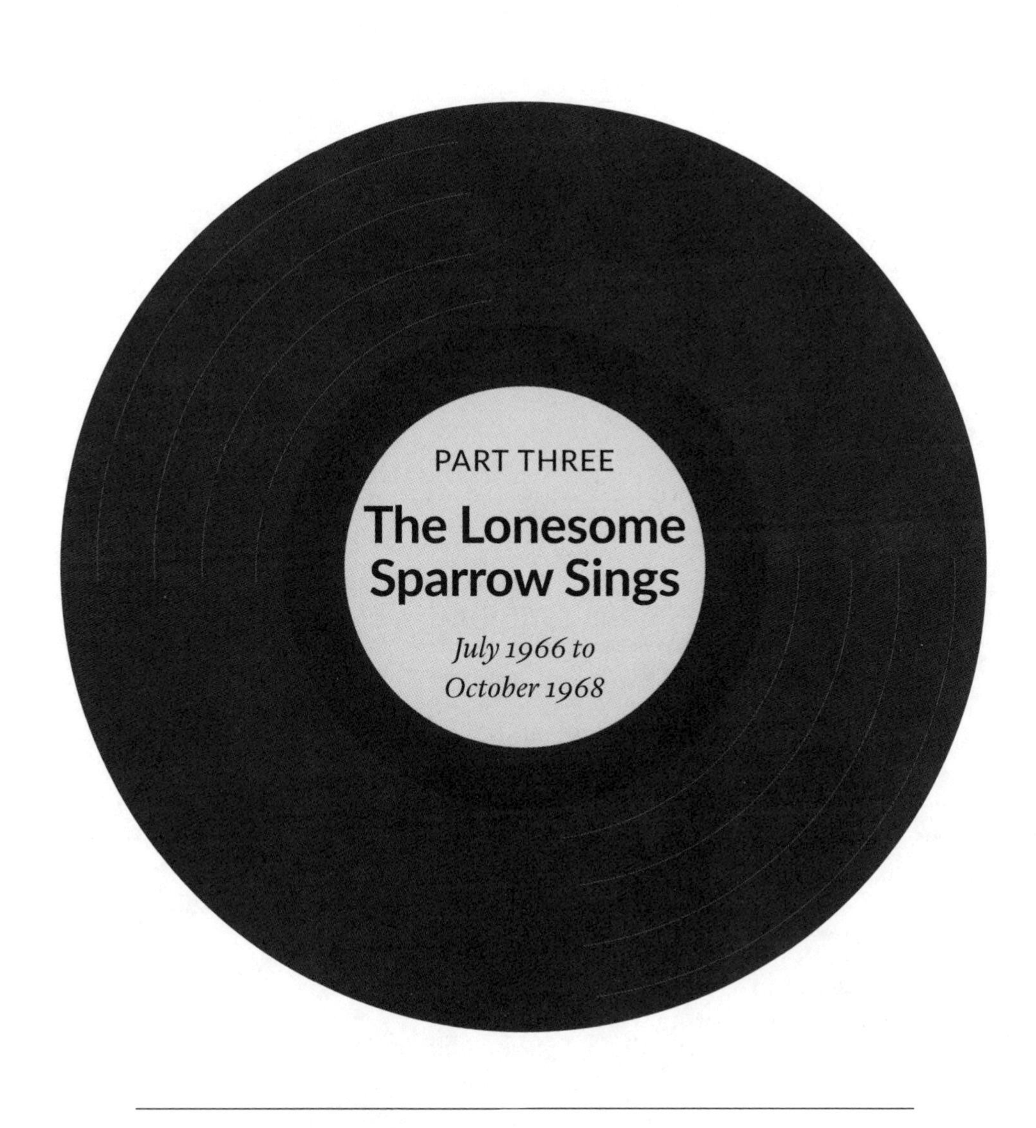

PART THREE

The Lonesome Sparrow Sings

July 1966 to October 1968

Bob Dylan, "Gates of Eden," *Bringing It All Back Home*, LP (Columbia, CS 9128, 1965), side 2, track 2.

THOMAS MERTON	BOB DYLAN
1966	
July 29: has medical checkup in Louisville and writes “Cancer Blues”	**July 29:** the motorcycle accident
Aug. 12: Margie’s commencement	
Aug. 13: Victor and Carolyn Hammer visit	
Sept. 8: is officially confirmed as hermit and receives package of Dylan records	
Sept.: *Conjectures of a Guilty Bystander* published	
Sept.–Oct.: writes most of *Cables to the Ace*	
Oct. 7–9: Jacques Maritain and others visit	
Oct. 11: Daniel Berrigan visits	
Oct. 28–30: Sidi Abdeslam visits	
Dec. 8: Joan Baez and Ira Sandperl visit	
1967	
Jan.: abandons Dylan article	
	March–May: Red Room Sessions (Basement Tapes)
	May 17: *Dont Look Back* released to theaters
late May: the Hammers visit John Jacob Niles	
	June–Oct.: Big Pink Sessions (Basement Tapes)
July 10: Victor Hammer dies	
	Oct.–Nov.: *John Wesley Harding* sessions
Oct. 28: hears Niles’s settings of three poems	
mid-November: last phone call to Margie	
Dec.: *Mystics and Zen Masters* published	**Dec. 27:** *John Wesley Harding* released
1968	
	Jan. 20: plays at Woody Guthrie tribute, NY
Jan. 29: buys *John Wesley Harding* and *Ascension* albums	
Feb.: visits jazz clubs in Louisville	
spring: *Cables to the Ace* published	
May: spends three weeks in California	
	June 5: Dylan’s father dies
Oct. 15: departs for Asia	
	Oct. 23: meets with Johnny Cash in New York
Nov. 4: meets the Dalai Lama	
Dec. 10: dies near Bangkok	
1969	
	April 9: *Nashville Skyline* released
	July: *Great White Wonder* bootleg released
	Aug. 15–18: Woodstock Festival
	Aug. 30–31: Dylan plays Isle of Wight Festival

Sort of a Bob Dylan Thing

Friday, July 29, 1966

As he sits in the waiting room of the Medical Arts Building in Louisville, he shuffles through the uneven stack of magazines on the side table. The cover of a recent *TIME* displays a drawing of Defense Secretary Robert McNamara with a map of Vietnam floating ominously behind him, and on the front of *Life* magazine, a dark-haired young actress is coyly posing outdoors in a wooden bathtub. The odd contrasts of American culture.

This morning, away from the abbey, he was finally able to post a candid, informative letter to Laughlin in which he recounted the recent events and enclosed some new Menendez poems along with a carbon copy of the lengthy *Midsummer Diary*. None of this, he knows, is likely to be published in his lifetime. But someday, perhaps.

More importantly, he was able to post a letter to Margie—a fairly unambiguous farewell at last. But now he feels torn and distraught. He can think of little else. She is somewhere in the nearby hospital, but unlike before, he didn't call her in advance. His four-month checkup was originally scheduled for next week, to coincide with her commencement, at which time they planned to meet again in Cherokee Park, but in the letter he mailed this morning, he canceled the rendezvous and said good-bye for good. To avoid any second-guessing, he had rescheduled the doctor's appointment for today. Though his love would continue, the affair was over.

Now, as he sits there, nearly in tears, the cover of *The Saturday Evening*

Post catches his eye. Dylan. He's on the cover under the banner "Rebel King of Rock 'n' Roll." There he is—in profile, in all his fuzzy-haired glory, head bowed, cigarette in mouth, scarf over his shoulder as he trudges through what looks like a post-apocalyptic New York cityscape. It's a romantic image, Byronic—the lone poet, turning his collar to the wind and wandering who-knows-where through an indifferent, monochromatic world. The cover also touts an article called "A Major Report on the New Nuns," which promises to be interesting. But the nuns will have to stand by. The Rebel King awaits.[1]

• • •

On that same morning, July 29, 1966—the morning of Dylan's motorcycle mishap—by some bizarre coincidence, some inscrutably cosmic happenstance, Thomas Merton and Bob Dylan, eight hundred miles apart, were consulting their doctors about back injuries at precisely the moment when each man was desperately trying to turn his life in a different direction. Even more strangely, Merton was thinking about Dylan that morning and by the end of the day would write a poem he described as "sort of a Bob Dylan thing."[2]

It might not have occurred to Merton to write such a poem that day if he hadn't stumbled across the *Post*. And though the cover headline read "Rebel King of Rock 'n' Roll," the article inside was titled "Bob Dylan: Well, What Have We Here?" written by Jules Siegel, a hip, thirty-year-old journalist who had spent some rare one-on-one time with Dylan on tour the previous year.[3] Siegel confirmed what Laughlin had written to Merton: Dylan's book, to be called *Tarantula*, was due out later that summer. Under the impression that the book would be a memoir, Merton knew it would be essential reading for his own article.

The *Post*'s cover photo was by Jerry Schatzberg, who also shot the quintessential Dylan image for the jacket of the recently released *Blonde on Blonde*. A week earlier, that record—the first double album in rock-music history—had appeared on *Billboard*'s Top LPs list, eventually climbing to number nine on the US charts. Merton, however, knew nothing about the new album because Siegel never mentioned it, nor would Merton hear about Dylan's accident until two months later.

As Merton sat in the waiting room, a song flashed through his head, a patter of words with a blues riff behind them. It gave him an idea. He took a pad of paper and a pencil from his pocket and jotted down some Dylan-esque lines for another Menendez poem, which at that point he called "A Blues for Margie," though he later retitled it "Cancer Blues."

But it was more than a Dylan pastiche. The poem was inspired by a specific song from *Highway 61*, which was still the only Dylan album Merton knew. Since Father Chrysogonus had toted the abbey's record player (a sturdy old portable with a fold-down lid) to the hermitage two weeks earlier, Merton had repeatedly listened to the album, anatomizing it with the same focused attention he reserved for writers like Camus and Edwin Muir, about whom he was currently writing major articles in addition to the one he hoped to tackle about Dylan.

Merton's template for "Cancer Blues" was Dylan's "From a Buick 6," in which Dylan extols his hip, scrappy, gun-toting woman as someone who "keeps [him] hid" and can "sew [him] up with a thread" after the singer crashes on the highway. At the end of each of the four verses, Dylan chants almost ecstatically, "Well, if I go down dyin', you *know* she bound to put a blanket on my bed"—those last ten syllables being delivered in a machine-gun-like iambic pentameter.[4] As swaggering and surreal as Dylan's song is, sounding for all the world as if it could have been the inspiration for the *Mad Max* movies, it is essentially a love song, albeit a visceral gut-punch of one, but oddly tender for all that. It is the only unambiguously adoring love song on the album. Its narrator fuses his own battered macho bluster with his awestruck reverence for his muse's magical healing arts and toughness. She is part shaman, part exorcist, able to "unload" the singer's head and "keep away the dead."

Over the past month, Merton could not have helped but hear echoes of Margie throughout "From a Buick 6." She was the woman who kept Merton and their relationship hid, who had sewn him up, or at least applied fresh bandages to his incision in the hospital; she frequently headed down the highway to see him; and she was the one who had literally put a blanket on his hospital bed.

Dylan uses a string of earthy epithets for his formidably streetwise nymph: "graveyard woman," "junk-yard angel," "steam-shovel mama," "dump-truck baby." This technique of applying cryptic epithets to one's lover appealed to Merton; in "Cancer Blues" he rolls out his own list. The poet's muse is a "magic Indian healer," a "punishment of dark sickness," a "sweet relentless punishing / INDIAN," his "photo-electric / CURE." So strong is the woman's healing power that she cleanses the town of its "racetrack vampires and sham aristocrats"—a line that Dylan himself might have envied.

In Merton's poem, he dramatizes himself as being bogged down amid "tree frogs and rain" in a hot "solitary swamp" (the hermitage) with the "cancer blues" (his depression and longing for Margie), while his healer continually "grows a little wiser" (Margie's medical training). Throughout the poem, he contrasts her "fiery gentle healing light" with the harsh, unforgiving city in which she lives, the city that he himself has just escaped after the doctor's appointment that day. Like the narrator in "From a Buick 6," the poet in "Cancer Blues" barrels down dangerous highways, a rebellious anti-hero on the verge of cracking up. Merton's narrator connects with the woman through his own "rush signals of emergency love and dread" (his letters and the *Midsummer Diary*), and his healer woman can only revive him through her "distant radio-electric loving glance" (phone calls). Near the end of the last stanza, he writes:

> You never miss you point right down to the
> ROOT CURE
> All the way down in the sweet summer earth to clean
> The hunted heart of the hell-blues because you are grown
> Into a healer.[5]

While infused with an electric-blues attitude, the poem is a touching commemoration of Margie's impending graduation from nursing school. She had indeed "grown / Into a healer."

• • •

That August, one year after telling the novices that in the solitary life "you no longer care about anything,"[6] Merton began to assess the collateral damage of his "affair"—a word that he himself used at this point.[7] His chief concern, of course, was Margie, and he grieved for her. But he also took stock of the many people who had facilitated the relationship, sneaking letters out of the abbey, finding payphones, driving him to and from Louisville, arranging meetings, and secretly archiving his poems. In various letters and journal entries, he began to acknowledge them.

He was aware of how close he had come to losing the hermitage. Dom James could easily have evicted him back in June, convinced, as he was, that Merton's unusually chaotic version of solitude had become almost more than either the monk or the abbot could bear. Merton scrambled to make concessions, which Dom James willingly accepted, while Merton chafed at the dominant position this put the abbot in.

But the threat of losing the hermitage didn't entirely go away. At the abbot's request, Merton had been counseling with Father John Eudes Bamberger, a trusted younger monk with psychiatric training—a substitute for James Wygal, whose relationship with Merton was slowly fraying. Father Eudes too began talking as if Merton's life outside the walls was a problem, to the point that Merton, in a sort of tactical flanking maneuver, wrote a series of letters to the abbot explaining why the hermitage was essential to his well-being. In one, he wrote somewhat threateningly, "If I could not stay in the hermitage, life would not be worth living and I would certainly create far more problems because I would be a burden to myself and to everyone else."[8] Again the abbot relented. He had a stake in keeping Merton content and productive.

Merton was also at a theological impasse with the abbot. While Merton took responsibility for his actions, he could not bring himself to regard his love for Margie as a moral failing. While ill-advised in light of his vows, the affair, Merton believed, had made him a more complete human being, more aware of his capacity for love and of God's immense love for him.

Having learned this, Merton was eager to face the future as a wiser, more loving individual, while the abbot simply wanted him to admit his failings, ask forgiveness, and get back to being the old Merton.

Merton was also aware that the affair had distanced him from his fellow monks even more severely than his move to the hermitage had; he was now "a priest who has a woman."[9] To make matters worse, the August 5 issue of *Life* magazine featured excerpts from Merton's forthcoming *Conjectures of a Guilty Bystander* as well as photos of Merton onsite at Gethsemani—the first time such photos had appeared in a glossy magazine. It wasn't good timing. Merton was now becoming a bigger celebrity for being a hermit. Doubly disconcerting was the fact that Merton, whom the church did not even allow to have his photo on his book jackets, had neglected to inform the abbot about the *Life* photos beforehand. The only good thing about the exposure was that Margie would see it and know that he was all right.

To mitigate some of the damage, Merton devised a plan. On August 12, the day of Margie's commencement, he came up with the idea of having a sort of graduation ceremony of his own in the near future. He proposed that he be allowed to make an official profession, to undergo a formal rite of "putting away a hermit." This simple act would communicate to the abbot and the brothers that after his one-year trial at the hermitage he was recommitting himself to the abbey, to solitude, and to stability. The abbot agreed. They scheduled the ceremony for Thursday, September 8.

• • •

The "old Merton" was never coming back, and few people were as aware of that fact as Victor and Carolyn Hammer. Victor, a retired artist-in-residence at Transylvania College in Lexington, was a well-known artist, typographer, and printer who had befriended Merton more than a decade earlier. He and his wife, Carolyn, a publisher and fine-press printer in her own right, had been frequent visitors to Gethsemani through the years. In the late 1950s and early '60s, the Hammers produced exquisite hand-printed editions of three of Merton's shorter contemplative works, among which was *What Ought I to Do?*, an early take on *The Wisdom of the Desert*. Featuring Victor's own medieval-style designs, these volumes were works of art, rich reinterpretations of fourteenth-century scribal manuscripts.

William Blake's maxim "Opposition is true Friendship"[10] summed up the nature of Merton's and Victor's relationship—for theirs was a bond founded in part upon a disagreement about aesthetics. In 1955, Hammer, in his first letter to Merton, outlined a complex theory of art that included the notion that three-dimensional, representational art, which Hammer called "classic art," was the hallmark of civilization. It was the only kind that accounted for the spiritual realm because it presented reality in a fully delineated, multilayered way. Merton disagreed. For years he gently tried to convince Victor of the equal value of "Byzantine art," painting that presented flat figures in two dimensions—the third, unseen dimension being an open door to spiritual reality. Among the arts, this included religious icons, abstract expressionism, and primitive art, such as Paleolithic cave painting.[11]

In the early 1960s, as Merton's interest in social issues paralleled his growing admiration for modern art, he himself experimented with free-form, Asian-inspired brush drawings. He shared these nonrepresentational shapes and swirls with the Hammers, and the couple saw them reproduced in Merton's recently published *Raids on the Unspeakable*.

As part of their ongoing dialogue, Merton had been trying since the late 1950s to arrange a meeting between the Hammers and artist Ad Reinhardt, the acclaimed abstract painter who had been one of Merton's friends at Columbia. Like Hammer, Reinhardt too had developed a complex aesthetic philosophy, which was a necessity in Reinhardt's case because his work was controversial and, in the opinion of many, needed a lot of explaining. He was famous for his "black-on-black" canvasses that looked from a distance as if they were solidly monochromatic but upon closer examination revealed subtle gradations of tone and pattern.

Reinhardt's New York exhibitions in the early 1960s were widely ridiculed in the popular press, though often praised by critics. (The *New Yorker*, among others, couldn't resist lampooning Reinhardt in its cartoons; one pictured an art student with her paints and easel, seated in front of an all-black Reinhardt painting. Her replica is nothing but a smaller painting, all black as well.) Reinhardt once explained that he wanted each of his paintings to be a "free, unmanipulated and unmanipulatable, useless, unmarketable, irreducible, unphotographable, unreproducible, inexplicable icon."[12]

Reinhardt's use of the word *icon* is significant for its religious connotations. Poet and critic John Yau suggests that Merton admired Reinhardt's black paintings because they were visual representations of the *via negativa*,[13] a way of coming to terms with God by contemplating what God is not, by meditating on the cloud of unknowing, the dark night of the soul.[14] Indeed, Merton once called Reinhardt the "Dean of the Great Quiet."[15] Far from being bleak negations of life, Reinhardt's paintings are invitations to the viewer to clear the mind of ordinary reality in order to focus on the vast, incomprehensible mystery of the divine. Yau quotes this passage from Merton's *New Seeds of Contemplation* by way of explanation:

> It is in this darkness that we find true liberty. It is in this abandonment that we are made strong. This is the night which empties us and makes us pure. Do not look for rest in any pleasure, because you were not created for pleasure: you were created for spiritual JOY. And if you do not know the difference between pleasure and spiritual joy you have not yet begun to live.[16]

Though Merton often referenced Reinhardt in his discussions with Victor, Merton failed to bring the two artists together. Had they met, Victor would have reiterated his opinion expressed to Merton in a letter in 1959: "To me abstract art is pure perversion. Reinhardt may be sincere, but as an abstractionist he is a sinner against the Holy Ghost. It is a travesty on creation Carolyn said."[17] Reinhardt, in response to Hammer's predilection for realism, might well have quoted something he wrote in an art journal: "The one thing to say about art and life is that art is not life and life is not art."[18] In theological terms, the discussion would have been a fascinating confrontation between the apophatic and the cataphatic, the negative and positive spiritual paths.

Traditionalist to the core, Victor was baffled by this increasingly modern Merton. The Hammers preferred instead the hermit monk who quoted the Desert Fathers and engaged in contemplative prayer; what had first attracted the couple to Merton was what they perceived as his unalloyed *contemptus mundi*—his disdain for the world. Merton did indeed criticize the modern world's destructive technologies, grotesque commercialism, and corrupting messages, but the Hammers failed to account for Merton's long-time, enduring engagement with modern art, music, literature, philosophy, and theology. He loved jazz, Beat poetry, and Albert Camus, after all. And now, Bob Dylan's music. Merton tended to see the spiritual in every honest artist, and it is a testimony to Merton's brilliance that he could befriend two people as different as Victor Hammer and Ad Reinhardt.

In the summer of 1966, however, Merton wasn't interested in engaging the Hammers in discussions about art. Instead, he asked them if they might be willing to produce a handmade, limited edition of his Menendez poems, the same ones he had been sending to Laughlin since early May. Merton knew it would have to be done discreetly, perhaps by using a pseudonym or by waiting a few years so as not to exacerbate his current problems, but the idea of an exquisite art-book edition of the poems for Margie captivated him.

When the Hammers came to see Merton on August 13, the three of them, caught in a rainstorm, ducked into a barn and sat on hay bales for a chat. The Hammers kindly declined Merton's proposal. The reasons were Victor's poor health (he was eighty-three) and their other commitments. But the subject matter itself may have been the greater problem. The Hammers, in whom Merton had confided details of his affair, were sympathetic, but they were disconcerted by his situation as well, and during their talk that day they expressed their relief that the relationship had ended. For them, the romance was another indication of Merton's devolution, paralleling his shift away from contemplative writing and his seemingly ardent embrace of modernism. Carolyn Hammer referred to it as Merton's transition "from cowl to blue jeans."[19]

• • •

Around the time of the Hammers' visit, the bursitis in Merton's elbow flared up, becoming so intense that he requested to see the doctor in Louisville. The appointment was scheduled for August 19. As before, he took advantage of this sojourn outside the abbey to post another confidential letter to Laughlin, updating him on the situation with Margie and his resolution to rededicate himself to the hermit life. Wistfully, Merton made this request: "In case of some important event like my death or my sudden transportation to the moon . . . I wish you would tip her off. No one here would." Toward the end of the letter, he adds, "Did the Bob Dylan book come out yet? I am perhaps going to write a piece on him for *Jubilee*."[20]

Though resolved that their affair was finished, Merton found it impossible not to place a long-distance call to Margie in Cincinnati. They hadn't spoken directly since their picnic in Cherokee Park a month earlier, so the emotions were intense. He wrote in his journal that the talk "was wonderful and in a way shattering," and before the end of the conversation he felt as if his heart had been "churned to pieces."[21] He learned that she had written him letters that apparently had been intercepted at the abbey. She also explained that she would be returning to Louisville for some exams in late October, hinting that they might find a way to see each other then. This posed a dilemma for Merton since he had already resolved to resist such temptations.

• • •

As Merton struggled to remind himself that the affair was over, he continued to write. He busied himself with the articles on Camus and Muir, he translated the poems of French surrealist René Char and the Spanish poems of Miguel Hernandez, and he contemplated a new direction in his own poetry—a non-Menendez, non-Margie direction. All the while, he listened to his single Dylan album, something he reserved for the evenings before going to bed, a routine that only increased his appetite for Dylan's music.

As far as the article Merton hoped to write, he knew he was handicapped by not having Dylan's book and access to more music. Realizing that two months had passed since he had requested the records from Ed Rice, he sent him a whimsical reminder on August 29:

> Do not hesitate at once to procure these gems instantly and at no matter what personal sacrifice. . . . This is a one shot expedition into the land of Nod for your old chum. I will be allowed a record player for this once only time in a lifetime to which I will be glued for half a day or so and then pfft. Further I wish to accomplish this spring rite before too long when I am to make profession as a hermit. Hurry then to your nearest drugstore with all possible patience and longanimity and if you can't get this just send me a bucket of LSD. . . .
>
> Or if you prefer those Dylan records. I am going to be the teen culture king of Trappist Nebraska.[22]

That last phrase deliberately echoes *The Post*'s "Rebel King of Rock 'n' Roll."

• • •

The first week of September was given over to a spiritual retreat in preparation for his official installation as a hermit. Merton rose early each morning to roam the hills around the abbey, saying prayers and praying the Rosary. Each afternoon he repeated these walks after Mass.

Then, on September 8, after Merton read aloud a short vow at the abbey, Abbot Dom James officially confirmed him as a hermit of the Roman Catholic Church. The ceremony was low-key. Although he didn't climb into a cave and pull the rope up after him, as he had joked with the novices a year ago, it was a milestone, a way of declaring that his solitary life was permanent and irrevocable. He had chosen solitude.

That same day, as fate would have it, a package arrived at the abbey. From its shape alone, Merton knew exactly who it was from, and he couldn't have been more delighted.

The American Villon

As promised, Ed Rice's package contained the three records: *Bringing It All Back Home*, *Another Side of Bob Dylan*, and *The Times They Are A-Changin'*, precisely as listed on the back of *Highway 61 Revisited*. But the package also contained a surprise, a fourth album that Merton hadn't been aware of. Although no name or title appeared on the cover, the photo said it all. When the gatefold cover was spread open, it displayed a slightly blurred, three-quarter-length photo of the musician staring disdainfully into the camera. He sported a brown-suede double-breasted coat with a scarf cinched at the neck. Inside the gatefold, in small type, were the titles of the album's fourteen songs and a collage of nine black-and-white photos, with Dylan in all but two of them. Noticeably heavier than the others, this album contained two vinyl records instead of one. Upon inspection, Merton would have discovered that words were indeed printed on the outside cover, small letters along the thin spine of the gatefold, right across the right breast of Dylan's coat: *Bob Dylan—Blonde on Blonde*.

At that point, a smile must have crossed Merton's face. For a second time, one of Dylan's album titles was making a sly, almost imperceptible allusion to someone Merton knew personally. Just as *Highway 61 Revisited* was a playful echo of Evelyn Waugh's *Brideshead Revisited*, the title of this new record was surely a tongue-in-cheek reference to Ad Reinhardt's notorious "black-on-black" paintings,[1] one series of which was even titled *Black on Black*.[2] Merton would soon discover that one of Dylan's songs on

Bringing It All Back Home refers to a mysterious woman who can "paint the daytime black."[3]

Dylan's song titles on the four albums provided playful appropriation of the device used by many modern artists of numbering their artworks in a series. On *Another Side*, for instance, Dylan calls one of his songs "I Shall Be Free No. 10"; on *Bringing* is "Bob Dylan's 115th Dream"; and the opening track on *Blonde* is "Rainy Day Women #12 & 35."

There was also poetry. Except for *Blonde on Blonde*, each album offered original poetry by Dylan himself. The back cover of *Times* provided the first four poems in a series called "11 Outlined Epitaphs," which continued on a sheet inserted into the record sleeve. The back of *Another Side* featured five poems under the title "Some Other Kinds of Songs." On the flip side of *Bringing* was an untitled, dissociative prose-poem, which began, "i'm standing there watching the parade/." Merton could now study some of Dylan's poetry while waiting for the memoir to be published.

Merton immediately took a deep dive into the music. By the next day, Friday, September 9, he had heard enough of *Blonde on Blonde* for one of its songs to become an earworm. While Merton was in Louisville for spinal X-rays, "I Want You," the first track on side 2, continually "rang through [his] head."[4] One can imagine why: with an infectious riff and doggedly symbolist lyrics, the song expresses the desperate longings of every lover. In the refrain, Dylan chants, "I want you, I want you / I want you so bad / Honey I want you."[5]

After humming the song to himself that day and thinking about Margie in such starkly yearning terms, Merton couldn't refrain from calling her from a payphone near the bus station in Bardstown on his way back to the abbey. In his journal, he described their conversation as "happy"; they discussed how much they missed each other, the demands of Margie's new job, and Merton's commitment ceremony the previous day. When Merton shared his enthusiasm for the new Dylan records, she said she had heard some of the new songs as well, which led to one moment of tension. Merton described it this way: "She was a little piqued that I liked B. Dylan's song 'Just Like a Woman.' [She said,] 'Well, it's *pretty*.' (Sort of distant tone.)"[6]

The reason for her pique isn't hard to fathom. The song is sung from the perspective of a man breaking off a romantic relationship. The lyrics hint that the woman, somewhat dismissively referred to as "Baby," is a spoiled socialite and drug user, and that her immaturity had doomed the affair from the start. While she "makes love just like a woman," she "breaks just like a little girl," and in the final verse, the singer addresses the child/woman directly in the second person, instructing her in the future not to tell anyone that she knew him back when "I was hungry and it was your world."[7] Margie had it right: the melody *is* pretty, one of Dylan's most plaintive, but a paean to former lovers it is not.

Back at the hermitage that evening, Merton continued his deep dive. By the next day he had absorbed all of the records, so that he was able to offer this assessment in his journal:

> Rich variety of things. I like best the "middle" (so far) protest songs like "Gates of Eden" which is full of a real prophetic ardor and irony. And power! But the newest baroque obscenities, the dead voice, the noise of rock, the crowding in of new fashion, this is very intriguing too. Intriguing is an extremely bad word. One does not get "curious" about Dylan. You are either all in it or all out of it. I am *in* his new stuff.[8]

Four days later, in a short note to a magazine editor, Merton couldn't resist tossing in a Dylan non sequitur: "I am with you and . . . I keep you in my prayers. Keep me in yours too. As Bob Dylan says, 'Everybody must get stoned.'"[9] That same day he jotted a gleeful note to Laughlin: "Have some fine records of Dylan . . . and am working on an article on him for *Jubilee*. Exciting stuff, very real, very good. New horizons in poetry opening up. Still expecting the book."[10]

The specific context for the phrase "new horizons in poetry" was the article Merton was currently writing about Scottish poet Edwin Muir. In his book *The Estate of Poetry*, Muir lamented the modern poet's lack of a wide audience; poets, he felt, were writing almost exclusively for critics and other poets. Muir looked back fondly to the by-gone days of traditional ballads, when poetry was the shared property of a community of working people, when poems were sung as often as spoken. In his essay on Muir, Merton responded:

> Muir apparently had no inkling of the possibilities that have since surprised us: the influence of young Soviet poets reading their works in the parks, or the power exercised by an admittedly unruly poet like Bob Dylan making use of modern media. Dylan may certainly have more in common with *Mad* comics than with Shakespeare but he is nevertheless definitely conscious of a poetic vocation and has communicated an authentic fervor to an audience that is deeply involved.[11]

• • •

Merton himself was among the "deeply involved," and throughout September he continued to absorb Dylan's music. At the end of the month, he wrote again to Laughlin:

> Having listened a bit to Bob Dylan's records I think that rock n' roll is rather essential to the poems: it is meant to bring out the shades of irony and all that: and his peculiar way of singing them too is part of it. Now that I am addicted, I think that just reading him on a printed page misses a lot of it, though it is good too.[12]

In that last sentence, Merton is referring to the poetry printed on four of the five records in his possession—poetry that was loose, iconoclastic, unafraid of being serious, surreal, and nonsensical all at the same time. Dylan's poems demonstrated a deliberate technique and often contained sublimely striking lines and images. Just imagine how this line from the back cover of *Bringing* would have caught the attention of the contemplative monk: "experience teaches that silence terrifies people / the most."[13]

But all this poetry got Merton thinking. What impact might his own poems have if set to music? He had even pondered that question in his *Midsummer Diary*.

• • •

The "authentic fervor" that Merton admired in Dylan's poetry was something Merton himself had been seeking in his own writing, especially since the affair's discovery in June. At that time, he had declared his intention to write "a new book now, in a new way, in a new language too."[14] Bob Dylan had opened that door for him. During the last three weeks of September and much of October, Merton experienced his most joyful, intense period of listening to Dylan's songs and reading Dylan's poems, absorbing the offbeat, avant-garde prosody, and relishing the eccentric phrasings. It was an artistic honeymoon. And now these "new horizons in poetry" were emerging to reenergize Merton's own.

During those same weeks, Merton composed most of a new collection of experimental verse, tentatively called *Edifying Cables*. The book contains eighty-eight poems—or, more precisely, it is one long poem in eighty-eight numbered sections—with a prologue and an epilogue. In a sense, the book began with Dylan in mind, for Merton had already written to Ed Rice that "The Prospects of Nostradamus," the first section of *Cables* to be written, would be ideal for Dylan to set to music.

Dylan-like images and poetic devices seep into nearly every corner of the new project, giving it a startling freshness and an unmistakable oral quality. The book's eventual title, *Cables to the Ace, or Familiar Liturgies of Misunderstanding* (published by New Directions two years later), has a Dylan-like mock earnestness to it, and, most tellingly, in the margin of one page of his working notebook for *Cables*, Merton scrawled, "Bob Dylan is one of the most important voices in the country . . . infinite variety."[15]

An "infinite variety" à la Dylan seems to have been Merton's intention for *Cables*, for each section plays with tone and voice and allusion in its own kaleidoscopic way, throwing out seemingly random shards of language and flashing wordplay. There are satirical bits of advertising lingo, an absurdist business memo, a mock news report, quotes from classic writers, oblique literary allusions, an entire section in French, spoofs of nursery rhymes and devotional verse, mock theology, the hilarious pastiche of Nostradamus's prophecies, nonsensical lists, and more. Like Dylan's songs, *Cables* is full of free-associative comic surrealism and high-camp cheekiness—elements not often found in Merton's earlier poetry.

There are passages of Dadaist dissociation in which Merton seems to imitate Dylan's liner notes to *Bringing* and *Highway 61*. In section 70 of *Cables*, for instance, he summarizes the plot of a TV show this way: "Riot woman transformed into savings bonds is traced to unforgettable swans for the entire ruin of one season."[16] And there is section 54, where Merton writes, "Amid the cries of gang walls and surprises the echoes come forward. They are nude. A brazen charm expands. It invests the unguarded senses. Twin stars rise over the library."

Just as Dylan always included love songs on his albums, Merton includes lyrics about Margie in *Cables*. In section 75, he tenderly writes, "I seek you in the hospital where you work. Will you be a patch of white moving rapidly across the end of the next hall?" And in section 58, which is more skewed and complex, he refers to the abbey's censoring of her mail: "All the mailmen study my friendless state holding back the letters." In that same piece, he humorously refers to the hermitage as his "house of grammar and of wine."

Cables also contains a couple of straightforward religious pieces. Few of Merton's devotional poems are as exquisite as section 80, which begins: "Slowly slowly / Comes Christ through the Garden / Speaking to the sacred trees." And one of the more mystical passages in all of his writings is section 84, headed with the German word *Gelassenheit*—"Serenity." In this prose poem, Merton once again connects his own longing for the desert with the *via negativa*, the seeking of God in emptiness, in primordial formlessness, with capitalized words signaling the presence of the divine:

> Desert and void. The Uncreated is waste and emptiness to the creature. Not even sand. Not even stone. . . . But the Uncreated is no

> something. Waste. Emptiness. Total poverty of the Creator: yet from this poverty springs *everything*. . . . Infinite Zero. Everything comes from this desert Nothing. Everything wants to return to it and cannot. For who can return "nowhere"?

The passage is as beautiful as anything in Saint John of the Cross's *Dark Night of the Soul*. And two sections later, in 86, Merton picks up that theme again by quoting Meister Eckhart: "The true word of eternity is spoken only in the spirit of the man who is himself a wilderness."

Merton's apprehension about the dehumanizing effects of technology threads its way throughout the collection, a theme that Dylan too wrote about in songs like "Gates of Eden" and "It's Alright, Ma (I'm Only Bleeding)." Just the year before, Merton had been fascinated by Jacques Ellul's seminal *Technological Society*, in which Ellul dissects the process by which new technologies—computers, electronics, automation, the media—desacralize religion to the point that technology itself becomes the de facto religion of our time. Section 8 of *Cables* begins, "Write a prayer to a computer? But first of all you have to find out how It thinks." The capitalization of *It*, as if the computer were the deity, is significant. In 34, Merton writes of "the radiograms of hymnody." In 35, a prose poem written in French, Merton talks of a blind captain who "sings the partaking of electric Communions." Section 83 refers to the *Sanctus* (the hymn beginning, "Holy, Holy, Holy, Lord God of hosts") being sounded "amid . . . / the golden fury of wires."

Cables is the book in which Merton *went electric*, every bit as much as Dylan did at Newport the previous year. *Cables* brims with images of electricity: "sandy electric stars" (13), "the electric world" (14), "the psycho- / Electric jump" (32), "blue electric palaces" (34), among many others. Merton associates the noise of electric guitars with societal collapse. In what might be a reference to Dylan, section 1 begins:

> Edifying cables can be made musical if played and sung by full-armed societies doomed to an electric war. A heavy imperturbable beat. . . . With the unending vroom vroom vroom of guitars we will

> all learn a new kind of obstinacy, together with massive lessons of irony and refusal . . .

That last sentence is an apt description of Dylan's own poetic calling.

As a bookend to section 1, the Epilogue of *Cables* reprises the theme of a musical soundtrack for the end of the world. "You will by your own free choice be locked in with Jack Sound and his final trumpet. The name of the day is Doom. . . . And now play it Jack! Give it that old-new sound." Whether Jack Sound is Dylan or Merton himself or some angelic final trumpeter is not clear, but "that old-new sound" is a fine description of Dylan's brand of folk-rock.

Dylan's clearest influence on *Cables* is seen in Merton's appropriation of Dylan's favorite literary devices, including inventing characters with bizarre names. The people who walk on and off the stage of Dylan's imagination often have monikers like "Captain Arab" ("Bob Dylan's 115th Dream"), "Mack the Finger" ("Highway 61 Revisited"), and "Madam John . . . Savage Rose & Fixable" (liner notes to *Highway 61*). Picking up on this technique, Merton populates his pieces with such characters as "Polo King" and "Mister Charlie" (28), "Uncle Sled" (31), "Senator Tolling Bell" (48), "Uncle Constellation" (63), and "Jack Sound" and "Miss Daisy" (Epilogue).

Not all of Dylan's characters have names. Many are portrayed with absurd or evocative epithets, like the "graveyard woman" in "From a Buick 6." Dylan's "Gates of Eden" trots out a parade of such unlikely people: "the cowboy angel," "the savage soldier," "the motorcycle black Madonna," and more. Merton too invents such epithets for his vividly absurd characters: section 70, which parodies *TV Guide*, is populated with the "clean-cut pirate," the "beautiful clever custard woman," the "subliminal engineer," the "rocket woman," and the "sham doctor." Elsewhere, Merton refers to the "basketface hero" (42), "Martian Doctors" (48), and "the Vegetable King" (74), among others.

Dylan also delights in transporting well-known cultural figures into improbable situations, what Merton had referred to as Dylan's "brave [jumbling] together all the mad collection of cultural ikons that have been stuffed into the heads of our kids in high school."[17] Dylan sings about "Einstein disguised as Robin Hood" ("Desolation Row") and "Ma Rainey and Beethoven . . . unwrap[ping] a bedroll" ("Tombstone Blues"). Merton jarringly displaces his own icons, among others: "Eve . . . visits a natural supermarket of naked fruits" (36), "Pocahontas a jungle nun" (68), "Little Red Riding Hood in chains" (70), "Coleridge . . . swimming in Walden Pond" (74), and "The midnight express / Bringing Plato, Prophets, Milton, Blake" (83).

While Dylan's lyrics and poetry can be mordant, absurd, and full of "irony and refusal," they are usually highly comic at the same time, a quality that Merton emulates. *Cables* is not only one of his most dense and eclectic works, it is one of his funniest. In the Prologue, Merton pugnaciously states, "The realm of the spirit is two doors down the hall. There you can obtain more soul than you are ready to cope with, Buster"; and in the Epilogue he interrupts the writing itself for "a word from our sponsor. . . . For a dollar ninety-nine you will have immortal longings here on the front porch." The humor is richer in light of the fact that Merton had experienced his share of immortal longings on his own front porch.

Merton also picks up on Dylan's penchant for badgering the reader. In the liner notes to *Highway 61*, Dylan introduces his record this way: "if you do not know where the Insanity Factory is located, you should hereby take two steps to the right, paint your teeth & go to sleep." Merton's Prologue to *Cables* takes this to the level of taunting: "You, Reader, need no prologue. Do you think these Horatian odes are all about you? . . . / Go shake hands with the comics if you demand a preface. . . . / Go write your own prologue."

Essential to an appreciation of *Cables to the Ace* is a familiarity with Dylan's music from 1965 and 1966. While one critic has argued that the book was Merton's way of engaging the philosophy of Herbert Marcuse, with its emphasis on the evils of mass culture and political repression,[18] Merton's personal writings make clear that Dylan's work was the ongoing frame for *Cables*. While Merton had absorbed Marcuse's philosophy years earlier, that great thinker is never mentioned in Merton's journals in 1966.

Other astute critics find in *Cables* clear echoes of Ernesto Cardenal's poetry as well as Nicanor Parra's antipoems, and while they do inform *Cables*, to cite those poets as the primary influence overstates the case. Merton wasn't reading them at the time.

And Merton was well aware of Dylan's influence. A year later, when a high school girl wrote to him offering to educate him about popular music, he responded by providing his own bona fides. He wrote that he liked the Beatles, especially "Taxman"; he then disclosed, with more than a hint of understatement, that his as-yet-unpublished *Cables* "is a bit Dylan-like in spots."[19]

• • •

Merton was eager to gauge others' responses to his new, long antipoem, and an opportunity arose the first week of October. Writer, photographer, and friend John Howard Griffin, best known for his book *Black Like Me*, arranged for Jacques Maritain to visit Gethsemani. A small entourage also tagged along, including Father Daniel Walsh, Elisabeth Manuel, a twenty-something assistant to Maritain, Griffin himself, and a few others—all of whom were excited by the prospect of witnessing the reunion of these two great Catholic thinkers.

Maritain, then eighty-three, was touring the US, seeing old friends and visiting family gravesites on what he believed would be his final visit. As one of the most influential Catholic philosophers of the twentieth century, the Frenchman had been a mentor to countless writers and thinkers, including Giovanni Montini, who was the current Pope Paul VI; and Maritain had shaped Merton's own approach to faith. They had maintained a correspondence through the years and had seen each other on Maritain's previous visits.

The group arrived on the evening of October 7. After dinner and a lively conversation, the company retired early so as to be fresh for next morning's meal and Mass, which Merton himself celebrated for the group. In deference to Maritain's frailty and a foot injury of Griffin's, the group was driven to the hermitage, and by 8:45 a.m. they had settled around the fireplace for a free-ranging conversation. The young Elisabeth Manuel was especially enchanted by the intellectual vigor of the discussion and vividly recalled the gathering thirty years later.[20]

Griffin shot scores of photos. One shows Merton serving coffee in glass tumblers to the group, and several show Maritain and Merton sitting on either side of the fireplace. Maritain, looking gaunt but engaged, smoked a pipe and sat to the left of the fire with a shawl on his lap. Merton sat to the right.

The conversation was often in French (which Merton spoke fluently), so as not to overtax Maritain, and it ranged from the new vernacular liturgy to the prospects for world peace. But when the subject turned to what each man was writing, Merton was ready with his *Cables*. The group encouraged him to read them aloud. Although the pieces were nothing like Merton's previous poems, the group seemed to respond positively.

Not surprisingly—and perhaps to put his poems in context—Merton brought up the subject of Bob Dylan, whom he characterized to Maritain as a modern American Villon, referencing the fifteenth-century French vagabond poet, who, like Dylan, had been a poetic innovator and artistic rebel. The description was not only apt, but it was sure to resonate with Maritain as a Frenchman and as a lover of poetry. Merton must also have known that Maritain's close friend, the philosopher Étienne Gilson, was an admirer of Villon and had written about the poet.

By way of demonstration, Merton brought out Ed Rice's copy of *Bringing It All Back Home*, placed it on the turntable, and set the volume on high. He started with side two. The first song, "Mr. Tambourine Man," was followed by "The Gates of Eden," both examples of Dylan's Villonesque traits—for, like Villon's poems, those songs are full of irony, earthy slang, astonishingly original images, religious references, and deliberate inversions of convention, both social and artistic. Merton himself had written in his journal two weeks earlier that "Gates of Eden" had "real prophetic ardor and irony. And power!"[21]—lending itself easily to a straightforward biblical interpretation, dealing in its symbolist way with themes of sin and redemption. In a life that is absurd, in a world that is fallen, "there are no truths outside the Gates of Eden."[22]

But Merton's intention was more than simply demonstrating that Dylan was the American Villon. That Merton played the record after reading *Cables* allowed his guests to understand that the rollicking, rebellious, dissociative quality of his pieces was quite contemporary. *Cables* was different; it was Merton's "new book . . . in a new language." He had gone electric.

We don't know how many Dylan songs Merton played that day, though Merton would certainly have wanted them to hear the third song, "It's Alright, Ma (I'm Only Bleeding)," if only because it touches on issues Merton himself was passionate about. The song could be interpreted as a rock 'n' roll take on Ellul's *Technological Society*. The fourth song, "It's All Over Now, Baby Blue," a man's edgy send-off of a former lover, Merton may have played for his own personal reasons.

As Griffin reported, "Played at full volume, the Dylan songs blasted the still atmosphere of Trappist lands with the wang-wang of guitars and voice at high amplification."[23] Elisabeth Manuel later wrote: "What a strange scene . . . these men listening, in the monastery of Gethsemani, to the hard and expressive voice of a young rebel poet." She wrote that Maritain was especially impressed with "Gates of Eden,"[24] though others later suggested he only responded out of courtesy. In any case, Maritain soon declared that they were wasting valuable time by listening to records, which quickly shut down further discussion of the modern Villon.

Yet it was a stunning moment. The renowned philosopher was, at that time, a month shy of his eighty-fourth birthday, which means that Merton was playing Bob Dylan songs for a man born in 1882—the year that Robert Ford killed Jesse James and Tchaikovsky premiered his *1812 Overture*.

Ever since his college days, Merton couldn't resist sharing his enthusiasms, whether he was rhapsodizing about Saint John of the Cross to the novices or trying to introduce Ad Reinhardt to Victor Hammer. Fervently communicating his passions was rooted in Merton's character and a major focus of his writing—perhaps *the* major focus. In addition to putting the language of *Cables* into context, he also revealed himself as a devoted Dylan fan—"addicted," as he wrote to Laughlin a week earlier.

Known for his playfulness, Merton also knew the French decadent poets well enough to appreciate their urge to *épater le bourgeois*, to "shock the bourgeoisie," and due to the awkwardness he felt after the affair with Margie, he may have enlisted Dylan as a way to shake things up a little among that august company of priests, writers, and mentors, a way of defusing any lingering embarrassment. He loved to play against expectations. Who would have thought that a visit to a hermit's peaceful forest hut would result in listening to an off-key, nasal-voiced rock icon? One can easily envision Merton peering up with raised eyebrows at Maritain and the others, gauging each one's reaction, as Dylan intoned these lines:

> With a time-rusted compass blade
> Aladdin and his lamp
> Sits with Utopian hermit monks
> Sidesaddle on the Golden Calf[25]

A New Consciousness

Late October brought cooler weather and a change of seasons. From the front windows of the hermitage, Merton could look across the clearing to see the leaves of a maple and two sweetgums turn from green to orange to dazzling red—so richly colored against the surrounding evergreens that he called them his "three small harlequins."[1] And he was sensing a change within himself as well. Things that had seemed so fresh and captivating the summer before were now beginning to fade as day-to-day realities brought about a reevaluation, a modest but important shift in perspective.

October began with reminders of life's fragility. Two days before Maritain's visit, Merton was among those who discovered one of the older brothers gasping for breath under a tree by the gatehouse. The monks knelt on the ground and prayed over him as he died. He was buried in the abbey's cemetery the next day. A few days later, Merton received a letter from Laughlin, informing him, more than two months after the fact, that Bob Dylan had been in a serious motorcycle accident. Though Dylan was expected to recover, the news was disconcerting.

On October 11, an old and valued friend arrived. Activist-priest Daniel Berrigan had just returned to the US after six months of semi-exile. His Jesuit order had sent him out of the country as a way of expressing their displeasure over an incident the year before: Berrigan had conducted a private memorial service for Roger LaPorte, the young antiwar activist who had set fire to himself in front of the United Nations the previous year.

While Berrigan's visit was welcome, it served as a yardstick against which to measure how far his own focus had veered recently from social concerns. After Berrigan's departure, Merton returned to work on his book *Faith and Violence* and wrote a foreword he had promised to provide for Thich Nhat Hanh's forthcoming book, *Vietnam: Lotus in a Sea of Fire*, a piece in which Merton harshly castigated the church for its complicity in the Vietnam war.

• • •

A week later, Merton was once again dispatched to the hospital in Louisville, this time for a stomach ailment—another reminder of life's unpredictability. Margie was in town for exams, and as she had promised, she managed to visit him—their first face-to-face meeting since their Cherokee Park rendezvous in July. Although their reunion was emotional, Merton was surprised that the intensity of his feelings had diminished. Although he cared for her still, much of the passion had ebbed, and he began to wonder whether their love had actually been "from God." He wrote in his journal, "Basically, I am much more ready now to admit that the whole thing was a mistake, a subtle and well-meant seduction to which I too easily and too completely yielded. . . . This must never happen again. Also it is clearly *over*."[2]

As so many time before, he overstated things. He wasn't quite over the relationship at that point, but his preoccupation with it certainly grew less intense. His feelings would reemerge from time to time, but he was now generally more clear-headed and able to focus on his many writing projects, especially on his "new book . . . in a new language."

• • •

During the last part of October, he tried to wrap up *Edifying Cables*, but he grew increasingly dissatisfied with it. The long poem felt scattered; it didn't ring true. "[I] can't say I like it," he wrote. "It is disturbing and false in many ways. It is not myself and I don't know who it is. A glib worldly spirit.

Empty voices."[3] In a letter to Maritain, Merton described it as "a solemn anti-language that people will not know what to do with,"[4] and in a note to Ping Ferry, he referred to *Cables* as "a long poetic retch," curiously similar to Dylan's reference, in an interview, to his first draft of "Like a Rolling Stone" as "a long piece of vomit."[5]

On the last weekend of October, he had yet another important visitor, someone who affected Merton even more deeply than the others. While Merton had summed up the visit from Maritain in a single journal paragraph, he expended fourteen paragraphs on this new visitor, and even then he wrote, "I can't begin to put everything down, I was so moved by the visit."[6] Merton sensed that this man was coming as "a messenger from God."[7]

That visitor was Algerian Sufi Muslim teacher and mystic Sidi Abdeslam. The meeting was Merton's first face-to-face encounter with a follower of the Sufi way, and it had had been arranged by Bernard Phillips, chairman and founder of the Religion Department at Temple University in Philadelphia.

For more than a decade, Merton had delved into Islam, partly through the writings of his friend Louis Masignon, an influential Catholic scholar of Islam. As a poet, Merton was enthralled by the great Sufi mystic poets, having translated some of them and having had his own poetry influenced by their direct and passionate openness to God. As Merton anticipated Abdeslam's arrival, he wrote a euphoric letter to the Argentinean poet Miguel Grinberg in which he let his own Sufi-like joy and mysticism emerge:

> Sun rises in mist with thousands of very soft explosions and I am entirely splashed with designs coming through the holes in the lace wall of trees. Everything in the world is transparent. The ferocities of mankind mean nothing to the hope of light. You are right, preserve your hopes. For this one must keep eyes open always and see. The new consciousness will keep awakening. I know it. Poets, designers, musicians, singers. Do you know Bob Dylan's songs? Won-

> derful poet. But he almost broke his neck on his motorcycle. Still he is getting better. He will bring out a book. But his records are the best thing. Now he is baroque. At first he was austere and social. . . .
>
> New consciousness. There has to be clean water in the mind for the spirit to drink.[8]

From the outset, Merton was thrown off balance by Abdeslam. As they strolled the hills surrounding the monastery, the Sufi suggested that Merton had "arrived" spiritually and was "very close to mystical union" with God,[9] that the slightest nudge might accomplish it. Merton was astonished by the man's insights and his devotion to God but also convicted by his own shortcomings. Merton longed to live up to Abdeslam's assessment of him.

To achieve "mystical union," said Abdeslam, Merton should abandon the monastery, which the Sufi viewed as a prison, and he recommended that Merton stop wasting his energy on writing. "The Prophets of the Book were illiterate," Abdeslam later wrote to Merton through a friend; "they *were* the book that others believed they were writing."[10] His prescription was for Merton to shun notoriety, to travel the world to meet with ordinary people on the streets and in small groups, and to preach a message of compassion, spiritual authenticity, and seeking the divine.

When Merton said he couldn't possibly leave the monastery, Abdeslam slyly responded that perhaps the abbot might die soon and Merton would then be free to leave. Mysteriously, Abdeslam added, "Within a year, there will be some change."[11]

• • •

Abdeslam's visit, along with the other recent events, sparked a rigorous self-examination, causing Merton to renew his determination to remain faithful to his vows, to do the work God had called him to, and to trust whatever the future offered.

On November 2, a blizzard blew in, and Merton welcomed the silence that came with it. It was the first month since March that required no medical checks or procedures. The newly installed gas heater in the hermitage smelled bad, but it obviated the need to chop firewood, a chore that inflamed his bursitis. And November brought no illustrious visitors needing to be entertained—only a priest wanting Merton to sign a document endorsing the idea of married priests and also a friend of Ernesto Cardenal's, bringing greetings from the Nicaraguan poet.

As the snow continued, Merton hunkered down, read, prayed, wrote, and relished the aloneness—all the things that had led him to the hermitage in the first place. The borrowed record player fell silent. His waning obsession with Dylan made room for new interests—notably, in the novels of William Faulkner.

Although Merton continued to wrestle with his feelings for Margie, he discovered a certain tranquility in the quiet. As winter progressed, he was finally able to find, if not complete serenity, at least a sense of detachment from the contradictions. Just as he believed that he could only achieve unity with humanity by being alone, so too he realized that he could only be true to Margie by remaining true to his vows of celibacy. This synthesis made him feel more settled, more at peace.

But the quiet wouldn't last: the second week of December brought more important guests—and unexpected upheaval. Although Ping Ferry had been unable to lure Bob Dylan to Gethsemani, he arranged for another visitor every bit as intriguing: singer Joan Baez, along with her friend and mentor Ira Sandperl.

• • •

Three years before Bob Dylan ever set foot in a Greenwich Village coffeehouse, Joan Baez had begun to establish herself as one of the brightest rising stars on the folk scene. At seventeen, she debuted at the Club 47 in Cambridge, Massachusetts, and one year later, in July 1959, she got a big break when folksinger Bob Gibson invited her to duet with him on the main stage at the first Newport Folk Festival. That appearance led to a recording contract and the release of her debut album in October 1960, the one that opens with "Silver Dagger." By the time she traveled to Kentucky in December 1966, she had recorded seven more albums.

While making the rounds of the folk clubs in 1961, she crossed paths with a scruffy twenty-year-old folksinger named Bob Dylan, on whom she developed a crush. Two years later, impressed by his innovative songwriting, she invited him to tour with her as a way of exposing him to a wider audience. In those concerts, after duetting with her on a couple of songs—sometimes including "Silver Dagger"—Dylan would sing a solo number or two, though his piercing, nasal voice and ragged appearance appalled many of her fans. They performed together on the podium at the March on Washington on August 28, 1963, the day Martin Luther King Jr. delivered his "I Have a Dream" speech.

Their affair began that summer, and the media hailed them as the new folkie "it" couple, "the king and queen of folk music." Although Dylan was recovering from a broken relationship and was still writing such bitter songs as "Boots of Spanish Leather" and "It Ain't Me, Babe," Baez seemed to inspire a new optimism in some of his other songs. He wrote the activist anthem "The Times They Are A-Changin'" that fall and the rapturously poetic "Chimes of Freedom" and "Mr. Tambourine Man" the following year. By the time she traveled to Gethsemani, Baez had recorded seven of Dylan's songs on various albums, and in 1968 she would release a double album, *Any Day Now*, made up entirely of his songs. She had been one of his most influential champions.

Now, in late 1966, a year and a half after her breakup with Dylan, Baez was championing another cause. She and Sandperl had sought out this chance to visit Merton, hoping he would give his blessing to their recently founded Institute for the Study of Nonviolence; perhaps he might even agree to teach there. The institute, in Carmel, California, was training human-rights workers and peace activists and had attracted the attention of Dr. King, alongside whom Baez and Sandperl had marched earlier that year. Their visit to Gethsemani was a stopover on their way to Atlanta to meet once again with King and other leaders of the Southern Christian Leadership Conference to discuss issues of organized protest and nonviolence.

Baez and Sandperl were not married, nor were they lovers, as some books suggest.[12] The two met at a Quaker meeting when she was eighteen and he was thirty-six. Sandperl lived in the Menlo Park area of California, where he worked at Keplar's Books. He was an institution among Bay-area activists. An indefatigable autodidact, he was a passionate follower of Mahatma Gandhi and known for vigorously engaging bookstore customers in thoughtful debate. He organized book readings, discussion groups, sit-ins, and peace gatherings. Baez once referred to him as "a rascal who longs to be a saint."[13] It's easy to see why he became a crucial mentor to the idealistic young folksinger and how their friendship blossomed into the founding of the institute.

After their plane landed at the Louisville airport early on December 8, Baez and Sandperl drove their rented car to Gethsemani, arriving just after lunch. At the gate, they were greeted by several of the brothers. Baez was delighted by the open-hearted reception and surprised that the monks seemed so ordinary, not austere or super-spiritual.

When Merton arrived a moment later, he announced that the first order of business was food—non-monastery food—so the visitors escorted him out of the front gate and drove him to a nearby fast-food joint where he ordered "two cheeseburgers, a chocolate milkshake, and a large order of fries" to go.[14] Upon returning with their carry-out sacks, Merton led his guests to an open field near the tobacco barn, where they feasted and talked. The weather was unseasonably mild and sunny for much of the afternoon.[15]

Merton hadn't been so elated with visitors since Maritain's visit. And in the open field, he and Sandperl drank beer, and the three of them argued, laughed, and had animated discussions about Gandhi and the peace movement. Conversation would have ranged from Merton's meeting with Berrigan, to the challenges to truly nonviolent protest, to Baez's work with the institute, her recent arrest at an antiwar protest, and her marching with Dr. King.

Like Abdeslam, Sandperl tried to convince Merton to leave Gethsemani, to broaden his experience and teach at the institute—the students needed him. This was the second time in as many months that someone had advised him to venture out into the world. Again, Merton kindly demurred, citing his vows.

At one point, Baez playfully compared their group to characters from *Winnie-the-Pooh*—she being the wide-eyed Piglet, Sandperl, the austere and wise old Owl, and Merton, the lovable Pooh.[16] As a world-renowned spiritual writer, Merton would have been delighted to be considered the cuddly one rather than the wise one.

Midafternoon, they walked back to the abbey, where they met Dom James. Merton noticed Baez's dislike of him and that she "saw through him at once and [the abbot] was visibly upset."[17] Even so, she gave the abbot a copy of her latest album.

Then, around dusk as a light rain fell, Merton, Baez, and Sandperl walked up to the hermitage accompanied by Father Chrysogonus. As rain dripped from the eaves, Merton lit a fire in the fireplace, and Baez pulled from her pack a copy of her newly released *Noël* album, a collection of seventeen multicultural Christmas songs. In the dim light, the four of them sat on the floor, listening to the album's first side. As a composer, Chrysogonus resonated with these simple folk melodies and with their lush orchestrations arranged by Peter Schickele, who, like Chrysogonus, had studied with Vincent Persichetti.

Later, after a lively discussion, Chrysogonus left, and Merton served his guests a light meal of "goat-milk cheese and bread and honey and . . . tea."[18] From somewhere he produced a bottle of Irish whiskey, and he and Sandperl proceeded to drink until they were, in Baez's phrase, "pie-eyed . . . like two old Russian convicts."[19]

At some point, Merton mentioned that he was hoping to write an article about Dylan. In her response, Baez told him that Dylan, with his new rock 'n' roll persona, was "destroying himself, and becoming mean, stupid etc."[20] Notably, on his 1965 tour of England, Dylan had agreed to have Baez accompany him with the implied intention of asking her to duet on a song or two at each concert, in that way introducing her to UK audiences just as she had introduced him to American audiences two years earlier.

But, although Baez accompanied Dylan's entourage, she was never asked to perform.

In several scenes of the documentary film of that tour, *Dont Look Back*, she can be seen sitting in song circles with Dylan or fading into the background. The most painful incident comes near the end. As Dylan taps out a new song on his typewriter, he and pal Bobby Neuwirth cruelly tease her about her appearance. When she's had enough, she quietly walks out—the last she saw of Dylan for nearly ten years.[21]

Since Merton, Baez, and Sandperl had spent much of the day discussing various approaches to nonviolence as practiced by Gandhi, the Civil Rights movement, and the peace marchers, Baez argued that Dylan exhibited violence in his lyrics, a notion Merton hotly disputed. Although the exchange was cordial, her jibe hit a nerve. In early September, poet Cid Corman had written Merton to say that he felt Merton had given in to violence in parts of *Raids on the Unspeakable*.[22] The comment baffled Merton. Was Corman accusing him of bullying, of "telling everybody what to do"?[23] Or was Corman accusing him of somehow using language in a violent way? Now, Joan Baez accused Bob Dylan of the same thing. For Merton, it was uncanny and unsettling.

But the discussion was part of a larger unsettling. The company of this attractive, articulate young woman not only energized Merton but caused his intense feelings for Margie to resurface unexpectedly. Baez and Margie were the same age, and in his journal, Merton repeatedly described Baez in terms similar to the ones he used for Margie. His description of Baez, in her parachute pants, "running down the wide field . . . her long hair flowing,"[24] is similar to his description of his meeting Margie outside Cunningham's in June, when she walked up to him "in a light dress, long hair flying in the wind."[25] Both women had black hair. Baez, like Margie, was "pure, honest." "She is an indescribably sweet girl," Merton wrote of Baez, "and I love her. I know she loves me too."[26]

Baez's presence, the stimulating conversation, and the alcohol made it inevitable that he would divulge the details of his affair. Although, curiously, he never mentioned that "Silver Dagger" had been a lover's charm for him and Margie, he did read aloud some Menendez poems. Impulsively—and with a bit of inebriated bravado—the trio formulated a plan, one they must have known was doomed from the start. Although conflicting accounts exist, the gist seems to be that Baez and Sandperl would drive Merton two and a half hours to Cincinnati that night so he could surprise Margie as she got off work at 11:30. Then they would drive Merton back to the abbey in the early morning hours in time for them to dash up to Louisville to catch their flight to Atlanta. Having resolved this, they hiked down to the abbey's parking lot in the rain, where they bundled themselves into the rented car and set off in the dark.

They got no farther than Bardstown before Merton began to have qualms. Perhaps he should call Margie first to warn her. The two had broken up, after all. By then, Baez too, who hadn't been drinking that day, was having second thoughts, for the implications of the misadventure were beginning to dawn on her. What if Merton got thrown out of the monastery? What if his reputation and career were ruined because she and Sandperl had gotten him drunk and smuggled him out of the abbey?

Injecting some realism into the situation, Baez said they couldn't possibly reach Cincinnati, return to Gethsemani, and make it to Louisville in time for their flight, the reservations for which couldn't be changed. The argument gave everyone the excuse they needed to simply extend their time together by driving on to the motel in Louisville, with a crisis averted.

Once in Louisville, Merton said his good-byes to Baez and Sandperl, then arranged for his friend Professor Jack Ford to pick him up. The two then drove to Ford's house, where they watched the last part of the CBS Playhouse television production of Tennessee Williams's *The Glass Menagerie*, starring Hal Holbrook and Barbara Loden. The drama would have been an emotionally charged experience for Merton after a day like the one he'd just had. The play's action is viewed through the eyes of a man who, because of his long absence and a certain impassiveness, was unable to protect his innocent younger sister, Laura. Because of a mild disability, she had escaped into a fantasy world. Among its many memorable passages is one that comes in the final scene, the famous "Blow out your candles,

Laura" soliloquy, which must have affected Merton powerfully. How could he not think of Margie as the play's older brother (whose name, coincidentally, is Tom) confronts the ghost of his sister's memory?

> It always comes upon me unawares, taking me altogether by surprise. Perhaps it was a familiar bit of music. . . . Then all at once my sister touches my shoulder. I turn around and look into her eyes . . . Oh, Laura, Laura, I tried to leave you behind me, but I am more faithful than I intended to be![27]

Late that night, Ford drove Merton back to Gethsemani, and two days later, Merton wrote in his journal, "Guilt next day for this wild impulsiveness, this night ride."[28]

• • •

The exhilaration and agitation of Baez's visit marked a new beginning for Merton, an exorcism of ghosts, after which his journal entries about Margie gradually became fewer. A short time later he wrote instructions that his journals should not be made public until twenty-five years after his death, a request honored by his executors; he also requested that all of his love letters to Margie, which he called "the silly stuff," be destroyed.[29] Only the Menendez poems were published earlier, when Laughlin's New Directions printed two hundred and fifty slipcased copies in 1985 under the title *Eighteen Poems*. Never reprinted, it is one of the rarest of all of Merton's books.

The journals were important to him. Merton wanted his readers and admirers to understand the story of the affair eventually, the temptations he faced, and the trials that solitude entailed. He explained, "I have always wanted to be completely open, and about my effort to make sense out of my life. The affair with M. is an important part of it."[30] But he wanted the publication delayed because so many of the people he wrote about were still alive.

Although his obsession with Dylan began to moderate, he still longed to hear his own poems set to music. A week after Baez's visit, he mailed her two poems, which, he hinted, were unusually "singable." She didn't take the hint.[31]

A short time later, Merton mailed a chapter from his book-in-progress, *Faith and Violence*, to the Catholic Peace Fellowship. In it, he articulated his concerns about the peace movement's sometimes questionable approach to nonviolence—the self-immolations, the self-righteousness, the coercive tactics, and the tendency to portray all opposition as evil. All these were issues he had discussed with Berrigan, Baez, Sandperl, and others. CPF published Merton's essay as a pamphlet that July and distributed it to its members. It was titled "Blessed Are the Meek: The Roots of Christian Nonviolence."[32]

Just before publication, he had an afterthought. He wrote to his friend Jim Forest, CPF's editor: "One thing I have been meaning to write about, and keep forgetting. I want a *dedication* somewhere. . . . Is there a little spot, where you might put: For Joan Baez."[33]

Prophetic Voices

Thomas Merton never wrote the article about Bob Dylan. At the end of January 1967, he wrote to Ed Rice, "Haven't done anything on Dylan, . . . and I guess it is useless waiting for his book. Besides I'll soon have to return the Abbot's record player."[1] In February he wrote to Baez and Sandperl, "Still haven't written anything on Dylan, and perhaps won't after all. I lack perspective."[2] In that last comment he seemed to acknowledge Baez's more personal connection with Dylan, while still pondering the issue of violence in Dylan's lyrics. Ultimately, he knew his article would be outdated the instant the book was published.

Little did Merton know that pirated copies of the book's rough galleys were available—if only Laughlin had known where to look, that is, in the hippie head shops and underground record stores springing up on both coasts. The official edition, published by Macmillan, wouldn't appear for another five years—three years after Merton's death.

What would Merton have made of *Tarantula*? Since he was expecting a memoir, he would have been disappointed—baffled, even—by its anarchic verbal deconstructions, and, like many critics, he might well have found it self-indulgent and silly. One writer described the book as "a foray into career suicide,"[3] though it had its admirers, one of whom called it "a high-art symphony of allegoric metaphor."[4]

But if Merton could have read *Tarantula* in the spirit in which Dylan had written it, the book would have reminded him of the French surrealist poets like André Breton, whom Dylan admired, and René Char, whom

Merton had been recently reading and translating. Merton was unusually responsive to the surrealists, for, in his words, they fomented a much-needed revolt against the contemporary world's "tidal wave of trademarks, political party buttons, advertising and propaganda slogans, and all the rest . . . an age of mass psychosis. . . . That is why some of the best poets of our time are running wild among the tombs in the moonlit cemeteries of surrealism."[5]

Merton might have been one of the few critics to approach *Tarantula* on its own terms, as an experimental foray into verbal dissociation along with a sort of strident playfulness. *Tarantula* might have led Merton to re-evaluate his own *Cables to the Ace*, a book that also explored some of the same surrealist terrain.

Although the article was never written, we can catch a glimpse of what it might have contained by considering the adjectives Merton had already used in his letters and journals to describe Dylan and his songs—"pointed and articulate,"[6] "prophetic . . . baroque,"[7] "exciting . . . very real, very good,"[8] "unruly . . . authentic,"[9] "blatant,"[10] "inspired, shamanic, and everything"[11]—all of which suggest that Merton's approach would have been adulatory and complex.

The core of the article would no doubt have been Dylan's "prophetic" voice—a word Merton applied to his favorite poets. For Merton, *prophetic* implied both a high level of truth-telling and the state of being ahead of one's time. The idea of poetry as a prophetic vocation recurred in several of Merton's essays written during the time of his Dylan infatuation. In an article about the early-twentieth-century Nicaraguan poet Rubén Darío, Merton stated, "All true poetic genius tends to generate prophetic insight. The poet cannot help but listen to awakening voices that are not yet audible to the rest of men."[12] In another essay of that time, comparing Milton and Camus, Merton wrote, "Poets and poetic thinkers—men who construct myths in which they embody their own struggle to cope with the fundamental questions of life—are generally 'prophetic' in the sense that they anticipate in their solitude the struggles and the general consciousness of later generations."[13]

At that time, Merton talked openly with his friends about Dylan's prophetic art. Professor Ron Seitz remembers Merton playing Dylan's "Rainy Day Women #12 & 35" for him in the hermitage, and Merton even had him sing along on the "Everybody must get stoned" refrain. As Merton explained, "This is the new American poetry! No kidding! It's that important!"[14] But the incident may also be an example of Merton's humor, for Seitz had told him about marching in a demonstration at which he'd had actual stones thrown at him—he'd been stoned!

Despite abandoning the article about Dylan, Merton had not abandoned his desire to hear his poems turned into Dylan-like songs. While he waited for Baez to respond to his poems, another musician was hard at work.

• • •

In late May 1967, Victor Hammer, who was then quite ill, and his wife, Carolyn, visited an old friend, performer and folk-song collector John Jacob Niles, who lived not far from Lexington. When the conversation turned to Niles's poetry, Carolyn told him bluntly, "Johnnie, you're wasting your time on a lot of nonsense. . . . Have you ever read Tom Merton's poetry?"[15] She then handed him copies of Merton's *Selected Poems* and *Emblems of a Season of Fury*.

Niles read the books and was fascinated. He set to work composing tunes for some of the poems, and over the next few years he would transform twenty-two of them into songs. They were first performed in public in 1971, and ten years later the set was published as *The Niles-Merton Songs, Opus 171/172*. The front cover displayed color reproductions of two portraits—one of Niles, one of Merton—both painted by Victor Hammer. That edition was a posthumous tribute to all three men, for by then all three of them were gone.

• • •

As a teenager, John Jacob Niles fell in love with Appalachia, its people and its music. In 1907, at the age of fifteen, he collected his first folk song, and over the next five decades he transcribed countless traditional songs, more than a hundred of which ended up in his seminal 1961 collection, *The Ballad Book of John Jacob Niles*.

But it was as a composer and performer that he earned his reputation. He is now mostly remembered for such original compositions as "Go 'Way from My Window" and the popular Christmas song "I Wonder as I Wander." So authentic-sounding were some of Niles's compositions that they would be collected in the field by other folklorists who mistook them for traditional songs. The confusion was unavoidable, of course, because Niles, like Woody Guthrie and, later, Bob Dylan, was a musical magpie, adapting bits of traditional songs to create new ones.

Niles's performances were unlike any other—regarded as bizarre by many. Accompanying himself on his handmade, oversized Appalachian dulcimer, he would dramatize the ballads as he sang them, often in a high falsetto. Greenwich Village folkie Dave Van Ronk remembered him this way: "There are a few things that make me glad I'm old, and one of them is that I saw John Jacob Niles perform 'Hangman, Slack Your Rope,' running around the stage with his dulcimer and playing all the roles. It was gorgeously awful."[16]

Niles's influence on younger singers was enormous. At age sixty-seven, he performed at the first Newport Folk Festival in 1959, the year that an eighteen-year-old Joan Baez got her big break there, and a short time later, Baez's manager arranged for her to sing two songs at one of Niles's own concerts. Blues-rock legend Janis Joplin started her musical career as a teenager playing autoharp and singing Niles's songs. Early on, Bob Dylan was mesmerized by Niles's musical persona, and if anyone was fascinated by musical personas, it was Dylan. He wrote:

> Niles was nontraditional, but he sang traditional songs. A Mephistophelean character out of Carolina, he hammered away at some harplike instrument and sang in a bone chilling soprano voice. Niles was eerie and illogical, terrifically intense and gave you goosebumps. Definitely a switched-on character, almost like a sorcerer. Niles was otherworldly and his voice raged with strange incantations.[17]

In Henry Miller's 1953 autobiographical novel, *Plexus*, a novel Merton likely read, Miller provides his own rhapsodic tribute to the folksinger. In one scene, the book's narrator and his wife listen repeatedly to one of Niles's records:

> Our favorite was "I Wonder as I Wander," sung in a clear, high-pitched voice with a quaver and a modality all his own. The metallic clang of his dulcimer never failed to produce ecstasy. . . . A sweep of the hand and the dulcimer gave forth magical sounds which caused the stars to gleam more brightly, which peopled the hills and meadows with silvery figures and made the brooks to babble like infants.[18]

Merton was already familiar with Niles's work, especially "I Wonder as I Wander," the fifth track on side one of Baez's *Noël* album. So the prospect of Niles's adapting his poems was more than promising—it was something he had been longing for.

• • •

To have a world-renowned composer transform one's words into songs is an honor that few poets experience, and Merton couldn't have been more exhilarated. But that exhilaration didn't last long, for it was soon lost among other significant events.

On June 20, Merton was once again at the doctor's in Louisville. Knowing that Margie was in town that day, he opted to call her rather than seeing her in person; the situation had changed. "No longer in love, and not even particularly in tune with each other,"[19] still, they spoke, and she urged him, for his own sake, to leave the monastery and "be [him]self,"[20] just as Abdeslam and Sandperl had recommended earlier. Similar exhortations also arrived in letters from Catholic feminist theologian Rosemary Radford Ruether, a friend and correspondent, one of the most anti-monastic thinkers Merton knew.

This time, however, rather than citing his vows as a defense, he wrote in his journal that perhaps it was time "to be a little more free of the system here, and able to circulate a little and find some other people who are awake and doing something."[21] This thought was a seed that would blossom the following year.

The first week of July 1967, a kitchen sink and cabinet were delivered to the hermitage, and running water was piped in, six months after the well had been drilled. Though no toilet was installed yet, forcing Merton to continue using the snake-infested outhouse, he no longer needed to tote jugs of water from the abbey each day. And a set of bookcases arrived, so he could finally organize his stacks of borrowed books.

All this brought him a step closer to greater independence from the abbey. With an unlimited supply of water, he would no longer have to keep buckets of rainwater to wash his dishes, and he could drink coffee and tea anytime he wanted. Tea was in fact his main source of nourishment while he fasted, which he did that first week of July after hearing that Victor Hammer was in the hospital as the result of a heart attack. Another step toward independence occurred when the abbot gave him permission to have a small altar built for the hermitage; that way, Merton could say Mass there instead of walking to the abbey each day.

While his independence from the abbey increased, Merton's solitude was still plagued by too many visitors—people with agendas unrelated to his vocation. The constant traffic left him little time to write. That summer he managed to complete the essays for *Faith and Violence*, and for Seabury Press he wrote a commentary and an introduction for their new edition of Camus's *The Plague*. But he felt he should be doing more.

On July 11, the news arrived that Victor Hammer had died the previous day. Merton was distraught. Not only had he lost a friend, but he felt that he had failed in some small way to guide Hammer, a lapsed Catholic, back to the faith. Of all Merton's visitors, the Hammers were among his favorites. They had created deluxe editions of his books and encouraged his writing. Victor's presence was always "reassuring, stabilizing,"[22] and he was someone Merton could confide in. "We belonged together,"[23] Merton wrote.

A week after Victor's death, Dom James appeared at the door of the hermitage. After a few minutes of conversation, Merton gingerly broached a subject they had discussed briefly in previous conversations: the abbot's retirement. Merton had encouraged such a move for the abbot's sake—and for his own; there was, after all, no requirement to stay on indefinitely.

In early September, to Merton's surprise, the abbot announced his resignation. Not only was he retiring, but he was planning to become a hermit. Another monk had found him a cabin about thirty minutes away by car, on a ridge with a stunning view. The structure was so cozy and secluded that Merton was envious. But more surprising was Dom James's suggestion that Merton join him by relocating to another cabin on a nearby hill. Merton wrote, "I can think of nothing worse! . . . just being in the same acreage. It would drive me crazy."[24]

By the end of 1967, Merton was discovering what many people in their fifties and sixties discover: that their friends and peers are dying at an alarming rate. In August, Merton was devastated to learn of Ad Reinhardt's death. Not only had he failed to introduce Reinhardt to Victor Hammer, but now both of them were gone within months of each other.

Two other friends from his Columbia days also died around this time. First was John Slate, the attorney who had been setting up the trust that would care for Merton's literary archives. Slate was also a humor writer who published in a number of major magazines.

A few months later, Merton received news of the death of Sy Freedgood, a writer and editor for *Fortune* magazine. In *The Seven Storey Mountain*, Merton had described Freedgood as someone who was "full of a fierce and complex intellectuality."[25] Tragically, Freedgood was burned to death in a house fire. Merton had even had a premonition of that death the previous year when he heard that Freedgood had been in a serious car accident.

It was a sad toll. These deaths hit close to home, and Merton wondered what his own future held. He was at the age when most people realize that their days are passing more quickly and that every life has an expiration date.

• • •

In October, Merton's friend Doris Dana drove him to Lexington, where they picked up Carolyn Hammer and proceeded to the home of John Jacob Niles and his wife, Rena. Boot Hill Farm, where they lived, was just north of Berea, Kentucky, and east of Highway 75. Now Niles had completed three of Merton's songs and was eager to premiere them.

The late-afternoon gathering began with imbibing Niles's homemade cider and listening to him sing some of his favorite songs on his dulcimer. Delighted, Merton found that their eccentric host fully lived up to expectations: "Niles is a character and I like him . . . ," Merton wrote. "He has a good weather-beaten, self-willed face, is a bit of a madman. . . . And he can carve messages on doors, besides play the lute and sing a toothy song in a metallic voice."[26]

At dinner, Merton mentioned that Joan Baez had visited him, and Niles abruptly declared that she was "a whore."[27] Merton leaped to her defense even as Niles complained about the many performers who sang his songs without crediting him. Baez had recorded two of his original songs: "Go 'Way from My Window" (*Joan Baez/5*) and "I Wonder as I Wander" (*Noël*). On the records, she credits the first as having been "arranged," not composed, by Niles, and lists the other as simply "traditional." She also recorded his version of the traditional "Black Is the Color of My True Love's Hair" (*Joan Baez in Concert*), though she credited him for the arrangement. In her autobiography, Baez, with no love lost, referred to Niles as "the well-known traditionalist and old crank."[28]

As dinner ended, two women arrived, musical associates of Niles. One was a singer, an operatic soprano named Jacqueline Roberts, and the other was her piano accompanist, Janelle Pope. They were there to sing Niles's settings of Merton's poems "Messenger," "Carol," and "Responsory (1948)." At this point Merton realized that Niles's settings weren't going to be in the folk idiom, nor sung by Niles. In fact, they were about as far from being Dylanesque—or even hummable—as they could be. Niles had transformed the poems into what are called "art songs," with complex, nuanced, somewhat meandering melodies meant to be sung by trained voices.

Unlike the more "singable" poems Merton had sent to Baez, the poems

Niles selected were free-verse, lacking the meter and rhyme of simple musical settings. Whether taken aback or not, Merton wrote that "it was really a moving experience . . . and I burst into tears at Jackie's singing."[29]

A few days later, Merton wrote to a friend a somewhat less glowing report. "I think he did a fine job, and is in any case a great person."[30] One wonders whether "a fine job" wasn't a bit of faint praise suggestive of Merton's own disappointment.

The following June, Merton traveled again to Lexington to hear more of Niles's settings, but at that time he wrote simply that it was an exceptionally tiring trip.[31] Whatever Merton thought of the *Niles/Merton Songs*, he certainly didn't regard them as "toothy," nor were they "inspired, shamanic, and everything," as Merton had said of Dylan's songs. They were, sadly, closer to what Merton had described to Margie the previous summer—new hymns that "nobody is ever going to sing."[32]

• • •

That fall, Seabury Press published their edition of Camus's *The Plague*, for which Merton had written the introduction and commentary. As part of their marketing push, the publicist sent Merton a questionnaire, asking him to list his favorite things, a list that would then be printed in *Publishers Weekly* as a way to pique interest in the book. In the issue dated November 6, 1967, that list appeared under the heading "A Hermit's Preferences": it was a neat summary of the last year and a half of Merton's life: "Zen. Indians. Wood. Birds. Beer. Anglican friends. Calligraphic abstract art. Ad Reinhardt. Subversive tape recordings for nuns. Tea. Bob Dylan. Nicaraguan folk art. Quakerism. Shakerism. Novels of Walker Percy. Myth in William Faulkner."[33]

• • •

In mid-November, Merton phoned Margie. She was moving to Miami to take a job, she said, and hinted that he might join her there, that he should "reach out for happiness." The phrase struck him, and it was the only part of their conversation that he quoted directly in his journal. But he knew that he "could not live happily with a woman," for the two of them would ultimately make each other miserable. Still, like so many of his other friends, she was encouraging him to venture beyond the monastery. It was their final conversation, and Merton described it as "a sad sort of call and in the end she was crying."[34]

But it was not their final communication. A month later, two days before Christmas, a card arrived from Margie, unleashing a flood of memories. Merton had been thinking about her recently—so intensely that he could "almost [see] her it was so vivid"—and he wrote in his journal that he felt "less real, somehow, without our constant communication, our sense of being in communion." Although he still recognized that marriage would have been impossible (he was too old anyway, he said), he admitted that he often felt tired of his solitude, or, as he phrased it, "the drab, futile silences of this artificial life."

Although the depression would pass within a few days' time, and he would energetically throw himself back into his routine of prayer and reading and writing, still, on the day that he received Margie's Christmas card—for that brief moment, at least—he reflected, "This afternoon I wondered if I'd really missed the point of life after all."[35]

DYLAN INTERLUDE NO. 3

Join the Monk

Even while John Jacob Niles was earnestly transforming Merton's three poems into songs, Bob Dylan, at his home in Woodstock, New York, was trying out chord progressions on his piano, just as he had done since high school. His intensely engaged demeanor belied the sparkling, Fellini-esque words, sounds, and images flashing through his mind. Like Niles, he too was busy composing. Though Dylan's output was not as meticulously wrought as Niles's, it was considerably larger. During that summer and fall of 1967, Dylan wrote more than sixty songs, as well as at least two dozen handwritten lyrics for which he never wrote tunes. It was the culmination of an astonishing six-year run of creativity, one of the most phenomenal spurts of songwriting in the history of popular music, not just in terms of volume but in terms of originality and influence.

For true fans of sixties culture, 1967 wasn't just the year of the Summer of Love and the Beatles' *Sgt. Pepper's*, it was the year of the Basement Tapes.

• • •

Hi Lo Ha was Bob Dylan's home and, in a sense, his hermitage.

In July 1965, he and Sara, his wife-to-be, had purchased the eleven-room house in the scraggy hills just north of Woodstock at the sugges-

---

Bob Dylan, "Tiny Montgomery," *The Bootleg Series, Vol. 11: The Basement Tapes Complete*, 6 CDs (Legacy Columbia, 88875016122 2014), disc 2, track 6.

tion of Dylan's manager, Albert Grossman, though Dylan spent little time there due to his heavy recording and touring schedules. That is, until the accident. As a place to recuperate, decompress, and chill with family and friends, Hi Lo Ha was ideal, being only two hours from New York City and just ten minutes from Grossman's house.

One of the first projects Dylan tackled after the accident was the editing of D. A. Pennebaker's footage of the European tour, which was scheduled to air on the *ABC Stage 67* television series that fall, though Dylan's vision for the film was considerably different from Pennebaker's—and ABC's, for that matter. Dylan's concept for the film, which he called *Eat the Document*, was closer in spirit to *Tarantula* than to *Dont Look Back*. He spliced and diced Pennebaker's footage with oddly jerky cuts and a sometimes perverse randomness.

ABC was not amused, and *Eat the Document* was never aired, though pirated copies still circulate on the bootleg video market. The title presumably alludes to Cold War spies who, when captured—in old movies, at least—eat the pieces of paper in their pockets containing top-secret information.

As with *Tarantula*, Dylan seemed to be reaching for a kind of artistic freedom that few famous artists, short of a Picasso or a Stravinsky, ever achieve. Dylan had told Grossman to put everything on hold—the fans, the tour, the new album, the book—so that he could simplify life, find space, and create.

Although neither *Tarantula* nor *Eat the Document* were unqualified successes, they cleared the creative channels for masterworks to follow. By jumbling together enough ideas and images, Dylan was able to achieve something almost superhumanly beyond the limits of normal creativity. You don't drive down *Highway 61* without passing through *Tarantula*, and you don't produce the best of the Basement Tapes (or the worst of them either, for that matter), without *Eat the Document*. The poet, as Lawrence Ferlinghetti once wrote, is "constantly risking absurdity / and death" to reach "that still higher perch / where Beauty stands and waits"[1]—or, as Merton put it, "There has to be clean water in the mind for the spirit to drink."[2]

Of course, total artistic freedom is usually illusory, if not counter-productive. So, in late 1966, Grossman, ever eyeing the bottom line, made a proposal. To keep the royalties flowing, Dylan wouldn't have to tour or record an album. Instead, the two of them could form a jointly owned music company so that Dylan could write songs at his own pace, commit rough versions to tape as demos, and then have Grossman find other musicians to record them. Voilà! New Dylan songs without the stress of studio time, producers, or paid musicians! It would all be icing on the cake. And so Dwarf Music was formed.

In spring 1967, Dylan and the members of his 1966 touring band, the Hawks, set up a makeshift recording studio in Hi Lo Ha—in what was called the Red Room. Grossman contributed a two-track tape recorder and borrowed some microphones from Peter, Paul and Mary. Hawks keyboardist Garth Hudson became the de facto recording engineer, and within weeks they had committed about four dozen songs, mostly rough jams, to tape. Their process was simple. It was one that Dylan has used repeatedly throughout his career, that is, "learning to go forward by turning back the clock"[3]—and go back they did. At these initial sessions, they played old country-western standards, folk and blues chestnuts, and pop tunes of bygone days—with a few Dylan originals mixed in.

The sessions in the Red Room were productive but noisy. Since Sara was pregnant once again, and since Jesse was a year old, the musicians agreed to find less disruptive quarters. In nearby West Saugerties, Hawks bassist Rick Danko, keyboardist Richard Manuel, and Garth Hudson shared a house that the locals called "Big Pink" due to its exterior paint job; and guitarist Robbie Robertson lived close by. Big Pink had a walk-out basement-garage on the south side that could easily accommodate the six musicians, their recording equipment, their many instruments, and an old dog to lie on the floor.

And so, the legendary Basement Tapes were born. From May to October, the group turned out scores of songs, including many of Dylan's most memorable; they were committed to tape, sometimes in multiple takes, and not without a fair amount of stimulant-induced silliness interspersed.

As planned, Grossman farmed out copies of fourteen of the best songs, known as the Big Ben Demos, to other artists. Peter, Paul and Mary, whom Grossman also managed, had a minor hit with Dylan's "Too Much of Nothing," and folk duo Ian and Sylvia recorded "Tears of Rage" and two others. Baez put three on her all-Dylan *Any Day Now* album.

The first to score a number-one hit with a Basement song was Manfred Mann in early 1968 with his version of "Quinn the Eskimo (The Mighty Quinn)," and Julie Driscoll with Brian Auger and the Trinity reached number five on the UK charts with a scorching version of "This Wheel's on Fire." The Byrds, who still relished doing Dylan covers, recorded "You Ain't Goin' Nowhere" and "Nothing Was Delivered" for their influential *Sweetheart of the Rodeo*, an album regarded as the granddaddy of country rock.

One year after the Basement sessions, the Hawks, now renamed the Band (as in *the* band who had backed Bob Dylan), released their own debut album, *Music from Big Pink*, on which their versions of "I Shall Be Released," "This Wheel's on Fire," and "Tears of Rage" appeared. Roger Waters of the group Pink Floyd ranked the Band's record as the second "most influential album in the history of rock 'n' roll," after only the Beatles' *Sgt. Pepper's Lonely Hearts Club Band*.[4]

Other Basement Tapes songs include the loopy "Million Dollar Bash"; "Crash on the Levee (Down in the Flood)"; "Tiny Montgomery," "Clothesline Sage," which is a sendup of Bobbie Gentry's "Ode to Billie Joe"; an impassioned south-of-the-border ballad called "Goin' to Acapulco"; "Sign on the Cross," which is a brilliantly macabre sendup of revival hymns; and the darkly stunning, half-mumbled "I'm Not There (1956)," which inspired Todd Haynes's 2007 Dylan biopic, *I'm Not There*.

But Dylan wasn't done. He made three trips to Nashville in October and November to record a new studio album—without the Band and without including any of the songs recorded at Big Pink. In a time of psychedelic overkill, elaborate overproduction, and concept albums, the new record was a starkly stripped-down affair. It was the anti-*Sgt. Pepper's*. With none of the provocative anarchy of *Highway 61 Revisited* or *Blonde on Blonde*, Dylan's twelve ethereal songs were a nod to some of his earlier symbolist lyrics, with swatches of religious imagery and mysticism overlaid. The album, released just after Christmas 1967, was called *John Wesley Harding*.

• • •

Among fans, the album aroused alarm. Why were none of the Basement songs, which other artists were recording, included? What happened to Dylan's versions? Had fans been cheated? One recently launched and soon-to-be-influential magazine, called *Rolling Stone* (so named, in part, as a tribute to Dylan), in their twelfth issue, featured an article that boldly declared, "Dylan's Basement Tape Should Be Released."[5] The zeal with which fans demanded the release was intense.

An answer of sorts appeared in the summer of 1969 in the form of an unauthorized double album, the first rock bootleg. It was available in head shops in major cities and by mail from various underground radio stations that were popping up on the relatively new FM frequency. The album, the cover of which was blank except for the words *Great White Wonder* crudely stamped in purple, contained seven of the fourteen Big Ben demos, along with more than a dozen other rare Dylan tracks. It was a cultural phenomenon, though it only served to whet fans' appetite for more. They would have to wait until 1975 for sixteen Basement songs to appear on the first official *Basement Tapes* album, and they would wait until 2014 before all 139 tracks were released on the 6-CD *Bootleg Series, Vol. 11: The Basement Tapes Complete*—more than six and a half hours of music. A critic for one major magazine described the set as "some of the most daring, creative and truly beautiful music ever recorded."[6]

• • •

The accident, the escape to upstate New York, and the mysterious subterranean recordings all fueled the myth of Dylan as a recluse, "the hermit of Woodstock."[7] Of course, no more a recluse than any celebrity forced to dodge meddlesome fans and far from being a hermit, Dylan was leading what most people would regard as a reasonably normal life. He was spending time puttering around his property, entertaining friends, and working on projects he was passionate about. Most of all, he spent time with his wife and his kids (he and Sara added another child to their family in 1968) and did the things that most dads do. One woman recalls attending a parent-teacher meeting at her child's elementary school in Woodstock, and there, sitting next to her in one of those undersized desks, was local parent Bob Dylan.

But the idyllic days at Hi Lo Ha were numbered. The place was becoming a porous kind of retreat, and again, the adulators, the wild-eyed devotees, despoiled paradise. They routinely sneaked onto the property, peered in the windows, and broke into the house, looking for souvenirs or clues to Dylan's mystifying charisma. As Dylan later wrote,

> What I was fantasizing about was a nine-to-five existence, a house on a tree-lined block with a white picket fence, pink roses in the backyard. . . . That was my deepest dream. After a while you learn that privacy is something you can sell, but you can't buy it back. Woodstock had turned into a nightmare, a place of chaos.[8]

This explains why Dylan opted not to perform at the Woodstock Festival in August 1969. Although the event was actually located more than an hour's drive from the village of Woodstock, it was still too close for comfort. Anticipating the arrival of hundreds of thousands of music fans, Dylan did the only rational thing: he got out of town. Two weeks later, he and the Band performed at the Isle of Wight Festival in England, only his third public appearance since the accident three years earlier.

• • •

Around that time (coincidentally, on the last day of the Woodstock Festival), Bob Dylan's contract with his manager expired, and a new era in their relationship began.

With a heaping dollop of understatement, Bob Dylan once wrote that Albert Grossman "was no hayseed." Grossman was one of the scrappiest, most aggressive music entrepreneurs of the 1960s. According to Dylan, Grossman carried a .45 pistol, had a voice "like war drums [and] didn't talk so much as growl."[9] A rabidly unapologetic capitalist, Grossman was despised by the more idealistic members of the folk community, but he made sure that he and his clients—people like Peter, Paul and Mary, Paul Butterfield, Mike Bloomfield, the Band, and Janis Joplin—received top dollar for their talents.

Early on, Grossman had essentially built Dylan's career from the ground up, negotiating contracts, scheduling concerts and recording sessions, and keeping close tabs on the finances. According to Pennebaker, Grossman "was kind of a father" to Dylan.[10] The two were a formidable pair, a confluence of powerful tidal currents. Both had talent, savvy, persuasive though difficult personalities, and ambition.

When it came time to renew their contract in 1969, Dylan sensed something was wrong. Over the years, through a series of complicated contractual maneuvers, a sort of legal shell game, Grossman had managed to assign to himself far more of Dylan's songwriting royalties than Dylan had been aware of. Dylan also discovered that some of Grossman's recently established companies were being secretly collateralized against older, jointly held companies.[11] The machinations resulted in Dylan firing Grossman. The two parted unamicably, and the complicated legal and financial wrangling would continue even after Grossman's death in 1986.

The fact is, Dylan no longer needed Grossman. How does one become more famous than famous? Rather than depending on someone else to develop his career, Dylan reclaimed his independence and the freedom to explore new directions—for instance, his foray into country music with his next album, *Nashville Skyline* (1969), and his first major acting role in Sam Peckinpah's western film *Pat Garrett and Billy the Kid* (1973), in which Dylan played a character named, ironically, Alias.

Had it not been for his so-called hermit years, during which he was raising his own children, Dylan might never have realized that he himself no longer needed a father figure. He was on his own.

• • •

So, Dylan was not a hermit in the way that Thomas Merton was.

And yet . . . in the summer of 1967, it would have been hard to tell which of them was the more unhermitlike.

A prisoner in solitary confinement experiences solitude. A monk in a mountain cave with the rope pulled up after him is a hermit by anyone's definition. But neither Thomas Merton nor Bob Dylan were solitaries at this point, despite the myths surrounding them. They were eminently sociable artists who depended almost entirely on others; they were creative thinkers with wide circles of stimulating friends and acquaintances to feed their creativity and help produce their work; and they had acquired huge audiences. They spent time alone, but no more nor less than most artists who carve out time to think and create. Otherwise, a steady stream of friends and visitors flowed through their lives.

Both were beset, however, with too many visitors of the unwanted kind. Dylan had to deal with the hippie invaders, while Merton had to cope with the unending parade of visiting priests and dignitaries.

Both were profiled in glossy magazines, interviewed by earnest journalists, their works reviewed in various publications; both had deadlines to meet and, to some degree, the business end of creativity to deal with.

Both were controversial and had acquired enemies, and both had to cope with the occasional hostility of their former fans.

Both had meddling father figures whom they struggled with and ultimately had to overcome, and Merton even addressed his as "Father."

Unlike Dylan, Merton had no family—though in another sense he did. It is not for nothing that monks are called *brothers*. For much of his time in the hermitage, Merton walked to the abbey every day for a meal and to attend Mass, he taught the novices on most Sundays despite no longer being their official novice master, and he personally counseled many of the monks, especially those considering leaving the monastery.

Merton would have resonated with Dylan's observation that "Privacy is something you can sell, but you can't buy it back."

• • •

Of course, on another level, "all men are solitary," wrote Merton. "Only most of them are so averse to being alone, or to feeling alone, that they do everything they can do to forget their solitude."[12] In one of his most beautiful Basement Tapes songs, "I Shall Be Released," Dylan refers to a man, perhaps a prisoner, standing by himself "in this lonely crowd" and plaintively longing to "be released."[13] As artists, Merton and Dylan had learned the trick of inhabiting that inner solitude even when surrounded by others. As spiritual thinkers, they accepted their basic existential aloneness before God. "This inner 'I,'" Merton wrote, "who is always alone, meets the solitude of every other man and the solitude of God. . . . This 'I' is Christ himself living in us: and we, in Him, living in the Father."[14]

In 1975, Bob Dylan, a year after returning to the concert stage, told an interviewer for *People* magazine,

> I don't think of my life as a reclusive life. I'm not a hermit. Exclusive, maybe, but not reclusive. I didn't consciously pursue the Bob Dylan myth. It was given to me—by God. Inspiration is what we're looking for. You just have to be receptive to it. . . . There is a voice inside us all that talks only to us. We have to be able to hear that voice.[15]

Thomas Merton would have known exactly what Dylan meant, though to describe that voice, he would have used another term: *prophetic*.

Ascension

Monday, January 29, 1968

It has been unseasonably warm for January, in the fifties all weekend—hardly enough for a jacket. In downtown Louisville, the day is bright, with only a few clouds, so there's no reason not to take a quick stroll before visiting a convalescing friend and heading back to the abbey. And anyway, he needs to shake off that aura of mortification that clings to you after a visit to the proctologist, "with your head down and your asshole up in the air," as he later wrote in his journal.[1]

Just down the street, at the corner of Preston and Broadway, is Vine Records, with its shop sign showing a stylized saxophone in place of the *V* in *Vine*. He's got money in his pocket, and his fifty-third birthday is only two days away, so why not take a peek? An indulgence, but it's not as though Dom James is still looking over his shoulder.

Inside, one of the first things that catches his eye is the new-releases rack, which displays a Bob Dylan record he's never seen, *John Wesley Harding*. The grainy black-and-white photo on the cover shows a bearded Dylan standing with three men, two of whom seem to be foreign—East Indians, maybe. And, oddly, Dylan is smiling. In all the other photos he's seen, Dylan is grimly poker-faced. He flips the record over and finds one of Dylan's typically surreal ramblings, which begins somewhat cheerily, "There were three kings and a jolly three too. . . ." It's encouraging to know that Dylan's recovered from the accident. As he tucks the album under his arm, he realizes this is the first Dylan record he's purchased rather than borrowed.

He checks the jazz bins. He's heard the flap about jazz's "New Thing"—by pioneers like Ornette Coleman, John Coltrane, Pharoah Sanders, and Charles Mingus. They're shaking things up right now, which is just what this society could use.

He stops at a Coltrane LP. The front cover shows the saxophonist sitting on a stool against a white background, soprano sax in hand, gazing into the distance like some Nubian prophet. *John Coltrane* is printed in black, and above it, in vivid multi-colors, is the album's title, *Ascension*. He flips the cover over. No tracks are listed, just photos of the musicians and an endorsement from poet LeRoi Jones: "Trane is now a scope of feeling. A more fixed traveler, whose wildest onslaughts are gorgeous artifacts not even deaf people should miss." Impressive. He takes the records to the sales desk.

In a world hell-bent on destroying itself, perhaps Bob Dylan and John Coltrane can offer some perspective.[2]

• • •

The first words Thomas Merton wrote in his journal in 1968 were "The year struggles with its own blackness."[3] The recent deaths of so many friends helped to inspire such forebodings about the New Year—forebodings that proved prophetic, since 1968 turned out to be one of the most tumultuous in American history, a genuine *annus horribilis*.

It would be the year in which nearly seventeen thousand Americans would be killed in Vietnam, more than in any other year of the war, and the year in which American soldiers would massacre five hundred unarmed civilians at My Lai. It would be the year in which riots would erupt in more than a hundred cities across America after the assassination of Dr. Martin Luther King Jr., and the progressive movement would falter with the assassination of presidential hopeful Robert F. Kennedy, who would be shot at point-blank range while campaigning. It would be the year in which police would beat student protesters bloody on the streets of Chicago during the Democratic Convention, and Richard M. Nixon would be elected president. In other parts of the world, "The Troubles" in Northern Ireland would begin, and it would be the second year of the war-induced famine in Biafra during which three million people would eventually starve to death.

Although distracted by the lengthy process of electing Dom James's replacement as abbot (Merton's friend and fellow hermit Father Flavian Burns was eventually chosen), Merton was profoundly troubled by the news of the world. It would dominate his journals and letters more than at any other time in his life.

At the end of January, he learned of the Pueblo Incident, in which North Korean ships commandeered an American spy vessel, killing one sailor and capturing the crew of eighty-three. Reminiscent of the Cuban Missile Crisis, the incident left the nation wondering whether the US was on the verge of another war. That the country was on high alert was personally evident to Merton, for on January 31, his fifty-third birthday, the earth rumbled beneath his feet and the windows of the hermitage rattled as the Army gunners at Fort Knox, thirty miles away, held artillery practice. "Will there never be any peace in our lifetime?" he wrote in his journal that day. "Really, what is ahead but the apocalypse?"[4]

• • •

Often in times of crisis, Merton sought out prophetic voices to put things into perspective—poets and novelists and theologians. Now, at the beginning of 1968, he tried reading several such writers—William Styron, Dietrich Bonhoeffer, and Martin Buber, among others—but none of them quite held his attention. The world seemed too unsettled.

To give context to the times, Merton decided to encourage new prophetic voices on his own by starting a literary magazine. It was a bare-bones affair, typed on a simple typewriter and mimeographed at the abbey. The four issues were published throughout the first half of 1968 and called, appropriately, *Monk's Pond*. While the production was humble, the caliber of the contributors was not. They included some of the most brilliant writers of the time, many of whom Merton knew personally, people like Nicanor Parra, Mark Van Doren, Czeslaw Milosz, Charles Simic, Jack Kerouac, Wendell Berry, Robert Lax, and dozens of others.

The two records that Merton had purchased in Louisville for his birthday also helped to put the chaotic times in perspective. They were prophetic in their own way. Merton relished Dylan's newest album, *John Wesley Harding*, most likely because it was his most self-consciously mystical album to date. In an odd twist, while many pop songwriters were now exploring their own inner Dylan, imitating his surrealism or social concerns, Dylan was exploring the Bible—though as Dylan told an interviewer at the time, "I have always read the Bible."[5] Scholars have tallied more than sixty biblical allusions among the album's twelve songs[6]—and Merton would certainly have caught many of them. The acoustic songs were mellow, most with dark, brooding undertones, and they spoke keenly to the spiritual hunger of the times. In his journal, Merton declared Dylan's new album to be "his best. Very encouraging."[7]

But that album's impact on Merton was negligible compared to that of the other record. He pronounced John Coltrane's *Ascension* to be "shattering. A fantastic and prophetic piece of music."[8] Beyond that, Merton didn't explain, but Coltrane seemed to capture Merton's feelings at the time. A few months later, when asked to conduct a workshop for some novice masters at the hermitage, Merton considered sharing Coltrane with them as a way to startle them, to wake them up to the state of the world.

• • •

Released in 1966, *Ascension* became a classic of "the New Thing," which eventually came to be called free jazz. Ahead of its time then as now, Coltrane's music was so controversial that he was booed on stage in 1965—just weeks after Dylan was booed at Newport. Many critics and fans found Coltrane's new sound, like Dylan's, chaotic and grating.

Coltrane's concept was to create a space in which the musicians were freed from as many constraints as possible, from standard rhythms, keys, tonalities, and chord structures. The ensemble on *Ascension* consisted of two trumpets, two alto saxes, three tenor saxes (including Coltrane's), a piano, two basses, and drums. The group recorded only two takes, each about forty minutes long, with the first take being selected and split over the two sides of the album.[9] After repeating a short opening theme, the musicians alternated relentlessly dissonant group improvisations with frenzied solos, Coltrane's main directive being that each solo should increase in volume and intensity as it progressed. So emotionally draining was the session that drummer Elvin Jones, at the end of the second take, hurled his drum kit against the studio wall. He left Coltrane's band a few months later.

The fact that Merton declared the album "prophetic" was itself prophetic. Few people would have used that word at the time—probably about as many as thought Bob Dylan was a major literary figure. Just as Merton could hear the protest in Dylan's poetry, he recognized the penetrating social commentary in the instrumental jazz of John Coltrane.

Coltrane may have helped Merton resolve his uneasiness about Cid Corman's and Joan Baez's accusations of violence in language. Here was Coltrane, fiercely exploring music's *terra incognita*, the farthest reaches of jazz's possibilities, as a way of saying something important about the nature of society and humanity. While pushing art to its extremes may be perceived as violent by some, it is actually the breaking of new ground—*shattering*, to use Merton's word.

Before entering the monastery, Merton had been a jazzophile when the big names were Tommy Dorsey and Benny Goodman, though Merton preferred black artists like Duke Ellington, Billie Holiday, and Louis Armstrong. After he became a monk, his relationship with the music grew ambivalent. At times he shunned it as unspiritual, while at other times he speculated that "the more 'hot' it is, the more spiritual it seems to be," at points connecting uninhibited jazz improvisation with religious ecstasy. Still, he added, "none of this can be played long, or make sense for more than a few minutes, anywhere near the monastery."[10]

In late 1957, while having a molar extracted, he sat in the dentist's chair in a daze, listening to "ancient jazz" piped into the room, music he had once enjoyed. It now made him feel "overcome with a sense of immense hopelessness and defilement."[11] One romantic ballad kept repeating itself in his sleep that night, causing him to wake in a cold sweat.

Three years later, some friends took him to a jazz club in Louisville, and again, his reaction was negative. "I am dead to it," he wrote. "It is finished long ago. You don't drag a corpse down to 4th street and set it up in a chair, at a table, and in polite society."[12]

But by 1968 the world had changed, and so had Merton. World events had forced themselves on him, literally "shaking his windows and rattling his walls," to paraphrase "The Times They Are A-Changin'." Now, more than ever, Merton was perceiving jazz's inseparable relationship to the Civil Rights movement, to black empowerment, and to political dissent. Jazz, which had helped the nation survive World War II, had matured and, along with rock 'n' roll, was in the vanguard of social change. In his 1964 book about the black struggle for civil rights, *Seeds of Destruction*, Merton wrote, "There is no revolution without poets who are also seers. There is no revolution without prophetic songs. . . . Hence the numinous force of the great and primitive art of the American Negro, a force that makes itself felt precisely where men have lost the habit of looking for art, for instance in that potent and mysterious jazz."[13]

In February 1968, Merton returned with friends to the jazz clubs in Louisville, but this time he was enthralled.

As with Dylan's music, Merton would have heard more than just the social context of Coltrane's free jazz; he would have heard the spiritual content as well. The album's title, *Ascension*, a reference to Christ's ascension to heaven, Merton would have interpreted as Coltrane's longing to be present with God, so powerfully did the music seem to yearn for transcendence. While most melodic lines in Western music tend to descend in pitch, starting high and moving incrementally lower, Coltrane seems to have coached his session players to do the opposite, to start their improvisations low and move higher—almost as if the musicians were climbing a ladder to heaven. Coltrane considered music a form of prayer and, on his earlier score for *A Love Supreme*, scratched this note to the musicians: "All paths lead to God."[14]

Coltrane's uncompromising, ecstatic sound validates those who revere him as one of the most mystical figures in jazz. In 1966, a year before Coltrane's death, an interviewer asked him what he planned to do in the next ten years. Coltrane answered, "Become a saint."[15] That ambition was fulfilled when he was later elevated to sainthood by the African Orthodox Church, and in the 1980s, one of their congregations in San Francisco renamed their fellowship the Saint John Will-I-Am Coltrane African Orthodox Church.

• • •

Coltrane's artistic fearlessness may have emboldened Merton to reassess *Cables to the Ace* more positively. In February 1968, while he was listening to Coltrane and visiting the jazz clubs, Merton announced in a group newsletter to friends that the book, soon to be issued by New Directions, would most likely baffle them. "It is obscure and indirect," he wrote almost proudly. "Perhaps some of the younger ones will intuitively pick up some of the short-hand. It does not preach. It does not have a 'message.' Maybe most of you better steer clear of it."[16] By "short-hand," he may have meant all those Dylanesque poetic devices he used. A few months later, Merton journaled that he wished he had spent more time writing creatively in the mode of *Cables* and his subsequent book of poetry, *The Geography of Lograire*, instead of writing so many of his other books, which he deemed "trivial, sanctimonious editorializing."[17]

Like Dylan and Coltrane, Merton was savagely booed in some circles, not before large audiences but in some religious journals. His antiwar writings and his books about Eastern religion drew heavy fire from both inside and outside the church, to the extent that one Catholic layperson burned his books. Some accused him of being a Communist, a radical, and a heretic, and, unbeknown to him, J. Edgar Hoover's agents at the FBI were diligently amassing a file on him. (This surveillance began ten years earlier when the FBI found that Merton was corresponding with Soviet writer Boris Pasternak, author of *Doctor Zhivago*.) How curious that a solitary poet-monk who seldom left rural Kentucky could be regarded as a threat to national security, and yet a threat he was. What Merton had once written about the Desert Fathers was now just as true of himself: they "were in a certain sense 'anarchists,' . . . men who did not believe in letting themselves be passively guided and ruled by a decadent state."[18]

Though distressed, he deflected the hostility with his customary wit. "I must be Godless," he wrote in his journal. "I wish to save lives rather than kill commies for Christ."[19] To poet and monk Robert Lax, his old friend from Columbia, he wrote (in the idiosyncratic jargon the two of them shared), "Frantics are burning my books . . . (have writ to papers, . . . 'Merton is commie red atheist contra vietnam war pitznik') . . . Catlick papers all full of turmoil over your friend. / Ho ho ho turmoils. / Ha ha ha burn the books."[20]

In April, three days before Palm Sunday, things became too grim for sarcasm. After spending the day at Shaker Village in Pleasant Hill, Merton and a group of friends drove to Lexington for dinner. During the meal, they distractedly watched the day's news flash across the screen of the restaurant's television: footage of Vietnam and Martin Luther King Jr. speaking to striking sanitation workers in Memphis. On the night drive back to Gethsemani, a crackling voice on the radio reported first that King had been shot, then that he was in critical condition, and then that he had died. The news was devastating. Merton felt as if "an animal, a beast of the apocalypse," was crouching on the roof of the car.[21]

In a sad irony, King's death occasioned the first opportunity for poems by Merton, transformed into songs, to receive national attention. In 1964, a young black singer, Robert Lawrence Williams, had asked Merton to write some poems inspired by African American spirituals, to be used in a tribute to the late President Kennedy. The plan was to have Catholic liturgical composer Alexander Peloquin write folk-gospel settings for them, which Williams would then perform, and the royalties would be donated to a scholarship fund for underprivileged students. But Peloquin's settings, called *Four*

Freedom Songs, like Niles's adaptations, turned out to be thoroughly classical, requiring an operatically trained lead singer and an orchestral choir. Merton and Williams were dismayed; the music was too "white," closer to Carl Orff than to Mahalia Jackson, and before long, wrangling arose over who actually owned the rights: Williams, Peloquin, or Merton.

Despite the controversy, the *Four Freedom Songs* were later performed by the Ebenezer Baptist Choir (from King's home church), conducted by the composer, at the National Liturgical Conference in Washington, D.C., as part of a national tribute to King. Catholic social activist Dorothy Day, a friend of Merton's, was in the audience, and she immediately wrote to him, "The songs were enough to break down the walls of Jericho. People wept with joy."[22]

Not long after King's assassination, Merton learned that Daniel Berrigan was facing criminal charges. In May, Berrigan and eight other Catholic activists stole nearly four hundred files from the draft board in Catonsville, Maryland, doused them with napalm, and burned them. On the day that the group burned the files, Berrigan wrote a quick note to Merton; it read simply, "Wish us luck."[23] The group, dubbed the Catonsville Nine, defined new tactics for the antiwar movement and upped the ante in protests against the government. Berrigan, who evaded capture for a time, ended up on the FBI's Ten Most Wanted List.

Then, in June, Robert Kennedy was assassinated, which only confirmed in Merton's mind that murder had become a political tool. After sending a telegram of condolence to Ethel Kennedy, he lamented privately that the country was now headed for "degradation and totalism," that the "law and order" crowd would be energized—not to prevent more murders, but to crack down on protest and dissent.[24]

• • •

Like monks everywhere, Merton redoubled his efforts to pray for the world. For that to occur, he needed a certain amount of solitude but found it difficult to come by. As Merton confessed in his journal,

> Real solitude: I do not have it here. I am not really living as a hermit. I see too many people, have too much active work to do, the place is too noisy, too accessible. People are always coming up here, and I have been too slack about granting visits, interviews, etc., going to town too often, socializing, drinking, and all that. All I have is a certain privacy, but real solitude is less and less possible here. Everyone knows where the hermitage is.[25]

To deal with the revolving door of visitors, he altered his daily routine—by practicing avoidance. He shifted his writing time to early morning so he could go on extended, prayerful walks among the wooded hills at midday, the time when most visitors knocked on his door. He was not above lurking in the woods, spying from afar, waiting for the intruders to leave. But the tactic was often ineffective.

For more than a year, friends had advised him to travel, to experience the world beyond the abbey. Joan Baez had invited him to her institute. And for years some had suggested that he leave altogether: Ira Sandperl and Rosemary Radford Ruether, as well as Sidi Abdeslam, who had also mysteriously prophesied that a big change was in store for Merton. Even Margie, in their final conversation, implored him to "reach out for happiness" by leaving.[26] So, perhaps now was the time—not to leave the order, but to accept invitations to speak. By getting out and speaking up, he thought, perhaps he might do some good.

As a trial, he flew to the Redwoods Monastery in California in May to address a conference of monks and nuns about monastic vocation. For three weeks, friends toured him around the deserts, valleys, and mountains of the Southwest, which left him thoroughly energized. Merton discovered he actually had more solitude while traveling than he had at Gethsemani, and he was inspired by the stimulating people he met.

On May 16 (coincidentally, the day before Daniel Berrigan napalmed the government files in Maryland), Merton found himself in a San Francisco café, sipping espresso with Beat poet and publisher Lawrence Ferlinghetti and watching the many attractive women walk past the window.[27]

Although the two had corresponded for years, this was their first face-to-face meeting, and the experience was invigorating. Merton spent the night in an office-guestroom on an upper floor of Ferlinghetti's famous City Lights Bookstore.

The trip was decisive. It paved the way for Merton to consider another, far more ambitious journey. Earlier in the year, he had been asked to address an international conference of monastics in December, a meeting organized by the Benedictines, to take place in Bangkok, Thailand. At first he was unsure; he felt it would be one more distraction to what little solitude he had, and he suspected that Father Flavian would be no more encouraging about such things than Dom James had been. So he put the decision on hold. But after the California trip, Father Flavian was willing to let Merton go. So, Merton accepted the invitation to travel to Asia, something he had dreamed of for years.

• • •

Merton's interest in Asia dated back to his days at Columbia, when he started thinking about the differences between the Eastern religions and Catholicism, but his interest intensified while he was at Gethsemani, when he began to see the similarities as well. As a monastic, he was intrigued by the contemplative practices of other religions and avidly studied a wide variety of books on Buddhism, Taoism, Hinduism, and Sufism to learn more. With a particular interest in Zen, he corresponded through the years with professor and Zen practitioner D. T. Suzuki, who was instrumental in explaining the "Zen mind" to Western readers in such books as *The Zen Doctrine of No-Mind* (1949) and *Zen and Japanese Culture* (1959). As a poet, Merton also found inspiration in the poets of those traditions, especially the Sufi poets of the Middle East.

Merton's nearly lifelong appreciation for Asian philosophy and religion found its fullest expression in his writings in the 1960s. His essays on Zen were published in two collections, *Mystics and Zen Masters* (1967) and *Zen and the Birds of Appetite* (1968). He also spent five years translating passages from the writings of the ancient Chinese Taoist philosopher Chuang Tzu, published as *The Way of Chuang Tzu* in 1965, and in that same year his influential book *Gandhi on Non-Violence* was issued.

These books are essential in understanding Merton's elation at the prospect of actually traveling to Japan, India, and Southeast Asia. His intense study of Buddhism and Sufism, not just in an academic way but as an adjunct and challenge to his own faith, had led to Thich Nhat Hanh's earlier astonishment at Merton's lack of Western dualism and to Sidi Abdeslam's declaration that Merton had spiritually "arrived." Even today, Merton is considered one of the three great explicators of Zen to the Western world, alongside philosopher Alan Watts and D. T. Suzuki himself.

Although many inside the church, then as now, accused Merton of syncretism, of believing that all religions are essentially compatible, his thinking was far more complex and nuanced, and more than a dozen books have been written on the subject of Merton's Eastern interests. While he readily acknowledged the differences between the world's religious systems, he reserved his greatest fascination for their similarities, for how a mutual understanding among the different faiths might not only enrich those faiths but bring people together as well—an especially hopeful aspiration at the time of the Vietnam War. Merton wrote that all religions agree "that there is more to human life than just 'getting somewhere,' . . . that the highest ambition lies beyond ambition, in the renunciation of the 'self,' . . . that a certain 'purification' of the will and intelligence can open man's spirit to a higher and more illuminated understanding of the meaning and purpose of life, or indeed of the very nature of Being itself."[28]

And now, in the fall of 1968, Merton would have a chance to discuss these ideas with the adherents of those religions themselves.

• • •

A rough itinerary was sketched out. He was to leave in September on what would become his most energizing and decisive spiritual journey. The trip was, in a sense, "Thomas Merton on tour," the most extended series of speaking engagements he would ever have, and his many appearances at monasteries and conferences along the way helped finance parts of the trip.

The second week of September, he flew to New Mexico, where he visited the Benedictine Monastery of Christ in the Desert, then being refurbished, and where he also spent time with artist Georgia O'Keefe. He then flew to Chicago, where he addressed a conference of Poor Clare sisters and celebrated Mass. The following week, he flew to Anchorage, Alaska, where he spoke at a conference at the Convent of the Sister Adorers of the Precious Blood in nearby Eagle River. From there he traveled to several other places in Alaska to meet bishops, sight-see, hike, and speak to various conferences and monastic gatherings, all the while toying with the idea of perhaps someday moving to a new hermitage in Alaska. The first week of October, he flew to California, where he returned to the Redwoods Monastery to conduct a three-day workshop and to meet with friends. At City Lights Bookstore he bought so many books that he had to pay extra baggage fees on his flights.

On October 15, his plane left San Francisco, and, after a stop in Honolulu, made its way to Japan. Merton then flew to Bangkok for two days, and then to Calcutta, India, where he experienced his first major bout of culture shock. The poverty and overcrowded conditions stunned him, and he found that despite being a monk with no possessions, he was still regarded as an affluent Westerner. He spoke at a four-day interfaith conference in South Calcutta, which proved to be an exhilarating experience; he was able to have extended discussions with delegates from many of the world's major faiths.

In New Delhi a few days later, he was notified that his request for an audience with the fourteenth Dalai Lama (the *tulku*, or "custodian," of Tibetan Buddhism) had been approved. Excitedly, Merton traveled to Dharamsala, spoke with Buddhist monks and spiritual leaders, and met with the Dalai Lama on November 4. The conversation was so stimulating that the Dalai Lama invited Merton to have two more audiences with him. They discussed monasticism, Marxism, contemplation, education, and the purpose of vows. When the two parted, they felt as if they were brothers, and two decades later, the Dalai Lama would write, "It was Merton who introduced me to the real meaning of the word 'Christian.'"[29]

Merton then returned briefly to Calcutta before journeying to Darjeeling and several other cities. All along the way he celebrated Mass at various Catholic churches, spoke at conferences, and met with Buddhist Rinpoches, hermit monks, bishops and priests, and ordinary people. The next stop was a return to Bangkok, where he was scheduled to speak at an international conference of monastics, the event that had launched his journey to Asia in the first place.

Everything about this trip had been extraordinary, from Anchorage to Dharamsala, from Georgia O'Keefe to the Dalai Lama. On the day he left San Francisco two months earlier, he knew that this would be a time of self-discovery, the fulfillment of a dream. While over the Pacific on his flight to Asia, he had written, "I am going home, to the home where I have never been in this body."[30]

• • •

Sunday, December 8, 1968

He can't help but be overwhelmed. Bangkok. The gaudy temples; the traffic noise; the markets with their brightly colored wares; the street vendors' carts loaded with flowers and incense and steaming food; the sampans and long-tail boats on the Chao Phraya River; and, most of all, the people. Children everywhere, orange-robed Buddhist monks, the disabled and disfigured begging by the gates, streetwalkers, students handing out political tracts, women bargaining at the stalls, and old men in chairs, talking and watching. Some national celebration is underway. It's hard to believe that Thailand isn't more affected by the war—only Laos and Cambodia separate it from Vietnam. He's closer now to the Demilitarized Zone than Louisville is to Minneapolis.

The sun slowly sets as he strolls northward from the Oriental Hotel to Chinatown, with its neon signs and food smells wafting from every doorway. Earlier today he met with a Dutch abbot and some of the conference delegates who, in a few hours, will drive him to the Red Cross Conference Center outside the city, where he will speak about Marxism and monasticism, a topic he'd discussed with the Dalai Lama. The Dutch delegation has a television crew in tow, convinced that a permanent record of the conference will be "good for the church."[31] A doubtful claim. Several weeks earlier he had promised Father Flavian that he would scrupulously avoid all publicity on this trip.

But he doesn't have to worry about that until tomorrow. For now, he shuffles through the bustling streets, relishing it all: the fragrances, the colors, the confusion of tongues. He feels awake and alive, full of joy and light-years away from the tiny cabin in Kentucky. This is a far cry from Louisville or New York or London, but he senses a solidarity with these people just the same. He is home at last—at home in the world.

EPILOGUE

The story is told much the same way in every biography of Thomas Merton. On December 10, 1968, twenty-seven years to the day after arriving at Gethsemani, Merton touched a malfunctioning floor fan in his room near the conference center in Samut Prakan on the outskirts of Bangkok and was electrocuted. Only minutes before, he had concluded his address with the words "I will disappear from view, and we can all have a Coke or something."[1] The Dutch television crew captured that final lecture with their cameras—the only footage of Merton speaking ever made.

His body was flown back to California on a US Air Force transport plane. Alongside his casket on that long flight were the caskets of American service members killed in Vietnam. He was buried in the cemetery at Gethsemani on December 17, and nineteen years later, Dom James was buried in the adjacent plot. Ten years after that, the Dalai Lama, during a visit to the United States, made a special point of visiting Gethsemani. He wanted to pray at Merton's grave.

• • •

Merton's journey to the hermitage had taken twenty-four years. He lived there only three. The many distractions—the medical problems, the affair, the visitors—were frequent reminders that he was a long way from the desert and far removed from the caves of the Camaldolese. As many times as he tried to "pull the rope up after him," he was unable.

In one sense, he shouldn't have been surprised. In his epiphany on the streets of Louisville ten years earlier, he discovered that solitude was the path to greater oneness with others. After settling into the hermitage, he found an ever-widening circle of relationships, and through his acquaintances old and new, through his journey to the East, and through his millions of readers, he did indeed find a fundamental unity with the world. And an ever-deepening love for God.

His editor Robert Giroux once wrote, "I don't think he ever found a home, but I think he found happiness."[2] The hermitage was simply a way station, not the destination. No wonder Merton was fascinated by the deer that wandered out of the woods and stared at him so soulfully two and a half years earlier. It was as if they were beckoning him to follow. And follow them he did, halfway around the world.

But in another sense, he never left home. He carried it with him everywhere, for as Thich Nhat Hanh once wrote, "Our true home is the present moment, whatever is happening right here and now."[3]

• • •

A week and a half before Thomas Merton met with the Dalai Lama in Dharamsala, Bob Dylan met with country-music star Johnny Cash. The two had dinner immediately after Cash's concert in New York City on October 23, 1968. Although they had met several times before, this was an important reconnection. A few months later, they would record together in the studio for Dylan's album of country songs, *Nashville Skyline*, and the following July, Dylan would perform on Cash's television variety show.

Dylan owed Cash a considerable debt. Not only had he cut his teeth on Johnny Cash songs as a teenager, but after Dylan's debut album failed to sell well, Cash encouraged Columbia Records executives to give the young folksinger another shot, which resulted in the successful *Freewheelin' Bob Dylan* album. And two years later, when fans complained that Dylan had abandoned protest music, Cash defended him publicly in *Sing Out!* magazine by writing, "SHUT UP! . . . AND LET HIM SING!"[4]

But just a few months before their dinner in New York, Cash, who struggled with amphetamine addiction, had attempted suicide by crawling into a deep, watery cave not far from Chattanooga, Tennessee. Waiting to die in the dark, he had an epiphany, a penetrating sensation of God's presence. In his autobiography, he wrote, "I felt something very powerful start to happen to me, a sensation of utter peace, clarity, and sobriety. . . . There in the Nickajack Cave I became conscious of a very clear, simple idea: I was not in charge of my own destiny."[5] This experience led to a major renewal of the Christian faith of his childhood.

To Dylan, Johnny Cash was both a peer and a mentor—someone Dylan respected and to whom he could turn for wisdom and understanding. Dylan once acknowledged that "Johnny Cash was more like a religious figure to me."[6] Like Cash, Dylan had his own inner demons to outrun, not the least of which were the drugs and the burden of fame. In 1979, prompted in part by his failing marriage, Dylan too would publicly embrace Christianity, to the surprise—and consternation—of many of his fans.

Merton, had he lived, wouldn't have been surprised. He would have been sixty-four at the time of Dylan's famous conversion and would have found Dylan's new faith fascinating, arguing that Dylan had always been a spiritual seeker and pilgrim. *John Wesley Harding* was replete with biblical allusions, and *Highway 61 Revisited* expressed our existential aloneness better than most clergy, as Merton had explained in his *Midsummer Diary*. Dylan's embrace of religious faith, Merton would have argued, was inevitable; his honest voice, his authenticity, and his artistic integrity had always been indications of something deeply prophetic.

But Thomas Merton didn't live to see Bob Dylan's conversion. Nor did he have a chance to hear Dylan's controversial sequel to *John Wesley Harding*, the quite un-mystical *Nashville Skyline*, released six months after Merton's death. Although Merton might have been baffled by Dylan's new good-old-boy country persona, he would certainly have agreed with Johnny Cash's assessment on the back of that album: "Here-in is a hell of a poet."[7]

• • •

The images we have in our minds of Thomas Merton and Bob Dylan are founded in large part on who they were in 1966.

Fans of Merton's books almost invariably picture him in his hermitage, reading by the light of his single lamp or praying by the fire, talking delightedly with famous visitors like Thich Nhat Hanh, Jacques Maritain, Daniel Berrigan, and Joan Baez; and writing . . . always writing. One of the most iconic photos of Merton shows him standing outside the hermitage with his hands in the pockets of his rough denim coat, a blue stocking cap on his head, and a compassionate, slightly impish smile on his face. As John Howard Griffin wrote, "He had . . . an unblemished happiness with the moment."[8]

And likewise, even though his career has spanned six decades, it is the Bob Dylan of 1965 and 1966 that immediately appears to our cultural mind's eye. Music fans will always associate him with the tangle of electric-wire hair on his head, the Ray-Ban sunglasses, and the Fender Stratocaster strapped across his shoulder. They will always remember his intense, inscrutable expression on the covers of *Bringing It All Back Home*, *Highway 61 Revisited*, and *Blonde on Blonde,* and his cutting-edge, culture-shifting electric performances from Newport in July 1965 to London in May 1966.

Although one of those men died a few years later, and the other continued to create and perform for decades, both achieved something of an apotheosis during that critical, chaotic time. "Bringing it all back home" meant something different to each of them. But it is to our benefit that these two men, artists of very different kinds, had enough vision to seek out that ideal home in the first place and, when they grew disenchanted with it, enough wisdom to keep on looking.

• • •

Finally, for a man who earnestly sought the silence of solitude for much of his adult life, Merton was curiously infatuated with music: not just Dylan's, but classical, chant, jazz, ethnic, folk, and rock. Merton realized that silence and music are entwined, fellow travelers, or, to quote *Cables to the Ace*, "La musique est une joie inventée par le silence"—"Music is a joy invented by silence."[9]

Why else would a hermit monk on his journey into the desert—to live alone, worship God, and pray for the whole world—take a record player along?

"Music," wrote Merton, "is pleasing not only because of the sound but because of the silence that is in it. . . . If we have no silence, God is not heard in our music."[10]

ACKNOWLEDGMENTS

As always, this is for Shelley. She first suggested that what started as a breezy article might be turned into a serious book. Thank you to my daughters—Abbie, Molly, and Lili—for their encouragement.

Thank you to:

Agent and scholar Tim Beals of Credo Communications, a bookman of extraordinary insight; and writer, painter, and editor Lil Copan—it's hard to describe what an honor it is to work with two such brilliant, talented people. Mary Hietbrink for her careful editing and patience. Gwyneth Findlay for her review of and detailed corrections to the first draft. David Dalton, master writer on all things music and an inspiration; our conversations helped shape this material. Rachel Brewer, a brilliant and tireless master of marketing. Jeff Rosen and David Beal of Special Rider Music, for their assistance and willingness to answer my questions. Bill and Beth Murphy of the West Michigan Thomas Merton Society, who provided valuable feedback and opened the doors of Gethsemani, and Brother Paul Quenon, who answered so many questions. Kim Tanner for her expertise and assistance in matters of rights and permissions. Professor and musician Ron Pen of the University of Kentucky, the world's foremost authority on the life and artistry of John Jacob Niles. Sue Johnson of Thomas Nelson Publishers, who first piqued my interest in the story of Merton's relationship with Margie Smith. James Doherty for his insights into Catholicism and psychology; he first directed me to Mark Leffert's research on Gregory Zilboorg. Mary Hassinger for her expertise in Roman Catholic customs and terminology. Tim Baker for his always meticulous proofreading. And poet Brian Phipps . . . every writer needs someone to ask regularly, "How's the book coming?"

Thanks also to:

Dr. Paul M. Pearson, director and archivist at the Thomas Merton Center, Bellarmine University in Louisville, and Albert Romkema at MertonArtifacts.com, both of whom helped in the research of this book; Sarah Gombis, Zondervan marketing director; John W. Whitehead, writer and president of the Rutherford Institute; Jon Pott, former editor in chief of Eerdmans; Dylan scholar Scott Marshall; musician and JFK scholar Tom DeVries; musician Scott Lally; professor Nancy Erickson; motorcyclists Ben Thompson and Marvin Rosenberger; and jazzman Bob "Stormhorn" Hartig.

• • •

Finally, I should acknowledge the indirect contribution of two women I knew in my twenties. The first, when she saw me reading Merton's *No Man Is an Island,* looked at me disdainfully and asked, "What are you reading *that* for?" The second, whom I was dating, informed me that I would eventually have to choose between her and my Bob Dylan obsession. I chose Dylan and never looked back.

CREDITS AND PERMISSIONS

The author and publisher of *The Monk's Record Player* would like to extend their gratitude to the following:

Special Rider Music for permission to quote portions of the following songs and liner notes by Bob Dylan:

From *The Times They Are A-Changin'*

- "The Times They Are A-Changin'"

From *Bringing It All Back Home*:

- "Bob Dylan's 115th Dream"
- "Gates of Eden"
- "Love Minus Zero/No Limit"
- "Maggie's Farm"
- "She Belongs to Me"

From *Bringing It All Back Home* liner notes:

CREDITS AND PERMISSIONS

From *Highway 61 Revisited*:

- “Ballad of a Thin Man”
- “Desolation Row”
- “From a Buick 6”
- “Highway 61 Revisited”
- “Just Like Tom Thumb’s Blues”
- “Like a Rolling Stone”
- “Tombstone Blues”

Copyright © 1965 by Warner Bros. Inc.; renewed 1993 by Special Rider Music. All rights reserved. International copyright secured. Reprinted by permission.

From *Highway 61 Revisited* liner notes:

Copyright © 1965 by Special Rider Music. All rights reserved. International copyright secured. Reprinted by permission.

From *Blonde on Blonde*:

- “I Want You”
- “Just Like a Woman”

Copyright © 1966 by Dwarf Music; renewed 1994 by Dwarf Music. All rights reserved. International copyright secured. Reprinted by permission.

From *The Basement Tapes Complete*:

- “I Shall Be Released”

Copyright © 1967, 1970 by Dwarf Music; renewed 1995 by Dwarf Music. All rights reserved. International copyright secured. Reprinted by permission.

- “Tiny Montgomery”

Copyright © 1967 by Dwarf Music; renewed 1995 by Dwarf Music. All rights reserved. International copyright secured. Reprinted by permission.

From *John Wesley Harding* liner notes:

Copyright © 1968 by Special Rider Music. All rights reserved. International copyright secured. Reprinted by permission.

From *World Gone Wrong* liner notes:

New Directions Publishing Corporation for permission to quote passages from the following poems by Thomas Merton:

"Cancer Blues" from *Eighteen Poems*:

"Cables to the Ace" from *The Collected Poems of Thomas Merton*:

HarperCollins Publishers and The Merton Legacy Trust for permission to quote passages from the following books by Thomas Merton:

From *Entering the Silence: The Journals of Thomas Merton: Volume Two, 1941–1952* by Thomas Merton and edited by Jonathan Montaldo. Copyright © 1995 by The Merton Legacy Trust. Reprinted by permission of HarperCollins Publishers.

From *A Search for Solitude: The Journals of Thomas Merton: Volume Three, 1952–1960* by Thomas Merton and edited by Christine Bochen. Copyright © 1997 by The Merton Legacy Trust. Reprinted by permission of HarperCollins Publishers.

From *Learning to Love: The Journals of Thomas Merton: Volume Six, 1966–1967* by Thomas Merton and edited by Lawrence S. Cunningham. Copyright © 1996 by The Merton Legacy Trust. Reprinted by permission of HarperCollins Publishers.

ABBREVIATIONS

Because *The Journals of Thomas Merton* were cited frequently, the following abbreviations were used after the first reference in the preceding chapters.

J1—Merton, *Run to the Mountain: The Journals of Thomas Merton: Volume One, 1939–1941*

J2—Merton, *Entering the Silence: The Journals of Thomas Merton: Volume Two, 1941–1952*

J3—Merton, *A Search for Solitude: The Journals of Thomas Merton: Volume Three, 1952–1960*

J4—Merton, *Turning Toward the World: The Journals of Thomas Merton: Volume Four, 1960–1963*

J5—Merton, *Dancing in the Water of Life: The Journals of Thomas Merton: Volume Five, 1963–1965*

J6—Merton, *Learning to Love: The Journals of Thomas Merton: Volume Six, 1966–1967*

J7—Merton, *The Other Side of the Mountain: The End of the Journey: Journals, Volume Seven, 1967–1968*

NOTES

NOTES TO THE INTRODUCTION

1. Bob Dylan, "The Times They Are A-Changin'," *The Times They Are A-Changin'* (Columbia, CS 8905, 1964), side 1, track 1.

2. Thomas Merton, *Conjectures of a Guilty Bystander* (Garden City, N.Y.: Doubleday, 1966), 318.

3. Pope Francis I, "Address of the Holy Father," *Libreria Editrice Vaticana*, https://w2.vatican.va/content/francesco/en/speeches/2015/september/documents/papa-francesco_20150924_usa-us-congress.html.

4. Eleanor Wachtel, "Christopher Ricks on Why Bob Dylan Is 'the Greatest Living User of the English Language,'" *CBC Radio* (October 16, 2016), http://www.cbc.ca/radio/writersandcompany/christopher-ricks-on-why-bob-dylan-is-the-greatest-living-user-of-the-english-language-1.3803292.

5. *Thomas Merton and James Laughlin: Selected Letters*, ed. David D. Cooper (New York: Norton, 1997), 299.

6. Thomas Merton, *Learning to Love: The Journals of Thomas Merton: Volume Six, 1966–1967*, ed. Christine M. Bochen (San Francisco: HarperSanFrancisco, 1997), 129 (emphasis in original).

7. Robert Bly, *The Sibling Society: An Impassioned Call for the Rediscovery of Adulthood* (New York: Vintage, 1996), 26.

8. Robert Shelton, *No Direction Home: The Life and Music of Bob Dylan* (Milwaukee: Backbeat Books, 2010), 209.

9. Bob Dylan, Press Conference, London Airport, April 26, 1965. D. A. Pennebaker, *Dont Look Back*, DVD (Docurama NVG 9824, 2007); transcribed in *Dont Look Back: A Film and Book by D. A. Pennebaker* (New York: Ballantine, 1968), 21.

10. *Dont Look Back* was chosen for preservation by the National Film Registry at the Library of Congress in 1998 and ranked best rock documentary of all time by *Rolling Stone* magazine: "40 Greatest Rock Documentaries," August 14, 2014, http://www.rollingstone.com/movies/lists/40-greatest-rock-documentaries-20140815/dont-look-back-1967-20140815.

11. Thomas Merton, *Dancing in the Water of Life: The Journals of Thomas Merton: Volume Five, 1963–1965*, ed. Robert E. Daggy (San Francisco: HarperSanFrancisco, 1997), 36.

12. *J5*, 210.

13. WBAI-FM Studios, New York, Broadside Radio Show interview, recorded May 1962. Bob Dylan, *The Great White Wonder* bootleg LP (unofficial recording, 1969), side 3, track 2.

14. Nat Hentoff and Bob Dylan, "The Playboy Interview: Bob Dylan," *Playboy*, vol. 13, no. 3 (March 1966): 41–46. The three albums are *Bringing It All Back Home*, *Highway 61 Revisited*, and *Blonde on Blonde*.

15. Dylan provided the art for *Self Portrait*, *Planet Waves*, *Blood on the Tracks* (original printing, back cover), and *The Bootleg Series, Volume 10: Another Self Portrait*, and he painted the cover for the Band's debut album, *Music from Big Pink*.

16. F. Douglas Scutchfield and Paul Holbrook Jr., eds., *The Letters of Thomas Merton and Victor and Carolyn Hammer: Ad Majorem Dei Gloriam* (Lexington, Ky.: University of Kentucky Press, 2014), 199.

17. John Howard Griffin, *Follow the Ecstasy: The Hermitage Years of Thomas Merton* (Maryknoll, N.Y.: Orbis, 1993), 2–3.

18. See Paul M. Pearson, *Beholding Paradise: The Photographs of Thomas Merton* (New York: Paulist Press, 2017).

19. Walt Whitman, "Myself and Mine," in *Whitman: Poetry and Prose* (New York: Library of America, 1982), 380.

20. Thomas Merton, *Thoughts in Solitude* (New York: Farrar, Straus & Giroux, 1958), 84–85.

21. Bob Dylan, "Interview with Nora Ephron and Susan Edmiston, *Positively Tie Dream*: August 1965," in *Bob Dylan: The Essential Interviews*, ed. Jonathan Cott (New York: Wenner, 2006), 50.

22. According to the notes on the Lenny Bruce CD collection *Live at the Curran Theater*, the comic frequented Lawrence Ferlinghetti's City Lights Bookstore in San Francisco after his shows because it was the only place open. There he found Merton's poem "Chant to Be Used in Processions around a Site with Furnaces" in volume 1 of Ferlinghetti's *Journal for the Protection of All Beings* (1961). Bruce adapted lines from it to create a new piece that began "My Name Is Adolf Eichmann." Merton's "Chant" is a portrait of the commandant of Auschwitz, Rudolf Höss, who was hanged as a war criminal in 1947. Bruce recast it in Eichmann's voice because the Nazi bureaucrat had been tried and executed in Israel in 1962, and Hannah Arendt's controversial 1963 book *Eichmann in Jerusalem* had kept his name in the news. For Merton's poem, see *The Collected Poems of Thomas Merton* (New York: New Directions, 1977), 345–49. Bruce's piece is in John Cohen, ed., *The Essential Lenny Bruce* (New York: Bell, 1970), 229–30. For an audio recording of Bruce reciting "My Name Is Adolf Eichmann," see Lenny Bruce, *Let the Buyer Beware*, 6 CDs (Shout! Factory, DK 37109, 2004), disc 6, track 14.

23. Suze Rotolo, *A Freewheelin' Time: A Memoir of Greenwich Village in the Sixties* (New York: Broadway Books, 2008), 261–62.

24. Bob Dylan, "7 February 1986, Stuart Coupe Interview, Regent Hotel, Auckland, New Zealand," *Every Mind Polluting Word*, http://content.yudu.com/Library/A1plqd/

BobDylanEveryMindPol/resources/765.htm, 932. This is the full quotation: "Yeah, I saw [Lenny Bruce] perform in the early sixties, around 1963, before he got caught up in all that legal stuff."

25. Dylan later wrote a song called "Lenny Bruce," in which he states he once shared a taxi ride with Bruce. The song was released on *Shot of Love*, LP (Columbia, TC 37496, 1981), side 1, track 4.

26. Bob Dylan, "Desolation Row," *Highway 61 Revisited*, LP (Columbia CS 9189, 1965), side 2, track 4.

27. Bob Dylan, "Gates of Eden," *Bringing It All Back Home*, LP (Columbia CS 9128, 1965), side 2, track 2.

28. The database of Dylan interviews, *Every Mind Polluting Word*, contains 1,384 pages; it contains no references to Merton; http://content.yudu.com/Library/A1plqd/BobDylanEveryMindPol/resources/765.htm.

29. These can be found in the volume *Learning to Love.*

30. Michael Mott, *The Seven Mountains of Thomas Merton* (Boston: Houghton Mifflin, 1984), xv.

NOTES TO THE PROLOGUE

1. Although Merton writes that he watched the full moon rise the previous evening, Saturday, March 5, the meteorological charts record that the full moon actually rose on Monday, March 7. Merton doesn't specify when he watched the deer on Sunday, March 6, other than it was in the evening. It must have been light enough to watch them from a distance, and since the sun set at 6:40 p.m., it would have taken place between 6:30 and 7:00 p.m. This prologue is based on Thomas Merton, *Learning to Love: The Journals of Thomas Merton: Volume Six, 1966–1967*, ed. Christine M. Bochen (San Francisco: HarperSanFrancisco, 1997), 25.

2. *J6*, 18.

3. *J6*, 25.

NOTES TO CHAPTER 1

1. This sign language faded from use during Merton's time at Gethsemani.

2. Adapted from "The Daily Schedule at Gethsemani During the 1940s," in Thomas Merton, *Entering the Silence: The Journals of Thomas Merton: Volume Two, 1941–1952*, ed. Jonathan Montaldo (San Francisco: HarperSanFrancisco, 1996), 489.

3. Thomas Merton, *Run to the Mountain: The Journals of Thomas Merton: Volume One, 1939–1941*, ed. Patrick Hart (San Francisco: HarperSanFrancisco, 1995), 334ff.

4. *J2*, 355.

5. Dom Frederic Dunne (1874–1948) was the first American-born Trappist abbot.

6. Thomas Merton, *The Seven Storey Mountain* (New York: Harcourt, Brace, 1948), 316, 318.

7. *The Rule of Saint Benedict*, chapter 6, paragraph 3.

8. Robert Giroux, "Introduction," in Thomas Merton, *The Seven Storey Mountain, Fiftieth Anniversary Edition* (Orlando, Fla.: Harcourt, Brace, 1998), xiii.

9. Thomas Merton, *The Wisdom of the Desert* (New York: New Directions, 1960), 4, 23 (emphasis in original).

10. Exodus 3:1, 4, Douay-Rheims (1899).

11. *J1*, 333.

12. Thomas Merton, *The Hidden Ground of Love: Letters on Religious Experience and Social Concerns*, ed. William H. Shannon (New York: Farrar, Straus & Giroux, 1985), 3.

13. *J1*, 326.

14. *The Seven Storey Mountain*, 371.

15. Thomas Merton, *The Secular Journal of Thomas Merton* (New York: Farrar, Straus & Cudahy, 1959), 183.

16. *J2*, 3.

17. Thomas Merton, *Search for Solitude: The Journals of Thomas Merton: Volume Three, 1952–1960*, ed. Lawrence S. Cunningham (San Francisco: HarperSanFrancisco, 1996), 293.

NOTES TO CHAPTER 2

1. Thomas Merton, "For My Brother: Reported Missing in Action, 1943," in *The Seven Storey Mountain* (New York: Harcourt, Brace, 1948), 404.

2. *Rule of Saint Benedict*, chapter 2, paragraphs 16–17.

3. Robert Giroux, *The Education of an Editor* (New York: Bowker, 1982), 30.

4. Thomas Merton, *The Sign of Jonas* (New York: Harcourt, Brace & Company, 1953), 110.

5. Thomas Merton, *Entering the Silence: The Journals of Thomas Merton: Volume Two, 1941–1952*, ed. Jonathan Montaldo (San Francisco: HarperSanFrancisco, 1996), 34.

6. *J2*, 34.

7. *J2*, 63.

8. The woman and the child are thought to have died in the London blitz during the war.

9. Augustine, *Confessions*, Book 4, section 2. Augustine was seventeen years old when his son, Adeodatus ("Gift of God"), was born.

10. *J2*, 187–88 (emphasis in original).

11. *J2*, 98.

12. *J2*, 98.

13. *J2*, 128.

14. *J2*, 129.

15. *J2*, 141.

16. *J2*, 328. The abbot at this point was Dom James Fox.
17. *J2*, 328.
18. *J2*, 329.
19. *J2*, 329.
20. Deuteronomy 34:4, Douay-Rheims (1899).

NOTES TO CHAPTER 3

1. Thomas Merton, *The Sign of Jonas* (New York: Harcourt, Brace, 1953), 91.
2. Robert Giroux, "Introduction," in Thomas Merton, *The Seven Storey Mountain, Fiftieth Anniversary Edition* (Orlando, Fla.: Harcourt, Brace, 1998), xvi. The *NYT*'s policy of not including religious book sales in the best-seller list didn't change until the mid-1990s.
3. Garry Wills, *Head and Heart: American Christianities* (New York: Penguin, 2007), 457.
4. Thomas Merton, *The Wisdom of the Desert* (New York: New Directions, 1960), 5.
5. Edward Gibbon, *History of the Decline and Fall of the Roman Empire*, Chapter 37, Part I, "Conversion of the Barbarians to Christianity" (London: Penguin, 1995 [1788]), 411.
6. William Edward Hartpole Lecky, *History of European Morals from Augustus to Charlemagne*, vol. 2, chapter 4, "The Saints of the Desert" (New York: Appleton, 1869), 114.
7. *The Wisdom of the Desert*, 4.
8. Thomas Merton, *Entering the Silence: The Journals of Thomas Merton: Volume Two, 1941–1952*, ed. Jonathan Montaldo (San Francisco: HarperSanFrancisco, 1996), 222–23.
9. *The Sign of Jonas*, 90.
10. *J2*, 228.
11. *J2*, 228.
12. *J2*, 235.
13. *J2*, 235.
14. *J2*, 323.
15. *J2*, 324. Although Merton did not go to Rome, he eventually wrote the book about Bernard: *The Last of the Fathers: Saint Bernard of Clairvaux and the Encyclical Letter,* Doctor Mellifluus (New York: Harcourt, Brace and Co., 1954).
16. Thomas Merton, *Search for Solitude: The Journals of Thomas Merton: Volume Three, 1952–1960*, ed. Lawrence S. Cunningham (San Francisco: HarperSanFrancisco, 1996), 16.
17. *J3*, 36.
18. C. S. Lewis, *The Collected Letters of C. S. Lewis: Narnia, Cambridge, and Joy, 1950–1963* (San Francisco: HarperSanFrancisco, 2007), 1305. This comment was in a December 20, 1961, letter to Dom Bede Griffiths, who had been a student of Lewis's in the late

1920s and briefly corresponded with Merton in 1966. Like Merton, Griffiths became an important figure in exploring the connections between Eastern and Western spirituality.

19. Henry Weihoffen, "The Psychology of the Criminal Act and Punishment, by Gregory Zilboorg," *Indiana Law Journal*, vol. 30, issue 2, article 9 (January 1, 1955): http://www.repository.law.indiana.edu/cgi/viewcontent.cgi?article=2609&context=ilj.

20. *J3*, 59.

21. Michael Mott (*The Seven Mountains of Thomas Merton* [Boston: Houghton Mifflin, 1984], 291), among others, refers to Zilboorg's having treated Ernest Hemingway, but I have doubts about the accuracy of that information. None of the major biographies of Hemingway mention Zilboorg.

22. Howard Pollack, *George Gershwin: His Life and Work* (Berkeley: University of California Press, 2006), 208.

23. The details of Zilboorg's possible misdiagnosis of Gershwin and his misrepresentation of his credentials are outlined in Mark Leffert's article "The Psychoanalysis and Death of George Gershwin: An American Tragedy," *The Journal of the American Academy of Psychoanalysis and Dynamic Psychiatry* 39 (3) (Bloomfield, Conn.: AAPDP, 2011): 420–51. It should be noted that Zilboorg has his defenders, who claim that Gershwin's symptoms did not present themselves until after he had completed his therapy with Zilboorg. Leffert, however, has collected evidence to suggest that Zilboorg may well have been aware of these symptoms.

24. Leffert, "The Psychoanalysis and Death of George Gershwin," 420–51.

25. Mott, *The Seven Mountains of Thomas Merton*, 297. The bishop to whom Dom James addressed this letter was Giovanni Montini, who, in 1963, became Pope Paul VI, successor to Pope John XXIII.

26. Sigmund Freud, *Leonardo da Vinci and a Memory of His Childhood*, trans. Alan Tyson (New York: Norton, 1989 [1916]). Thank you to Dr. James Doherty for this insight.

27. *J3*, 59–60.

28. Thomas Merton, *The Courage for Truth: Letters to Writers*, ed. Christine M. Bochen (New York: Farrar, Straus & Giroux, 1993), 122.

29. *J3*, 60.

30. Mott, *Seven Mountains*, 297.

31. Merton's essay was posthumously published as "The Neurotic Personality in the Monastic Life," in Robert E. Daggy, Patrick Hart, et al., eds., *The Merton Annual*, Volume 4 (New York: AMS Press, 1991), 5–19.

32. Merton, "The Neurotic Personality," *The Merton Annual*, 6, 19.

33. Francis J. Braceland, "Gregory Zilboorg—A Memorial, 1891–1959," *American Journal of Psychiatry* 116 (January 1, 1960): 672.

NOTES TO CHAPTER 4

1. Thomas Merton, *Conjectures of a Guilty Bystander* (Garden City, N.Y.: Doubleday, 1966), 140.

2. Walnut is now Muhammad Ali Boulevard. The marker was presented to the city by the Thomas Merton Center Foundation.

3. "Thomas Merton (1915–68) (Marker Number: 2004)," *Kentucky Historical Marker Database*, https://archive.is/mvoJU.

4. Merton, *Conjectures of a Guilty Bystander*, 140, 141.

5. Merton, *Conjectures of a Guilty Bystander*, 142.

6. Thomas Merton, *New Seeds of Contemplation* (New York: New Directions, 1961), 53.

7. Thomas Merton, *Search for Solitude: The Journals of Thomas Merton: Volume Three, 1952–1960*, ed. Lawrence S. Cunningham (San Francisco: HarperSanFrancisco, 1996), 181–82.

8. T. S. Eliot, "Little Gidding," in *The Complete Poems and Plays of T. S. Eliot* (London: Faber and Faber, 1969), 197.

9. *J3*, 181, 182.

10. *J3*, 289.

11. *J3*, 297.

12. *J3*, 370–71.

13. The letters were posthumously published as *Cold War Letters*, ed. Christine M. Bochen and William H. Shannon (Maryknoll, N.Y.: Orbis, 2006).

14. *Cold War Letters*, 27.

15. James W. Douglass, *JFK and the Unspeakable: Why He Died and Why It Matters* (New York: Touchstone, 2008), 17–20.

16. Thomas Merton, *The School of Charity: The Letters of Thomas Merton on Religious Renewal and Spiritual Direction* (New York: Farrar, Straus & Giroux, 1990), 166.

17. Thomas Merton, *Turning Toward the World: The Journals of Thomas Merton: Volume Four, 1960–1963*, ed. Victor A. Kramer (San Francisco: HarperSanFrancisco, 1996), 6 (emphasis in original).

18. *J4*, 58 (emphasis in original).

19. *J4*, 63.

20. Thomas Merton, *Dancing in the Water of Life: The Journals of Thomas Merton: Volume Five, 1963–1965*, ed. Robert E. Daggy (San Francisco: HarperSanFrancisco, 1997), 151 (emphasis in original).

21. Thomas Merton, *The Wisdom of the Desert* (New York: New Directions, 1960), 5.

22. *J5*, 153, 159.

23. Thomas Merton, "Solitary Life: A Life without Care (8/20/1965)," *Thomas Merton on Contemplation*, 4 CDs (Now You Know Media, 2014), disc 4, track 2.

24. *J5*, 286.

25. The building was square as originally built, with an overhanging eave, supported by three posts, over the front porch. A later extension to the left of the kitchen contained a small chapel and washroom.

26. Thomas Merton, *Selected Essays* (Maryknoll, N.Y.: Orbis, 2013), 237.

27. *J5*, 275. Merton is quoting Søren Kierkegaard, *The Present Age*, trans. Alexander Dru (New York: Harper & Row, 1962), 56. As it appears in *Dancing in the Water of Life*, the line incorrectly reads ". . . if he courageously drinks it . . ." rather than ". . . if he coura-

geously desires it . . ." I suspect that whoever transcribed Merton's handwritten journal mistook "desires" for "drinks."

28. This performance is commercially available on the DVD *The Other Side of the Mirror: Bob Dylan Live at the Newport Folk Festival, 1963–1965*, directed by Murray Lerner (Columbia Music Video, Legacy, 8869714466 9, 2007).

NOTES TO DYLAN INTERLUDE NO. 1

Bob Dylan, *Bringing It All Back Home,* LP (Columbia, CS 9128, 1965).

1. From a personal conversation with writer David Dalton, who attended the Dylan concert at Newport.

2. Video footage of four of the five songs Dylan performed is available on Bob Dylan, *The Other Side of the Mirror: Bob Dylan Live at the Newport Folk Festival, 1963–1965*, directed by Murray Lerner, DVD (Columbia Music Video, Legacy, 8869714466 9, 2007). The missing song is the third and last one performed with the band: "It Takes a Lot to Laugh, It Takes a Train to Cry." Audio of all five songs can be heard on Bob Dylan, *1965 Revisited, Vol. 6*, 14 CDs (Great Dane, CD 9419/1-14, 1995).

3. Portions of Paul Butterfield Blues Band's 1965 performance at Newport are on Murray Lerner's documentary *Festival!* (Eagle Rock Entertainment, 2005).

4. Many of these details are from David Dann's chronology: "Mike Bloomfield at Newport," *Mike Bloomfield: An American Guitarist*, May 11, 2014, http://www.mikebloomfieldamericanmusic.com/newport.htm.

5. Robert Shelton, *No Direction Home: The Life and Music of Bob Dylan* (Milwaukee: Backbeat, 2011), 256.

6. Bob Dylan in a 1987 *Us* magazine interview, quoted in Paul Williams, *Bob Dylan: Performing Artist, 1986–1990 and Beyond: Mind Out of Time* (London: Omnibus, 2004), 43.

7. Fifty years later, in his mid-sixties, Dylan began sporting a pencil mustache that looked suspiciously like Little Richard's. In a Twitter interview, filmmaker John Waters, who also wears such a mustache, was asked what he thought of Dylan's stealing his mustache. Waters replied, "He could steal my wallet and I wouldn't be mad." http://www.theguardian.com/stage/live/2014/nov/07/john-waters-webchat-carsick#block-5460bcbde4b0a13a737c127b.

8. Don McLean, "American Pie," *American Pie*, LP (United Artist, UAS-5535, 1971), side 1, track 1. Coincidentally, Paul Griffin, who played piano at Dylan's *Highway 61 Revisited* sessions, also played piano on Don McLean's "American Pie."

9. Shelton, *No Direction Home*, 37.

10. Howard Sounes, *Down the Highway: The Life of Bob Dylan* (New York: Grove, 2001), 41.

11. Bobby Vee tells this story in an interview in *Goldmine* magazine: see "Elston

Gunnn: Early Alias for Robert Zimmerman/Bob Dylan," *Expecting Rain.com*, http://expectingrain.com/dok/who/g/gunnnelston.html.

12. Bob Dylan, in Ian Bell, *Time Out of Mind: The Lives of Bob Dylan* (New York: Pegasus, 2013), 414.

13. Bob Dylan, "13 June 1984: Robert Hilburn Interview, West Berlin," *Every Mind Polluting Word*, 794, http://content.yudu.com/Library/A1plqd/BobDylanEveryMindPol/resources/794.htm. "Highway 51" was written by Curtis Jones and released in 1938.

14. Damien Cave et al., "Truck Driver Invents Rock," *Rolling Stone* no. 951 (June 24, 2004), 84–85. "That's Alright, Mama" is the only song to have been recorded in common by Elvis, the Beatles, and Dylan.

15. Three takes of "That's Alright, Mama" and seven takes of "Mixed Up Confusion" were released on the 4-CD-R set: Bob Dylan, *The 50th Anniversary Collection: The Copyright Extension Collection, Vol. 1* (Sony Music Europe 8876546022, 2012). One version of "Mixed Up Confusion" became Dylan's first 45 rpm single release in December 1962.

16. Until thirty years later, that is. In the 1990s he recorded two throw-back albums of acoustic folk covers—*Good as I Been to You* (Columbia, CK 53200, 1992) and *World Gone Wrong* (Columbia, CK 57590, 1993).

17. Tim Riley, *Hard Rain: A Dylan Commentary* (New York: Knopf, 1992), 85.

18. Bob Dylan, "House of the Rising Sun" (1964 Tom Wilson overdub), *Highway 61 Interactive* CD-ROM (Columbia/Graphix Zone CDAC 085700, February 1995).

19. Although Dylan released "Mr. Tambourine Man" on *Bringing It All Back Home* (side 2, track 1), the Byrds based their version on an earlier unreleased take from the *Another Side* sessions. One hint of this is that the Byrds sing, ". . . there ain't no place I'm going to . . . ," just as Dylan does on the *Another Side* outtake. On the official *Bringing* version, Dylan sings, ". . . there *is* no place I'm going to . . ."

20. Although some writers state that neither Mayall nor Clapton was present, Clapton has stated in interviews that he was there; see Clinton Heylin, *Behind the Shades Revisited* (New York: Morrow, 2001), 194. Heylin believes Mayall was the one who commented, "Haven't worked much with bands, have ya?"

21. Bob Dylan, *Thin Wild Mercury Music*, CD (unofficial recording, Spank Records, SP-105, 1994), tracks 17–18.

22. Bob Dylan, interview with Martin Bronstein, February 20, 1966, Montreal, Quebec, Canada, on the 4-CD set *On the Crest of the Airwaves, Vol. 1* (Music Melon, MMLTD-BOX12, 2012). In June 2014, forty-nine years after the lyrics were written, Dylan's four-page manuscript of the first draft for "Like a Rolling Stone" sold at auction for two million dollars to an anonymous buyer.

23. Bob Dylan, "A Candid Conversation with the Iconoclastic Idol of the Folk-Rock Set," interview with Nat Hentoff, *Playboy* (March 1966), in Jonathan Cott, ed., *Bob Dylan: The Essential Interviews* (New York: Wenner, 2006), 97.

24. *Rolling Stone* magazine ranked "Like a Rolling Stone" number one in its list of the "500 Greatest Songs of All Time," May 31, 2011.

NOTES TO CHAPTER 5

1. Thomas Merton, *Learning to Love: The Journals of Thomas Merton: Volume Six, 1966–1967*, ed. Christine M. Bochen (San Francisco: HarperSanFrancisco, 1997), 25.

2. Writer and Merton scholar Thérèse Lentfoehr, SDS (1902–1981), was in the Sisters of the Divine Savior, headquartered in Milwaukee. As a poet, she corresponded with Merton before he entered the monastery. She collected his manuscripts and eventually gave them to the Merton archives at Columbia University.

3. Thomas Merton, *An Introduction to Christian Mysticism: Initiation into the Monastic Tradition* 3, ed. Patrick F. O'Connell (Kalamazoo, Mich.: Cistercian Publications, 2008), 122.

4. Meister Eckhart, *Meister Eckhart's Sermons*, trans. Claud Field (New York: Cosimo, 2007 [1909]), 32.

5. Thomas Merton, *The Courage for Truth: Letters to Writers*, ed. Christine M. Bochen (New York: Farrar, Straus & Giroux, 1993), 47.

6. Merton, *The Courage for Truth*, 47–48.

7. Thomas Merton, *Dancing in the Water of Life: The Journals of Thomas Merton: Volume Five, 1963–1965*, ed. Robert E. Daggy (San Francisco: HarperSanFrancisco, 1997), 291. Monica Weis in her book *The Environmental Vision of Thomas Merton* (Lexington, Ky.: University of Kentucky Press, 2011) devotes her afterword to Merton's relationship with the deer. She counts twenty-two references to deer in his journals between 1963 and 1968 and refers to the sixteen references between January 1965 and June 1966 as "a symphony of meaning" (157–58).

8. Psalm 41:2; Pontifical Bible Institute, *The Psalms: A Prayer Book* (New York: Benziger Brothers, 1947). This follows the Catholic numbering of the Psalms as given in the Septuagint and Vulgate; this psalm is number 42 in most Protestant Bibles.

9. *J6*, 25.

10. Thomas Merton, *Praying the Psalms* (Collegeville, Minn.: Liturgical Press, 1956), 25.

11. Thomas Merton, *Turning toward the World: The Journals of Thomas Merton: Volume Four, 1960–1963*, ed. Victor A. Kramer (San Francisco: HarperSanFrancisco, 1996), 235.

12. Isaac of Nineveh, *Ascetic Treatises*, quoted in Olivier Clément, *The Roots of Christian Mysticism: Texts from the Patristic Era with Commentary* (London: New City, 1993), 213.

13. Song of Solomon 2:9, Douay-Rheims (1899).

14. Thomas Merton, *The Road to Joy: Letters to New and Old Friends*, ed. Robert E. Daggy (New York: Farrar, Straus & Giroux, 1989), 203.

15. *J6*, 24.

16. Rainer Maria Rilke, *Letters to a Young Poet*, trans. M. D. Herter Norton (New York: Norton, 1993 [1934]), 27. Although Merton read German with aids, this is most likely the translation he found in the university library.

17. *J6*, 31.

18. Thomas Merton, "With the World in My Blood Stream," in *In the Dark Before Dawn*, ed. Lynn R. Szabo (New York: New Directions, 2005), 188.

19. *J6*, 32.

20. *J6*, 33.

21. Merton most likely took Claud Field's translation to the hospital: *Meister Eckhart's Sermons* (London: Allenson, 1909).

22. Thomas Merton, "First Lesson about Man," in *The Collected Poems of Thomas Merton* (New York: New Directions, 1977), 624–26.

23. St. Joseph's Infirmary, run by the Sisters of Charity of Nazareth, was built on Preston Road, Louisville, in 1926 and torn down in the early 1980s, when its facilities were moved to what is now known as the Norton Audubon Hospital. The grotto and its adjacent garden still stand.

24. Thomas Merton, *A Search for Solitude: The Journals of Thomas Merton: Volume Three, 1952–1960*, ed. Lawrence S. Cunningham (San Francisco: HarperSanFrancisco, 1996), 184.

25. Merton, "With the World in My Blood Stream," in *In the Dark Before Dawn*, 188.

26. *J6*, 92.

27. Merton, "With the World in My Blood Stream," in *In the Dark Before Dawn*, 188.

28. Thomas Merton, "Preface to the Japanese Edition of *Thoughts in Solitude*, March 1966," in *"Honorable Reader": Reflections on My Work* (New York: Crossroad, 1989), 112, 116.

29. Merton, "Preface," in *"Honorable Reader,"* 118.

NOTES TO CHAPTER 6

1. Paul Wilkes, ed., *Merton by Those Who Knew Him Best* (San Francisco: Harper & Row, 1984), 3.

2. *J6*, 38.

3. *J6*, 77.

4. *J6*, 52.

5. *J6*, 52.

6. "The Menendez file" poems were published posthumously in a slipcased, limited edition of 250 copies nearly twenty years after they were written: Thomas Merton, *Eighteen Poems* (New York: New Directions, 1985). Thirteen of the poems are available in Thomas Merton, *In the Dark Before Dawn: New Selected Poems of Thomas Merton*, ed. Lynn R. Szabo (New York: New Directions, 2005).

7. *J6*, 52–53.

8. William Shakespeare, *Romeo and Juliet*, Act 1, scene 5, lines 93–110.

9. *J6*, 53.

10. *J6*, 81.

11. *J6*, 56.

12. *Time* magazine, cover story, November 23, 1962.

13. Jim Forest, *Living with Wisdom: A Life of Thomas Merton* (Maryknoll, N.Y.: Orbis, 1991), 197.

14. Henry Fielding, *Tom Jones* (New York: Random House, 2002 [1749]), 436.

15. Joan Baez, *The Joan Baez Songbook* (New York: Amsco Publications, 1964), 76–77. Public domain.

16. No one is sure where Merton listened to the Baez record that week. The library is possible, but so is the infirmary. A third location has also been suggested: a small brick building, referred to as the Red House, on the grounds just outside the infirmary. Each place had a record player with headphones. (The Red House has since been torn down.)

17. Joan Baez, *Joan Baez* (Vanguard, VSD 2070, 1960). The album was chosen for permanent archiving at the Library of Congress in 2015.

18. Bob Dylan, *Chronicles: Volume One* (New York: Simon & Schuster, 2004), 256.

19. *J6*, 305.

20. Joan Baez makes this comment before performing the song at the War Memorial Auditorium in Plymouth, Massachusetts, as part of Bob Dylan's Rolling Thunder Revue, on October 31, 1975; from *The Rolling Thunder Revue: Plymouth 1975*, 2 CDs (unofficial recording). She also says it was one of the first songs she ever learned.

21. *J6*, 305.

22. *J6*, 305.

23. John T. Elson, "Toward a Hidden God," *Time* (April 8, 1966).

24. Paul Tillich, *The Courage to Be* (New Haven, Conn.: Yale University Press, 1952), 190.

NOTES TO CHAPTER 7

1. These details are extrapolated from Merton's journal entry for that night. The moon set at 10:40 p.m.

2. Thomas Merton, *Learning to Love: The Journals of Thomas Merton: Volume Six, 1966–1967*, ed. Christine M. Bochen (San Francisco: HarperSanFrancisco, 1997), 68.

3. *J6*, 66–67.

4. *J6*, 72.

5. *J6*, 76.

6. For Nhat Hanh's poems to his brother, see Thich Nhat Hanh, *Tho Viet Nam (Vietnam Poems)* (Santa Barbara: Unicorn Press, 1967).

7. *J6*, 76.

8. King delivered this sermon on April 4, 1967, in Riverside Church, New York, one year to the day before King was assassinated.

9. Thomas Merton, *The Nonviolent Alternative*, ed. Gordon C. Zahn (New York: Farrar, Straus & Giroux, 1980), 263–64.

10. Dr. Martin Luther King Jr. also nominated Thich Nhat Hanh for the 1967 Nobel Peace Prize, but the Nobel Committee decided to award no Peace Prize that year.

11. *J6*, 79.

12. "On This Day: 31 May, 1966: Vietnam Buddhist Burns to Death," *BBC Home*, http://news.bbc.co.uk/onthisday/hi/dates/stories/may/31/newsid_2973000/2973209.stm.

13. The photograph was taken by American photojournalist Malcolm Browne (1931–2012). In 1963 the World Press Photo Foundation named Browne's image its World Press Photo of the Year.

14. Thomas Merton, *Dancing in the Water of Life: The Journals of Thomas Merton: Volume Five, 1963–1965*, ed. Robert E. Daggy (San Francisco: HarperSanFrancisco, 1997), 213.

15. Lyndon B. Johnson, *Lyndon B. Johnson: 1966 (In Two Books): Containing the Public Messages, Speeches, and Statements of the President* (Washington, D.C.: The Office of the Federal Register, National Archives and Records Service, General Services Administration, n.d.), Book 1, 246.

16. James H. Forest, *Thomas Merton's Struggle with Peacemaking* (Erie, Penn.: Pax Christi, 1983), 32.

17. Thomas Merton, *The Hidden Ground of Love: Letters on Religious Experience and Social Concerns* (New York: Farrar, Straus & Giroux, 1985), 149.

18. Thich Nhat Hanh, *Vietnam: Lotus in a Sea of Fire* (New York: Hill and Wang, 1967), 106.

19. Nhat Hanh, *Vietnam*, 110.

20. *J6*, 76.

21. Merton, "Certain Proverbs Arise Out of Dreams," *J6*, 65.

22. *J6*, 71.

23. *J6*, 77, 78.

24. *J6*, 78.

25. *J6*, 79.

26. Thomas Merton, *The Seven Storey Mountain* (New York: Harcourt, Brace, 1948), 88–89.

27. Albert Camus, *The Myth of Sisyphus* (New York: Knopf, 1955), 69.

28. *J6*, 81.

29. *J6*, 82.

30. *J6*, 84.

31. *J6*, 84.

32. *J6*, 84. The quote is from chapter 1 of Walter Lowrie's translation of Kierkegaard's *The Sickness Unto Death* (Princeton, N.J.: Princeton University Press, 1941).

33. In a July 3, 1965, letter to Giroux, Merton praises Karl Stern's *The Flight from Woman* for its psychoanalysis of Kierkegaard's relationship with Regine; Patrick Samway, ed., *The Letters of Robert Giroux and Thomas Merton* (Notre Dame, Ind.: University of Notre Dame Press, 2015), 343.

34. "il n'était pas mon père: il était avec les autres"; Albert Camus, *L'étranger* (London: Routledge, 1988 [1942]), 155.

35. *J6*, 85.

36. *J6*, 84.

37. Bob Dylan, "Like a Rolling Stone," *Highway 61 Revisited*, LP (Columbia, CS 9189, 1965), side 1, track 1.

38. *J6*, 83, quoting Bob Dylan, "Ballad of a Thin Man," *Highway 61 Revisited*, side 1, track 5.

NOTES TO CHAPTER 8

1. Thomas Merton, *Conjectures of a Guilty Bystander* (Garden City, N.Y.: Doubleday, 1966), 149.
2. The three albums are *Noël* (1966), *Joan* (1967), and *Baptism: A Journey Through Our Time* (1968).
3. The discographic information is from Barry Kowal, "*Billboard* Magazine Weekly Singles Charts from 1965," *Hits of All Decades: Rock and Roll*, http://hitsofalldecades.com/chart_hits/index.php?option=com_content&task=view&id=1941&Itemid=52.
4. Chrysogonus Waddell, *Christ Is Risen, Truly Risen!* CD (World Library Publications, 2007).
5. Many of the details about Father Chrysogonus are from Bradford Lee Eden, "The Sounds of Vatican II: Musical Change and Experimentation in Two US Trappist Monasteries, 1965–1984," *ValpoScholar* (Valparaiso University, Fall 2014): 86–93.
6. Thomas Merton, *Learning to Love: The Journals of Thomas Merton: Volume Six, 1966–1967*, ed. Christine M. Bochen (San Francisco: HarperSanFrancisco, 1997), 129.
7. Thomas Merton, *The Literary Essays of Thomas Merton*, ed. Patrick Hart (New York: New Directions, 1981), 315.
8. Bob Dylan, "Highway 61 Revisited," *Highway 61 Revisited*, LP (Columbia, CS 9189, 1965), side 2, track 2.
9. Bob Dylan, *Highway 61 Revisited*, LP liner notes.
10. Thomas Merton, *The Road to Joy: Letters to New and Old Friends*, ed. Robert E. Daggy (New York: Farrar, Straus & Giroux, 1989), 289.
11. *J6*, 85.
12. *J6*, 85.
13. *Thomas Merton and James Laughlin: Selected Letters,* ed. David D. Cooper (New York: Norton, 1997), 282–83; letters of June 1 and 9, 1966, respectively.
14. *Selected Letters*, 283–84.
15. *Selected Letters*, 285.
16. *J6*, 309.
17. Michael Mott, *The Seven Mountains of Thomas Merton* (Boston: Houghton Mifflin, 1984), 451. Merton added "The Prospects of Nostradamus" to *Cables to the Ace* as section 68.
18. Galatians 6:2, Douay-Rheims (1899).
19. *J6*, 325.
20. *Selected Letters*, 286.
21. *J6*, 89.
22. *J6*, 89.
23. *J6*, 92.

24. *J6*, 97.

25. Gregory J. Ryan, "Death of a 'Mertoniac': An Appreciation of W. H. 'Ping' Ferry," *Merton Seasonal*, vol. 20, no. 4 (Autumn 1995): 20.

NOTES TO DYLAN INTERLUDE NO. 2

Bob Dylan, "Just Like Tom Thumb's Blues," *Highway 61 Revisited*, LP (Columbia, CS 9189, 1965), side 2, track 3.

1. Peter Egan, a writer for *Cycle World*, studied photos of Dylan's motorcycle and determined it was either a 1963 or 1964 Triumph Speed Tiger T100SR. See Peter Egan, "The Great Dylan Crash," *Cycle World*, February 1998, 14. In an interview in *The Telegraph* 44 (Winter 1992), John Hammond Jr. believes the motorcycle was actually Rambling Jack Elliott's AJS 500, which Elliott had stored in Dylan's garage.

2. Bob Dylan, interview with Scott Cohen, "Don't Ask Me Nothin' about Nothin', I Just Might Tell You the Truth," *Spin* magazine (December 1985), 40.

3. Victor Maymudes and Jacob Maymudes, *Another Side of Bob Dylan: A Personal History on the Road and off the Tracks* (New York: St. Martin's, 2014), 128–29.

4. Daniel Mark Epstein, *The Ballad of Bob Dylan* (New York: HarperCollins, 2011), 180.

5. Elliott's AJS 500 was thirty pounds heavier than the Triumph. Even if that were the bike Dylan was riding, John Hammond affirms that the tires were flat and Dylan was taking it for repairs; John Hammond Jr., "Was Dylan Riding His Motorcycle?: John Hammond Jr. Speaks," *EDLIS: After a War*, http://afterawar.yolasite.com.

6. Interview with Peter Howell, "Fifty Years Later, the Truth behind Dylan's Motorcycle Crash," *TheStar.com* (November 21, 2016), https://www.thestar.com/entertainment/2016/11/21/fifty-years-later-the-truth-behind-dylans-motorcycle-crash.html.

7. Robbie Robertson, *Testimony* (New York: Crown/Archetype, 2016), 242.

8. David Dalton, "How Bob Dylan and the Holy Trinity Changed Music Forever," *Teamrock.com* (December 31, 2015), http://teamrock.com/feature/2015-12-31/bob-dylan-and-the-holy-trinity-revisited.

9. Ron Rosenbaum, "*Playboy* Interview: Bob Dylan: A Candid Conversation with the Visionary Whose Songs Changed the Times," *Playboy* (March 1978).

10. Kurt Loder, "The *Rolling Stone* Interview: Bob Dylan," *Rolling Stone* 424 (June 21, 1984), http://www.rollingstone.com/music/features/the-rolling-stone-interview-bob-dylan-19840621.

11. Bob Dylan, *Chronicles: Volume One* (New York: Simon & Schuster, 2004), 114.

12. Controversy surrounds the dating of *Blonde on Blonde*'s release. The date usually given is May 16, 1966, but nearly all media outlets at the time listed a later date, sometime around the end of June or beginning of July. See Jack Brown, "When Was *Blonde on Blonde* Released? Nobody Knows," *Glorious Noise* (May 18, 2016), http://gloriousnoise.com/2016/when-was-blonde-on-blonde-released-nobody-knows.

13. Snippets of these unfinished songs, informally recorded in a Glasgow hotel room, may be heard on Bob Dylan, *The Bootleg Series, Vol. 12: The Cutting Edge—Collector's Edition, 1965–66*, 18 CDs (Columbia 888751240218, 2015), disc 18, tracks 14; 9 and 10; and 11, respectively.

14. Bob Dylan, "The Rome Interview," July 2001, trans. Dave Flynn, originally published in the Italian newspaper *La Repubblica* (September 8, 2001), http://expectingrain.com/dok/cd/2001/romeinterview.html.

15. Bob Dylan, "3 May 1966, Press Conference, London, England," *Every Mind Polluting Word*, http://content.yudu.com/Library/A1plqd/BobDylanEveryMindPol/resources/765.htm.

16. Bob Dylan, *Tarantula* (New York: Macmillan, 1971), 68.

17. Jack Newfield, "Mods, Rockers Fight over New Thing Called Dylan," *The Village Voice* (September 2, 1965), 10.

18. These incidents are recounted in Clinton Heylin, *Bob Dylan: A Life in Stolen Moments: Day by Day from 1941–1995* (New York: Schirmer, 1996), 100–103.

19. This performance was captured on video: Bob Dylan, "'Like a Rolling Stone' (1966) (*Live* in the Manchester Free Trade Hall)," YouTube, https://www.youtube.com/watch?v=yUyL83KAsKc.

20. Partial or complete recordings of twenty-three of the 1966 concerts were officially released on Bob Dylan, *The 1966 Live Recordings*, 36 CDs (Columbia, Legacy, Sony, 889853581924, 2016).

21. Bob Dylan, "San Francisco Press Conference, December 3, 1965," *The Classic Interviews, Vol. 1, 1965–1966*, CD (*Isis* magazine, 2005).

NOTES TO CHAPTER 9

1. Exactly where Merton saw the *Post* article is unknown. We know he read it on this day, and the waiting room of the Medical Arts Building seems as likely a place as any, but it's speculative. Whether he saw the other magazines mentioned is also speculative, though those were the issues currently available. The actress on the cover of *Life* was Claudia Cardinale, who, coincidentally, is also pictured inside the gatefold of the original "nine-photo" issue of *Blonde on Blonde*. Her picture was later removed for copyright reasons.

2. Thomas Merton, *Learning to Love: The Journals of Thomas Merton: Volume Six, 1966–1967*, ed. Christine M. Bochen (San Francisco: HarperSanFrancisco, 1997), 104.

3. Jules Siegel, "Bob Dylan: Well, What Have We Here?" *Saturday Evening Post* (July 30, 1966), 32–39.

4. Quotes from Bob Dylan, "From a Buick 6," *Highway 61 Revisited*, LP (Columbia, CS 9189, 1965), side 1, track 4.

5. Quotes from Thomas Merton, "Cancer Blues," in *In the Dark Before Dawn: New Selected Poems of Thomas Merton*, ed. Lynne R. Szabo (New York: New Directions, 2005), 207–9.

6. Thomas Merton, "Solitary Life: A Life without Care (8/20/1965)," *On Contemplation*, 4 CDs (Now You Know Media, 2014).

7. *J6*, 90, 108, 114, 122, 151, and others.

8. Thomas Merton, *Witness to Freedom: Letters in Times of Crisis*, ed. William H. Shannon (New York: Farrar, Straus & Giroux, 1994), 238.

9. *J6*, 79.

10. William Blake, "The Marriage of Heaven and Hell," in *Complete Writings* (London: Oxford University Press, 1972), 157.

11. Their correspondence can be found in F. Douglas Scutchfield and Paul Holbrook Jr., eds., *The Letters of Thomas Merton and Victor and Carolyn Hammer: Ad Majorem Dei Gloriam* (Lexington: University of Kentucky Press, 2014).

12. Ad Reinhardt, quoted in Dorothy C. Miller, ed., *Americans 1963* (New York: Museum of Modern Art, 1963, exhibition catalog), 80.

13. John Yau, "Ad Reinhardt and the *Via Negativa*," *The Brooklyn Rail* (January 16, 2014), http://www.brooklynrail.org/special/AD_REINHARDT/ad-and-spirituality/ad-reinhardt-and-the-via-negativa.

14. *The Cloud of Unknowing* is an anonymous fourteenth-century book of meditation. *The Dark Night of the Soul* is a sixteenth-century mystical text by Saint John of the Cross. Both are classics of the Christian *via negativa*.

15. Thomas Merton, *The Road to Joy: Letters to New and Old Friends*, ed. Robert E. Daggy (New York: Farrar, Straus & Giroux, 1989), 282.

16. Thomas Merton, *New Seeds of Contemplation* (New York: New Directions, 1961), 258.

17. Scutchfield and Holbrook, *Letters of Thomas Merton and Victor and Carolyn Hammer*, 277–78.

18. Reinhardt in Miller, *Americans 1963*, 82.

19. David Cooper, "Victor Hammer and Thomas Merton: A Friendship *Ad Maiorem Dei Gloriam*," *The Kentucky Review*, vol. 7, no. 2 (Summer 1987): 24.

20. *Thomas Merton and James Laughlin: Selected Letters*, ed. David D. Cooper (New York: Norton, 1997), 293–94.

21. *J6*, 116.

22. Merton, *The Road to Joy*, 289–90.

NOTES TO CHAPTER 10

1. Among writers who make this connection, see Jim Curtis, *Rock Eras: Interpretations of Music and Society: 1954–1984* (Bowling Green, Ohio: Bowling Green State University Popular Press, 1987), 154.

2. Reinhardt's 1953 painting *Black on Black No. 8* sold at auction in 1983 to a private collector for $143,000.

3. Bob Dylan, "She Belongs to Me," *Bringing It All Back Home*, LP (Columbia, CS 9128, 1965), side 1, track 2.

4. Thomas Merton, *Learning to Love: The Journals of Thomas Merton: Volume Six, 1966-1967*, ed. Christine M. Bochen (San Francisco: HarperSanFrancisco, 1997), 130.

5. Bob Dylan, "I Want You," *Blonde on Blonde*, 2 LPs (Columbia, C2S 841 CS 9316, 1966), side 2, track 1.

6. *J6*, 130.

7. Bob Dylan, "Just Like a Woman," *Blonde on Blonde*, side 2, track 4.

8. *J6*, 129.

9. Thomas Merton, *Witness to Freedom: Letters in Times of Crisis*, ed. William H. Shannon (New York: Farrar, Straus & Giroux, 1994), 252. The song quoted is Bob Dylan, "Rainy Day Women # 12 & 35," *Blonde on Blonde*, side 1, track 1.

10. *Thomas Merton and James Laughlin: Selected Letters,* ed. David D. Cooper (New York: Norton, 1997), 295.

11. Thomas Merton, "The True Legendary Sound: The Poetry and Criticism of Edwin Muir," in *The Literary Essays of Thomas Merton*, ed. Patrick Hart (New York: New Directions, 1981), 35.

12. *Selected Letters*, 299.

13. Dylan, back-cover notes, *Bringing It All Back Home.*

14. *J6*, 84.

15. Sister Thérèse Lentfoehr, *Words and Silence: On the Poetry of Thomas Merton* (New York: New Directions, 1979), 100. Ellipsis in original.

16. Thomas Merton, *Cables to the Ace* (New York: New Directions, 1967), 48. Hereafter, quotations from *Cables to the Ace* will be referenced by section number in the text.

17. Thomas Merton, "Rafael Alberti," in *The Literary Essays of Thomas Merton*, 315.

18. David Cooper, *Thomas Merton's Art of Denial: The Evolution of a Radical Humanist* (Athens: The University of Georgia Press, 1989).

19. Thomas Merton, *The Road to Joy: Letters to New and Old Friends*, ed. Robert E. Daggy (New York: Farrar, Straus & Giroux, 1989), 308.

20. James and Tyra Arraj, directors, "Jacques Maritain's Farewell to America: A Visit with Elisabeth [Manuel] Fourest" (Inner Growth Videos, 1996).

21. *J6*, 129.

22. Dylan, "Gates of Eden," *Bringing It All Back Home*, LP, side 2, track 2.

23. John Howard Griffin, *A Hidden Wholeness: The Visual World of Thomas Merton* (Boston: Houghton Mifflin, 1970), 103.

24. Elisabeth Manuel Fourest, quoted in Jean-Luc Barré, *Jacques and Raïssa Maritain: Beggars for Heaven*, trans. Bernard E. Doering (Notre Dame, Ind.: University of Notre Dame Press, 2005), 436. Manuel mistakenly refers to the song as "Gates of Heaven."

25. Dylan, "Gates of Eden," *Bringing It All Back Home*, side 2, track 2.

NOTES TO CHAPTER 11

1. Thomas Merton, *Learning to Love: The Journals of Thomas Merton: Volume Six, 1966-1967*, ed. Christine M. Bochen (San Francisco: HarperSanFrancisco, 1997), 150.

2. *J6*, 154.

3. *J6*, 152.

4. Thomas Merton, *The Courage for Truth: Letters to Writers*, ed. Christine M. Bochen (New York: Farrar, Straus & Giroux, 1993), 49.

5. Thomas Merton, *The Hidden Ground of Love: Letters on Religious Experience and Social Concerns*, ed. William H. Shannon (New York: Farrar, Straus & Giroux, 1985), 229; Bob Dylan, "Marvin Bronstein Interview," CBC, Montreal (February 20, 1966): https://www.youtube.com/watch?v=JozbOTHdAUQ.

6. *J6*, 152.

7. *J6*, 152.

8. *The Courage for Truth*, 204.

9. *J6*, 153.

10. Rob Baker and Gray Henry, *Merton and Sufism: The Untold Story* (Louisville, Ky.: Fons Vitae, 2005), 189.

11. Thomas Merton, *The Other Side of the Mountain: The End of the Journey: The Journals of Thomas Merton: Volume Seven, 1967–1968*, ed. Patrick Hart (San Francisco: HarperSanFrancisco, 1998), 112.

12. Joan Baez, *Daybreak: An Autobiography* (New York: Dial, 1968), 80–81.

13. Baez, *Daybreak*, 77.

14. Joan Baez, *And a Voice to Sing With: A Memoir* (New York: Summit Books, 1987), 131.

15. Other books suggest the day was cold and threatening snow, but *Weather Underground*'s data for Bardstown, Louisville, and Fort Knox states that the afternoon of December 8, 1966, was in the sixties and sunny. Rain fell that evening. See "Fort Knox, KY," *Weather Underground* (Thursday, December 8, 1966), https://www.wunderground.com/history/airport/KFTK/1966/12/8/DailyHistory.html?req_city=Bardstown+Junction&req_state=KY&req_statename=Kentucky&reqdb.zip=40165&reqdb.magic=4&reqdb.wmo=99999.

16. Baez, *And a Voice to Sing With*, 131.

17. *J6*, 167.

18. *J6*, 167.

19. Joan Baez interview in Mark Shaw, *Beneath the Mask of Holiness* (New York: Palgrave Macmillan, 2009), 177.

20. *J6*, 167.

21. *Dont Look Back* was released in May 1967; it's now available on 2 DVDs (Docurama, NVG 9824, 2007). In 2009, Dylan publicly apologized to Baez.

22. *The Courage for Truth*, 249.

23. *The Courage for Truth*, 263.

24. *J6*, 167.

25. *J6*, 78.

26. *J6*, 167.

27. Tennessee Williams, *The Glass Menagerie* (New York: New Directions, 1970), 97.

28. *J6*, 168.

29. *J6*, 234.

30. *J6*, 234.

31. Although she never set the poems to music, more than a decade after Merton's death, she composed a setting for his poem about his brother's death, "The Bells of Gethsemani." She has not released a recording of it.

32. Thomas Merton, *Faith and Violence: Christian Teaching and Christian Practice* (Notre Dame: University of Notre Dame Press, 1968).

33. Thomas Merton, *The Hidden Ground of Love*, 303–4.

NOTES TO CHAPTER 12

1. Thomas Merton, *The Road to Joy: Letters to New and Old Friends*, ed. Robert E. Daggy (New York: Farrar, Straus & Giroux, 1989), 291.

2. Thomas Merton, *Witness to Freedom: Letters in Times of Crisis*, ed. William H. Shannon (New York: Farrar, Straus & Giroux, 1994), 117.

3. Rich Thane and Paul Bridgewater, "Bob Dylan's Top Ten Forays into Career Suicide," *The Line of Best Fit* (July 3, 2012), http://www.thelineofbestfit.com/features/listomania/bob-dylans-top-ten-forays-into-career-suicide-100459.

4. Mark Spitzer, "Bob Dylan's *Tarantula*: An Arctic Reserve of Untapped Glimmerance Dismissed in a Ratland of Clichés," *Jack* magazine, vol. 2, no. 3 (2003), http://www.jackmagazine.com/issue7/essaysmspitzer.html.

5. Thomas Merton, *The Literary Essays of Thomas Merton*, ed. Patrick Hart (New York: New Directions, 1981), 333.

6. Thomas Merton, *Learning to Love: The Journals of Thomas Merton: Volume Six, 1966–1967*, ed. Christine M. Bochen (San Francisco: HarperSanFrancisco, 1997), 83.

7. *J6*, 129.

8. *Thomas Merton and James Laughlin: Selected Letters,* ed. David D. Cooper (New York: Norton, 1997), 295.

9. Merton, *The Literary Essays of Thomas Merton*, 35.

10. *Selected Letters,* 299.

11. *The Road to Joy*, 309.

12. *The Literary Essays of Thomas Merton*, 305.

13. *The Literary Essays of Thomas Merton*, 252.

14. Timothy English, *Popology: Music of the Era in the Lives of Four Icons of the 1960s* (North Charleston, S.C.: CreateSpace, 2013), 207.

15. Ron Pen, *I Wonder as I Wander: The Life of John Jacob Niles* (Lexington: University of Kentucky Press, 2010), 261.

16. Dave Van Ronk with Elijah Wald, *The Mayor of McDougal Street: A Memoir* (Cambridge, Mass.: Da Capo, 2006), 46.

17. Bob Dylan, *Chronicles: Volume One* (New York: Simon & Schuster, 2004), 239.

18. Henry Miller, *Plexus* (New York: Grove Press, 1965), 366–67.

19. *J6*, 248.

20. *J6*, 254.

21. *J6*, 254.

22. *J6*, 271.
23. *J6*, 270.
24. *J6*, 286.
25. Thomas Merton, *The Seven Storey Mountain* (New York: Harcourt, Brace, 1948), 182.
26. Thomas Merton, *The Other Side of the Mountain: The End of the Journey: The Journals of Thomas Merton: Volume Seven, 1967–1968*, ed. Patrick Hart (San Francisco: HarperSanFrancisco, 1998), 7.
27. *J7*, 7.
28. Joan Baez, *And a Voice to Sing With: A Memoir* (New York: Summit, 1987), 63.
29. *J7*, 7.
30. *The Road to Joy*, 268.
31. *J7*, 128.
32. *J6*, 309.
33. Thomas Merton, "A Hermit's Preferences," *Publisher's Weekly* (November 6, 1967).
34. *J7*, 11.
35. *J7*, 29.

NOTES TO DYLAN INTERLUDE NO. 3

1. Lawrence Ferlinghetti, "15," *A Coney Island of the Mind* (New York: New Directions, 1958), 30.
2. Thomas Merton, *The Courage for Truth: Letters to Writers*, ed. Christine M. Bochen (New York: Farrar, Staus & Giroux, 1993), 204.
3. Bob Dylan, liner notes to the song "Two Soldiers" on *World Gone Wrong*, CD (Columbia, CK 57590, 1993).
4. Tom Pinnock, "The Band, Bob Dylan and Music from Big Pink—The Full Story," *Uncut* (July 31, 2015), http://www.uncut.co.uk/features/the-band-bob-dylan-and-music-from-big-pink-the-full-story-69989/5.
5. Jann S. Wenner, "Dylan's Basement Tape Should Be Released," *Rolling Stone* 12 (June 22, 1968): http://www.rollingstone.com/music/news/dylans-basement-tape-should-be-released-19680622.
6. Douglas Heselgrave, "Bob Dylan and The Band: The Basement Tapes Complete," *Paste* (November 11, 2014), https://www.pastemagazine.com/articles/2014/11/bob-dylan-and-the-band-the-basement-tapes-complete.html.
7. Roger Doughty, "Dylan Dirt," *LaCrosse Tribune* (December 26, 1970), 27.
8. Bob Dylan, *Chronicles: Volume One* (New York: Simon & Schuster, 2004), 117–18.
9. Dylan, *Chronicles*, 97.
10. Fred Goodman, *The Mansion on the Hill* (New York: Vintage, 1998), 95.
11. The best overview of these complex contractual issues can be found in Goodman, *Mansion on the Hill*, 102–5.

12. Thomas Merton, *Disputed Questions* (New York: Farrar, Straus & Giroux, 1960), 164.

13. Dylan, "I Shall Be Released," *The Basement Tapes Complete*, disc 3, track 20.

14. Merton, *Disputed Questions,* 193.

15. Jim Jerome, "Exclusive or Reclusive?" *People* magazine (November 10, 1975), http://people.com/archive/cover-story-exclusive-or-reclusive-vol-4-no-19/.

NOTES TO CHAPTER 13

1. Thomas Merton, *The Other Side of the Mountain: The End of the Journey: The Journals of Thomas Merton: Volume Seven, 1967–1968*, ed. Patrick Hart (San Francisco: HarperSanFrancisco, 1998), 48.

2. January 26 through February 6 was one of the warmest spells on record for that period in Louisville. Though the scene is dramatized, Merton purchased these records on this day, most likely at Vine Records, which was within a block of the medical center.

3. *J7*, 32.

4. *J7*, 47.

5. Bob Dylan, "June/July 1968, John Cohen and Happy Traum Interview, Woodstock, New York," *Every Mind Polluting Word*, http://content.yudu.com/Library/A1plqd/BobDylanEveryMindPol/resources/765.htm, 408.

6. Scott Marshall, *Bob Dylan: A Spiritual Life* (Washington, D.C.: BP/WND Books, 2017), 11.

7. *J7*, 48.

8. *J7*, 48.

9. The original 1966 release featured take 2. Coltrane preferred take 1, so the album was quickly re-released with that take, which is the one Merton would have purchased.

10. Thomas Merton, *A Search for Solitude: The Journals of Thomas Merton: Volume Three, 1952–1960*, ed. Lawrence S. Cunningham (San Francisco: HarperSanFrancisco, 1996), 225.

11. *J3*, 141.

12. Thomas Merton, *Turning Toward the World: The Journals of Thomas Merton: Volume Four, 1960–1963*, ed. Victor A. Kramer (San Francisco: HarperSanFrancisco, 1996), 18.

13. Thomas Merton, *Seeds of Destruction* (New York: Farrar, Straus & Giroux, 1964), 72–73.

14. John Coltrane, *A Love Supreme*, handwritten score, a jpg of which can be found at http://cdn8.openculture.com/wp-content/uploads/2013/09/love-supreme-manuscripts.jpg.

15. Eric Nisenson, *Ascension: John Coltrane and His Quest* (New York: Da Capo, 1995), 212.

16. Thomas Merton, *The Road to Joy: Letters to New and Old Friends*, ed. Robert E. Daggy (New York: Farrar, Straus & Giroux, 1989), 111.

17. *J7*, 156.

18. Thomas Merton, *The Wisdom of the Desert* (New York: New Directions, 1960), 5.

19. *J7*, 67.

20. Merton, *The Road to Joy*, 182.

21. *J7*, 78.

22. Anne Klejment and Nancy L. Roberts, *American Catholic Pacifism: The Influence of Dorothy Day and the Catholic Worker Movement* (Westport, Conn.: Praeger, 1996), 119.

23. *J7*, 110.

24. *J7*, 127.

25. *J7*, 82.

26. *J7*, 11.

27. Ferlinghetti remarked on this in Paul Wilkes and Audrey L. Glynn, *Merton: A Film Biography*, television documentary (New York: First Run Features, 1984; DVD, 2004).

28. Thomas Merton, *Mystics and Zen Masters* (New York: Farrar, Straus & Giroux, 1967), viii.

29. Dalai Lama, *Freedom in Exile: The Autobiography of the Dalai Lama* (New York: HarperCollins, 1990), 189.

30. Thomas Merton, *The Asian Journal of Thomas Merton* (New York: New Directions, 1975), 5.

31. *J7*, 328.

NOTES TO THE EPILOGUE

1. Thomas Merton, "Last Lecture," YouTube, https://www.youtube.com/watch?v=ywE6bhApcSk.

2. Robert Giroux, in Paul Wilkes, ed., *Merton by Those Who Knew Him Best* (San Francisco: Harper & Row, 1984), 25.

3. Thich Nhat Hanh, *Together We Are One: Honoring Our Diversity, Celebrating Our Connection* (Berkeley, Calif.: Parallax, 2010), 13.

4. Johnny Cash, "A Letter from Johnny Cash," *Sing Out!* no. 38 (March 10, 1964).

5. Johnny Cash, *Cash: The Autobiography* (New York: HarperCollins, 1997), 171.

6. Bob Dylan, *No Direction Home* (A Martin Scorsese Picture), 2 DVDs (Paramount Pictures, 03105), 2005.

7. Johnny Cash, liner notes to Bob Dylan, *Nashville Skyline*, LP (KCS 9825, 1969).

8. John Howard Griffin, *Follow the Ecstasy: The Hermitage Years of Thomas Merton* (Maryknoll, N.Y.: Orbis, 1993), 2–3.

9. Thomas Merton, *Cables to the Ace, or Familiar Liturgies of Misunderstanding* (New York: New Directions, 1967), 26.

10. Thomas Merton, *No Man Is an Island* (New York: Harcourt, Brace, 1955), 127.

BIBLIOGRAPHY

THOMAS MERTON

Baker, Rob, and Gray Henry. *Merton and Sufism: The Untold Story: A Complete Compendium*. Louisville, Ky.: Fons Vitae, 2005.

Coady, Mary Frances. *Merton and Waugh: A Monk, A Crusty Old Man, and* The Seven Storey Mountain. Brewster, Mass.: Paraclete Press, 2015.

Cooper, David, ed. *Thomas Merton and James Laughlin: Selected Letters*. New York: Norton, 1997.

———. *Thomas Merton's Art of Denial: The Evolution of a Radical Humanist*. Athens: The University of Georgia Press, 1989.

———. "Victor Hammer and Thomas Merton: A Friendship *Ad Maiorem Dei Gloriam*." *The Kentucky Review*, vol. 7, no. 2 (Summer 1987): 5–28.

Dart, Ron, ed. *Thomas Merton and the Counterculture: A Golden String*. Abbotsford, B.C.: St. Macrina Press, 2016.

Forest, James H. *Living with Wisdom: A Life of Thomas Merton*. Maryknoll, N.Y.: Orbis, 1991.

———. *Thomas Merton: A Pictorial Biography*. New York: Paulist Press, 1980.

———. *Thomas Merton's Struggle with Peacemaking*. Erie, Pa.: Pax Christi, 1983.

Fox, Matthew. *A Way to God: Thomas Merton's Creation Spirituality Journey*. Novato, Calif.: New World Library, 2016.

Griffin, John Howard. *Follow the Ecstasy: The Hermitage Years of Thomas Merton*. Maryknoll, N.Y.: Orbis, 1993.

———. *A Hidden Wholeness: The Visual World of Thomas Merton*. Boston: Houghton Mifflin, 1970.

Higgins, Michael W. *Heretic Blood: The Spiritual Geography of Thomas Merton*. Toronto: Stoddart, 1998.

King, Robert H. *Thomas Merton and Thich Nhat Hanh: Engaged Spirituality in an Age of Globalization*. New York: Continuum, 2001.

Kramer, Victor A. *Thomas Merton: Monk and Artist*. Kalamazoo, Mich.: Cistercian Publications, 1987.

Lentfoehr, Sister Thérèse. *Words and Silence: On the Poetry of Thomas Merton*. New York: New Directions, 1979.

Merton, Thomas. *The Asian Journal of Thomas Merton*. New York: New Directions, 1975.

———. *Cables to the Ace, or Familiar Liturgies of Misunderstanding*. New York: New Directions, 1967.

———. *Cassian and the Fathers: Initiation into the Monastic Tradition 1*. Ed. Patrick. F. O'Connell. Kalamazoo, Mich.: Cistercian Publications, 2005.

———. *Cold War Letters*. Ed. Christine M. Bochen and William H. Shannon. Maryknoll, N.Y.: Orbis, 2006.

———. *The Collected Poems of Thomas Merton*. New York: New Directions, 1977.

———. *Contemplation in a World of Action*. New York: Image, 1973.

———. *Conjectures of a Guilty Bystander*. Garden City, N.Y.: Doubleday, 1966.

———. "Conjectures of a Guilty Bystander: From a New Book by Thomas Merton." *Life* magazine (August 5, 1966), 60–73.

———. *The Courage for Truth: Letters to Writers*. Ed. Christine M. Bochen. New York: Farrar, Straus & Giroux, 1993.

———. *Dancing in the Water of Life: The Journals of Thomas Merton: Volume Five, 1963–1965*. Ed. Robert E. Daggy. San Francisco: HarperSanFrancisco, 1996.

———. *Day of a Stranger*. Salt Lake City: Gibbs M. Smith, 1981.

———. *Disputed Questions*. New York: Farrar, Straus & Giroux, 1960.

———. *Eighteen Poems*. New York: New Directions, 1985.

———. *Emblems of a Season of Fury*. New York: New Directions, 1963.

———. *Entering the Silence: The Journals of Thomas Merton: Volume Two, 1941–1952*. Ed. Jonathan Montaldo. San Francisco: HarperSanFrancisco, 1996.

———. *Faith and Violence: Christian Teaching and Christian Practice*. Notre Dame, Ind.: University of Notre Dame Press, 1968.

———. *The Geography of Lograire*. New York: New Directions, 1969.

———. *The Hidden Ground of Love: Letters on Religious Experience and Social Concerns*. Ed. William H. Shannon. New York: Farrar, Straus & Giroux, 1985.

———. *"Honorable Reader": Reflections on My Work*. Ed. Robert E. Daggy. New York: Crossroad, 1989.

———. *In the Dark Before Dawn: New Selected Poems of Thomas Merton*. Preface by Kathleen Norris. Ed. Lynn R. Szabo. New York: New Directions, 2005.

———. *An Introduction to Christian Mysticism: Initiation into the Monastic Tradition 3*. Ed. Patrick. F. O'Connell. Kalamazoo, Mich.: Cistercian Publications, 2008.

———. *The Last of the Fathers: Saint Bernard of Clairvaux and the Encyclical Letter,* Doctor Mellifluus. New York: Harcourt, Brace and Co., 1954.

———. *Learning to Love: The Journals of Thomas Merton: Volume Six, 1966–1967*. Ed. Christine M. Bochen. San Francisco: HarperSanFrancisco, 1997.

———. *The Literary Essays of Thomas Merton*. Ed. Patrick Hart. New York: New Directions, 1981.

———. *Monastic Observances: Initiation into the Monastic Tradition 5*. Ed. Patrick. F. O'Connell. Kalamazoo, Mich.: Cistercian Publications, 2010.

———. *Mystics and Zen Masters*. New York: Farrar, Straus & Giroux, 1967.

———. *New Seeds of Contemplation*. New York: New Directions, 1961.

———. *No Man Is an Island*. New York: Harcourt, Brace and Company, 1955.

———. *The Nonviolent Alternative*. Ed. Gordon C. Zahn. New York: Farrar, Straus & Giroux, 1980.

———. *Original Child Bomb: Points for Meditation to Be Scratched on the Walls of a Cave*. New York: New Directions, 1962.

———. *The Other Side of the Mountain: The End of the Journey: The Journals of Thomas Merton: Volume Seven, 1967–1968*. Ed. Patrick Hart. San Francisco: HarperSanFrancisco, 1998.

———. *Passion for Peace: Reflections on War and Nonviolence*. New York: Crossroad, 1995.

———. *Peace in the Post-Christian Era*. Ed. Patricia A. Burton. Maryknoll, N.Y.: Orbis, 2004.

———. *Praying the Psalms*. Collegeville, Minn.: Liturgical Press, 1956.

———. *Preview of the Asian Journey*. Ed. Walter Capps. New York: Crossroad, 1989.

———. *The Road to Joy: Letters to New and Old Friends*. Ed. Robert E. Daggy. New York: Farrar, Straus & Giroux, 1989.

———. *Run to the Mountain: The Journals of Thomas Merton: Volume One, 1939–1941*. Ed. Patrick Hart. San Francisco: HarperSanFrancisco, 1995.

———. *A Search for Solitude: The Journals of Thomas Merton: Volume Three, 1952–1960*. Ed. Lawrence S. Cunningham. San Francisco: HarperSanFrancisco, 1996.

———. *The Secular Journal of Thomas Merton*. New York: Farrar, Straus & Cudahy, 1959.

———. *Seeds of Destruction*. New York: Farrar, Straus & Giroux, 1964.

———. *Selected Essays*. Ed. Patrick F. O'Connell. Maryknoll, N.Y.: Orbis, 2013.

———. *The Seven Storey Mountain*. New York: Harcourt, Brace, 1948.

———. *The Seven Storey Mountain, Fiftieth Anniversary Edition*. Introduction by Robert Giroux. Orlando, Fla.: Harcourt, Brace, 1998.

———. *The Sign of Jonas*. New York: Harcourt, Brace, 1953.

———. *Thomas Merton on Peace*. Introduction by Gordon C. Zahn. New York: McCall, 1971.

———. *Turning Toward the World: The Journals of Thomas Merton: Volume Four, 1960–1963*. Ed. Victor A. Kramer. San Francisco: HarperSanFrancisco, 1996.

———. *The Waters of Siloe*. New York: Harcourt, Brace, 1949.

———. *The Way of Chuang Tzu*. New York: New Directions, 1965.

———. *What Are These Wounds? The Life of a Cistercian Mystic: Saint Lutgarde of Aywières*. Milwaukee: Bruce, 1950.

———. *The Wisdom of the Desert*. New York: New Directions, 1960.

———. *Witness to Freedom: Letters in Times of Crisis*. Ed. William H. Shannon. New York: Farrar, Straus & Giroux, 1994.

———. *Zen and the Birds of Appetite*. New York: New Directions, 1968.

Merton, Thomas, interview with Thomas P. McDonnell. "An Interview with Thomas Merton." *Motive* (October 1967): 32–41.

Middleton, Arthur. "The World in a Grain of Sand." *The Merton Annual*, Vol. 2. Ed. Robert E. Daggy, Patrick Hart, Dewey Weiss Kramer, and Victor A. Kramer. New York: AMS Press, 1989: 131–42.

Mott, Michael. *The Seven Mountains of Thomas Merton*. Boston: Houghton Mifflin, 1984.

Nugent, Robert. *Thomas Merton and Thérèse Lentfoehr: The Story of a Friendship*. Staten Island, N.Y.: St. Paul's, 2012.

Pearson, Paul M. *Beholding Paradise: The Photographs of Thomas Merton*. New York: Paulist Press, 2017.

Pennington, M. Basil. *A Retreat with Thomas Merton*. Rockport, Mass.: Element, 1991.

Pramuk, Christopher. *At Play in Creation: Merton's Awakening to the Feminine Divine*. Collegeville, Minn.: Liturgical Press, 2015.

Rice, Edward. *The Man in the Sycamore Tree: The Good Times and Hard Life of Thomas Merton: An Entertainment*. New York: Doubleday, 1970.

Samway, Patrick, ed. *The Letters of Robert Giroux and Thomas Merton*. Notre Dame, Ind.: University of Notre Dame Press, 2015.

Sandoval, Jessie. *From the Monastery to the World: The Letters of Thomas Merton and Ernesto Cardenal*. Washington, D.C.: Counterpoint, 2017.

Scutchfield, F. Douglas, and Paul Holbrook Jr., eds. *The Letters of Thomas Merton and Victor and Carolyn Hammer: Ad Majorem Dei Gloriam*. Lexington: University of Kentucky Press, 2014.

Shaw, Mark. *Beneath the Mask of Holiness: Thomas Merton and the Forbidden Love Affair That Set Him Free*. New York: Palgrave Macmillan, 2009.

Spencer, Thomas. "Joan Baez, Ira Sandperl, and Thomas Merton's Non-Violent Activism." *The Merton Seasonal*, vol. 34, no. 1 (Spring 2009): 21–28.

Tardiff, Mary, ed. *At Home in the World: The Letters of Thomas Merton and Rosemary Radford Ruether*. Maryknoll, N.Y.: Orbis, 1995.

Waddell, Chrysogonus. "Merton and the Tiger Lily." *The Merton Annual*, Vol. 2. Ed. Robert E. Daggy, Patrick Hart, Dewey Weiss Kramer, and Victor A. Kramer. New York: AMS Press, 1989: 59–84.

Waldron, Robert. *Thomas Merton: The Exquisite Risk of Love: The Chronicle of a Monastic Romance*. London: Darton, Longman and Todd, 2012.

____. *The Wounded Heart of Thomas Merton*. Mahwah, N.J.: Paulist, 2011.

Wilkes, Paul, ed. *Merton by Those Who Knew Him Best*. New York: Harper & Row, 1984.

Zuercher, Suzanne. *The Ground of Love and Truth: Reflections on Thomas Merton's Relationship with the Woman Known as "M."* Chicago: In Extenso, 2014.

BOB DYLAN

Bauldie, John. *The Ghost of Electricity: Bob Dylan's 1966 World Tour*. Privately published, 1988.

———. *Wanted Man: In Search of Bob Dylan*. New York: Citadel, 1991.

Bell, Ian. *Time Out of Mind: The Lives of Bob Dylan*. New York: Pegasus, 2013.

———. *Once Upon a Time: The Lives of Bob Dylan*. New York: Pegasus, 2014.

Björner, Olof. *Olof's Files: A Bob Dylan Performance Guide: Volume 1: 1958–1969: Bob Dylan All Alone on a Shelf*. Edinburgh: Herdinge Simpole, 2002. Continually updated at Olof Björner, *Still on the Road*, http://www.bjorner.com/still.htm.

BIBLIOGRAPHY

Cott, Jonathan, ed. *Bob Dylan: The Essential Interviews*. New York: Wenner, 2006.

Dalton, David. *Who Is That Man? In Search of the Real Bob Dylan*. New York: Hyperion, 2012.

Dunn, Tim. *The Bob Dylan Copyright Files, 1962–2007*. Bloomington, Ind.: AuthorHouse, 2008.

Dylan, Bob. *Chronicles: Volume One*. New York: Simon & Schuster, 2004.

———. *Lyrics, 1962–1985*. New York: Knopf, 1985.

———. *Lyrics Since 1962*. Ed. Christopher Ricks, Lisa Nemrow, Julie Nemrow. New York: Simon & Schuster, 2014.

———. *Tarantula*. New York: Macmillan, 1971.

———. *Writings and Drawings*. New York: Knopf, 1973.

Epstein, Daniel Mark. *The Ballad of Bob Dylan: A Portrait*. New York: HarperCollins, 2011.

Foulk, Ray, with Caroline Foulk. *When the World Came to the Isle of Wight, Volume 1: Stealing Dylan from Woodstock*. Surbiton, Surrey, UK: Medina Publishing, 2015.

Griffin, Sid. *Million Dollar Bash: Bob Dylan, the Band, and the Basement Tapes*. 2nd edition. London: Jawbone, 2014.

Hajdu, David. *Positively 4th Street: The Lives and Times of Joan Baez, Bob Dylan, Mimi Baez Fariña and Richard Fariña*. New York: Farrar, Straus & Giroux, 2001.

Harvey, Todd. *The Formative Dylan: Transmission and Stylistic Influences, 1961–1963*. Lanham, Md.: Scarecrow, 2001.

Heylin, Clinton. *Bob Dylan: Behind the Shades Revisited*. New York: Morrow, 2001.

———. *Bob Dylan: A Life in Stolen Moments: Day by Day from 1941–1995*. New York: Schirmer, 1996.

———. *Bob Dylan: The Recording Sessions (1960–1994)*. New York: St. Martin's, 1995.

———. *Judas! From Forest Hills to the Free Trade Hall: A Historical View of the Big Boo*. Pontefract, England: Route, 2016.

———. *Revolution in the Air: The Songs of Bob Dylan, 1957–1973*. Chicago: A Cappella, 2009.

Hoskyns, Barney. *Small Town Talk: Bob Dylan, The Band, Van Morrison, Janis Joplin, Jimi Hendrix and Friends in the Wild Years of Woodstock*. Boston: Da Capo, 2016.

Irwin, Colin. *Bob Dylan: Highway 61 Revisited*. Legendary Sessions Series. New York: Billboard, 2008.

Lee, C. P. *Like the Night: Bob Dylan and the Road to the Manchester Free Trade Hall*. London: Helter Skelter, 1998.

Marcus, Greil. *Bob Dylan by Greil Marcus: Writings, 1968–2010*. New York: PublicAffairs, 2010.

———. *Invisible Republic: Bob Dylan's Basement Tapes*. New York: Henry Holt, 1997.

———. *Like a Rolling Stone: Bob Dylan at the Crossroads*. New York: PublicAffairs, 2005.

Marshall, Scott. *Bob Dylan: A Spiritual Life*. Washington, D.C.: BP/WND Books, 2017.

Maymudes, Victor, and Jacob Maymudes. *Another Side of Bob Dylan: A Personal History on the Road and Off the Tracks*. New York: St. Martin's, 2014.

Pennebaker, D. A. *Dont Look Back: A Film Book by D. A. Pennebaker*. New York: Ballantine, 1968.

Renehan, Edward. *Dylan at Newport, 1965: Music, Myth, and Un-Meaning*. Wickford, R.I.: New Street Communications, 2015.

Ricks, Christopher. *Dylan's Vision of Sin*. New York: Ecco, 2003.

Riley, Tim. *Hard Rain: A Dylan Commentary*. New York: Knopf, 1992.

Scaduto, Anthony. *Bob Dylan: An Intimate Biography*. New York: Grosset & Dunlap, 1971.

Shelton, Robert. *No Direction Home: The Life and Music of Bob Dylan*. Rev. and updated. Ed. Elizabeth Thomson and Patrick Humphries. Milwaukee: Backbeat, 2011.

Siegel, Jules. "Bob Dylan: Well, What Have We Here?" *The Saturday Evening Post* 239, no. 16 (July 30, 1966): 32–39.

Sounes, Howard. *Down the Highway: The Life of Bob Dylan*. New York: Grove, 2001.

Spitz, Bob. *Dylan: A Biography*. New York: McGraw-Hill, 1989.

Trager, Oliver. *Keys to the Rain: The Definitive Bob Dylan Encyclopedia*. New York: Billboard, 2004.

Wald, Elijah. *Dylan Goes Electric: Newport, Seeger, Dylan, and the Night That Split the Sixties*. New York: Dei St./HarperCollins, 2015.

Wilentz, Sean. *Bob Dylan in America*. New York: Doubleday, 2010.

Williams, Paul. *Bob Dylan: Performing Artist, The Middle Years: 1974–1986*. Novato, Calif.: Underwood-Miller, 1992.

———. *Performing Artist: The Music of Bob Dylan: Volume One, 1960–1973*. Novato, Calif.: Underwood-Miller, 1990.

———. *Watching the River Flow: Observations on Bob Dylan's Art-in-Progress, 1966–1995*. London: Omnibus, 1996.

GENERAL

Alberti, Rafael. *Concerning the Angels*. San Francisco: City Lights, 1995.

Backhouse, Stephen. *Kierkegaard: A Single Life*. Grand Rapids, Mich.: Zondervan, 2016.

Baez, Joan. *And a Voice to Sing With: A Memoir*. New York: Summit, 1987.

———. *And Then I Wrote . . .* New York: Big 3 Music, 1979.

———. *Daybreak: An Autobiography*. New York: Avon, 1969.

———. *The Joan Baez Songbook*. New York: Amsco, 1964.

Barré, Jean-Luc. *Jacques and Raïssa Maritain: Beggars for Heaven*. Trans. Bernard E. Doering. Notre Dame, Ind.: University of Notre Dame Press, 2005.

Bly, Robert. *The Sibling Society*. New York: Vintage, 1996.

Bruce, Lenny. *The Essential Lenny Bruce*. Ed. John Cohen. New York: Bell, 1970.

Camus, Albert. *The Myth of Sisyphus and Other Essays*. Trans. Justin O'Brien. New York: Knopf, 1955.

———. *The Stranger*. New York: Vintage, 1989.

Cash, Johnny. *Cash: An Autobiography*. New York: HarperCollins, 1997.

Clément, Olivier. *The Roots of Christian Mysticism: Texts from the Patristic Era with Commentary*. London: New City, 1993.

Colegate, Isabel. *A Pelican in the Wilderness: Hermits, Solitaries and Recluses*. Washington, D.C.: Counterpoint, 2002.

Douglass, James W. *JFK and the Unspeakable: Why He Died and Why It Matters*. New York: Touchstone, 2008.

Eliot, T. S. *The Complete Poems and Plays of T. S. Eliot*. London: Faber and Faber, 1969.

Ellul, Jacques. *The Technological Society*. Trans. John Wilkinson. New York: Vintage, 1964.

English, Timothy. *Popology: The Music of the Era in the Lives of Four Icons of the 1960s*. North Charleston, S.C.: CreateSpace, 2013.

Giroux, Robert. *The Education of an Editor*. Ninth R. R. Bowker Memorial Lecture, New Series, December 16, 1981. New York: Bowker, 1982.

Helm, Levon, with Stephen Davis. *This Wheel's on Fire: Levon Helm and the Story of the Band*. Updated edition. Chicago: A Cappella, 2013.

Howison, Don E. *God's Mind in That Music: Theological Explorations through the Music of John Coltrane*. Eugene, Ore.: Cascade, 2012.

Kierkegaard, Søren. *The Present Age*. Trans. Alexander Dru. New York: Harper & Row, 1962.

King, Ursula. *Christian Mystics: Their Lives and Legacies throughout the Ages*. Mahwah, N.J.: Hidden Spring, 2001.

Klejment, Anne, and Nancy L. Roberts. *American Catholic Pacifism: The Influence of Dorothy Day and the Catholic Worker Movement*. Westport, Conn.: Praeger, 1996.

Leffert, Mark. "The Psychoanalysis and Death of George Gershwin: An American Tragedy," *The Journal of the American Academy of Psychoanalysis and Dynamic Psychiatry* 39(3) (Bloomfield, Conn.: AAPDP, 2011): 420–51.

Lynskey, Dorian. *33 Revolutions Per Minute: A History of Protest Songs, from Billie Holiday to Green Day*. New York: Ecco/HarperCollins, 2011.

MacNiven, Ian S. *"Literchoor Is My Beat": A Life of James Laughlin, Publisher of New Directions*. New York: Farrar, Straus & Giroux, 2014.

Muir, Edwin. *The Estate of Poetry*. Cambridge, Mass.: Harvard University Press, 1962.

Nhat Hanh, Thich. *Living Buddha, Living Christ*. New York: Riverhead, 2007.

———. *Tho Viet Nam (Vietnam Poems)*. Santa Barbara: Unicorn Press, 1967.

———. *Vietnam: Lotus in a Sea of Fire*. Foreword by Thomas Merton. New York: Hill & Wang, 1967.

Niles, John Jacob. *The Ballad Book of John Jacob Niles*. Boston: Houghton Mifflin, 1961.

Nisenson, Eric. *Ascension: John Coltrane and His Quest*. New York: Da Capo, 1995.

Parra, Nicanor. *Poems and Antipoems*. Ed. Miller Williams. New York: New Directions, 1966.

Pen, Ron. *I Wonder as I Wander: The Life of John Jacob Niles*. Lexington, Ky.: The University of Kentucky Press, 2010.

Rilke, Rainer Maria. *Letters to a Young Poet*. Trans. M. D. Herter Norton. New York: Norton, 1993 (1934).

Robertson, Robbie. *Testimony*. New York: Crown/Archetype, 2016.

Rotolo, Suze. *A Freewheelin' Time: A Memoir of Greenwich Village in the Sixties*. New York: Broadway Books, 2008.

Savage, Jon. *1966: The Year the Decade Exploded*. London: Faber & Faber, 2015.

BIBLIOGRAPHY

Van Ronk, Dave, with Elijah Wald. *The Mayor of MacDougal Street: A Memoir*. Cambridge, Mass.: Da Capo, 2006.

Waddell, Helen, trans. *The Desert Fathers*. Preface by M. Basil Pennington, OCSO. New York: Vintage, 1998.

Wills, Garry. *Head and Heart: American Christianities*. New York: Penguin, 2007.

DISCOGRAPHY/FILMOGRAPHY

Baez, Joan. *Any Day Now*, 2 LPs. Vanguard, VSD 79306/7, 1968.

———. *Joan Baez*, LP. Vanguard, VSD 2077, 1960.

———. *Noël*, LP. Vanguard, VSD 79230, 1966.

Bruce, Lenny. *Let the Buyer Beware*, 6 CDs. Shout! Factory, DK 37109, 2004.

Byrds, The. *Mr. Tambourine Man*, LP. Columbia, CS 9172, 1965.

Coltrane, John. *Ascension*, LP. Impulse! AS 95, 1965.

Dylan, Bob. *1965 Revisited*, 14 CDs. Unofficial recording, Great Dane, CD 9419/1-14, 1995.

———. *The 1966 Live Recordings*, 36 CDs. Columbia, Legacy, Sony, 889853581924, 2016.

———. *The 50th Anniversary Collection: The Copyright Extension Collection, Vol. 1* (1962), 4 CDRs. Sony Music Europe, 8876546022, 2012.

———. *The 50th Anniversary Collection, 1964*, 9 LPs. Sony Music Europe, 88875040861, 2014.

———. *Another Side of Bob Dylan*, LP. Columbia, CS 8993, 1964.

———. *The Basement Tapes*, 2 LPs. Columbia, C2 33682, 1975.

———. *The Basement Tapes Complete*, 6 CDs. Legacy Columbia, 88875016122, 2014.

———. *Blonde on Blonde*, 2 LPs. Columbia, C2S 841 CS 9316, 1966.

———. *Bob Dylan*, LP. Columbia, CS 8579, 1962.

———. *The Bootleg Series, Vols. 1–3: Rare and Unreleased, 1961–1991*, 3 CDs. Columbia, C3K 47382, 1991.

———. *The Bootleg Series, Volume 6: Bob Dylan Live 1964: Concert at Philharmonic Hall*, 2 CDs. Columbia Legacy, C2K 86882, 2004.

———. *Bringing It All Back Home*, LP. Columbia, CS 9128, 1965.

———. *The Classic Interviews, Vol. 1, 1965–1966*, CD. *Isis* magazine, 2005.

———. *The Cutting Edge, 1965–1966: Bootleg Series, Volume 12*, 18 CDs. Columbia, 888751240218, 2015.

———. *Dont Look Back*, 2 DVDs. Docurama, NVG 9824, 2007.

———. *The Freewheelin' Bob Dylan*, LP. Columbia, KCS 8786, 1963.

———. *The Great White Wonder*, 2 LPs. Unofficial recording, no label, 1969.

———. *Highway 61 Revisited*, LP. Columbia, CS 9189, 1965.

———. *John Wesley Harding*, LP. Columbia, CS 9604, 1967.

———. *Nashville Skyline*, LP. Columbia, KCS 9825, 1969.

———. *No Direction Home: Bob Dylan* (A Martin Scorsese Picture), 2 DVDs. Paramount, 03105, 2005.

———. *On the Crest of the Airwaves, Vol. 1* (interviews), 4 CDs. Music Melon, MMLTD-BOX12, 2012.

———. *The Other Side of the Mirror: Bob Dylan at the Newport Folk Festival, 1963–1965*, DVD. Columbia Music Video, Legacy, 8869714466 9, 2007.

———. *Thin Wild Mercury Music*, CD. Unofficial recording, Spank Records, SP-105, 1994.

———. *The Times They Are A-Changin'*, LP. Columbia, CS 8905, 1964.

Merton, Thomas. *Thomas Merton on Contemplation*, 4 CDs. Now You Know Media, 2014.

Niles, John Jacob. *I Wonder as I Wander: Carols and Love Songs*, LP. Tradition, TLP 1023, 1958.

Peter, Paul and Mary. *In the Wind*, LP. Warner Bros. Records, WS 1507, 1963.

Runyon, Chad, and Jacqueline Chew. *Sweet Irrational Worship: The Niles-Merton Songs, Opus 171 and 172*, CD. MSR Classics, MS 1174, 2006.

Various artists. *Festival!—The Newport Folk Festival*, DVD. Directed by Murray Lerner. Eagle Vision, EREDV499, 2005.

Waddell, Chrysogonus. *Christ Is Risen, Truly Risen: Easter Chants and Anthems*, CD. World Library Publications, 2007.

Wilkes, Paul, and Audrey L. Glynn. *Merton: A Film Biography*, television documentary. New York: First Run Features, 1984; DVD, 2004.

Williams, Paul. *Bob Dylan: Performing Artist, 1986–1990 and Beyond: Mind Out of Time*. London: Omnibus, 2004.

INDEX